The State House from Main Street

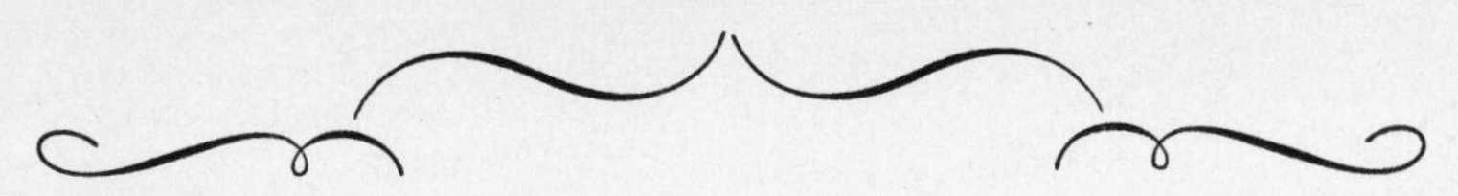

ANNAPOLIS

Anne Arundel's Town

by

WILLIAM OLIVER STEVENS

Illustrated by

THE AUTHOR

DODD, MEAD & COMPANY
NEW YORK 1937

PRINTED IN THE UNITED STATES OF AMERICA
BY THE VAIL-BALLOU PRESS, INC., BINGHAMTON, N. Y.

TO

HUGO AND MASON

NATIVE SONS

OF

THE ANCIENT CITY

ACKNOWLEDGMENTS

For the preparation of this descriptive chronicle of Annapolis, various books and articles have been consulted, some of which are mentioned in the following pages, but a complete list of which would be tedious. I should like to express my obligation to the friends who have contributed an anecdote here and there. In particular, I should like to mention Mr. R. T. Haines Halsey, formerly of the New York Metropolitan Museum staff and later, for a time, on the faculty of St. John's College. Mr. Halsey has kindly supplied me with important information about the old houses of Annapolis and especially about the architect, William Buckland, of whom he has made a special study.

Most of all, I am indebted to Mr. Peter H. Magruder, Secretary of the Company for the Restoration of Colonial Annapolis, and an outstanding authority on the history of both the city and the Naval Academy. On the one side his ancestors have contributed much to the annals of Annapolis from the earliest times. On the other, his own record of thirty-one years of service as Secretary of the Naval Academy gives him an intimate knowledge of that institution, a knowledge which he has kindly put at my disposal. The drawings in this book marked "after a photograph" were made from his priceless collection of old photographs. The historic map on the inside of the covers was drawn by permission from data on a recent map prepared under his direction for the Company for the Restoration of Colonial Annapolis. Finally, he has topped off his kindnesses by writing a preface. My thanks, therefore, are due him in great measure.

William Oliver Stevens

FOREWORD

Upon the green banks of the Severn, near the place where the little river lazily runs its waters into the blue Chesapeake Bay, slumbers picturesque old Annapolis, the Colonial Capital of Maryland, still enshrined in the glories of its past—a past full of historic richness, which has helped to mould America of today.

The flavor of the past has not entirely gone from Annapolis, and one soon realizes that there must be an ancient and romantic story about this quaint old town on the Severn. And there is a story, both ancient and romantic.

The Severn was first explored by Captain John Smith in 1608. As early as 1649, at the invitation of Governor Stone of Maryland, ten families came north from Virginia and built rude huts for themselves on the banks of this river. They called their tiny town Providence. These people were Puritans, who had been opposed by the Churchmen of Virginia. So it was to Maryland that the Puritans of Virginia came. In 1652, the settlers and the Indians made a treaty of peace, which tradition tells us took place under the famous Liberty Tree, now standing on the campus of St. John's College.

During the next half century, the little settlement on the Severn bore five different names: Providence, Town of Proctor's, Town at the Severn, Anne Arundel's Town, and finally, in 1694, Annapolis. The last name was given in honor of Princess Anne, at that time heir to the British throne. It was in this same year that Annapolis was made the capital of Maryland, in place of St. Mary's City. This meant that the Royal

Governors, who had been sent to Maryland after the Revolution of 1688 in England, would reside in Annapolis, which they did until our Revolution in 1776. This quaint town has also had in its time five different fancied names: The Athens of America (known throughout the Colonies as such), The Ancient City, The Finished City, The City of Chimneys, and finally The Home of the Navy.

Mr. Stevens, in his book, *ANNAPOLIS—ANNE ARUNDEL'S TOWN* has brought to light many heretofore unpublished incidents in connection with the picturesque surroundings, historic setting and background of old Annapolis, which he portrays in a most vivid and fascinating way, and in a different vein from those accounts previously published. For this reason, the lovers of Colonial Annapolis will find a keen interest in the very lively manner in which he presents his story; indeed, it should be accepted as a valuable addition to the cherished records of the past, appearing at a moment when a group of interested Marylanders are endeavoring with an organized Company to preserve and restore Colonial Annapolis.

PETER HAGNER MAGRUDER

Annapolis, Md.

CONTENTS

CHAPTER I

INTRODUCING THE "ANCIENT CITY"

ONE of the unique distinctions of Annapolis, the one that may strike the traveler even before he arrives there, is that this city is the one state capital in the nation which cannot be reached by a steam railroad. But it was not ever thus. As a person of color once expressed it to an agitated man on the station platform whose watch proved to be slow, "Yas, suh, the train's done been and gone." In the Good Old Days, a vague epoch with which this book will deal extensively, there were two steam railroads. On one of them the startled passenger would have recognized no less a personage than Rudyard Kipling punching the tickets. At any rate, he was the identical image of Rudyard. Strangers, fascinated, would eye him during the entire journey from Baltimore, wondering if it really could be the author incognito, making an honest living on the railroad, and half expecting him to murmur that there's a Burma girl a-settin' or that they're hangin' Danny Deever in the mornin'. But despite the amazing resemblance—glasses, walrus moustache and all—you came to the reluctant conclusion that he must be someone else, for he spake neither in prose nor in verse. Only as the little train slid into the station at the end of the route he would open the door of the car and announce the name twice in a mild tone, the first with a rising inflection like a question, the second, as a reply: "Nap-liss? Nap-liss." He never varied this formula in thirty years.

After the sooty trains had outlived their usefulness, both the lines took to electricity. One, the Washington route, even sent huge cars thundering through the streets of the Ancient City like some fearful Brontosaurus intent on its prey. Now, also like the Brontosaurus, the electric road has gone extinct, on account of small and more nimble enemies; to wit, the automobiles. Its bones are dust, its good rails rust, its soul is with the saints, we trust. At least, if a corporation has no soul, it has gone to "join the martyr throng"—all those other interurban railways which the motor car has done to death.

The other railroad, the Short Line, still shuttles an electric car back and forth from Baltimore, but how long that will last, against what Henry Ford and General Motors are doing, is a question. And, alas, Rudyard Kipling is punching tickets no longer.

The chances are that at least nine out of ten visitors come to Annapolis behind their own wheels. The most popular route is from Washington via the Defense Highway, but this offers a very drab introduction to the city, running first through a scrummy negro settlement and then along the dullest street in all Annapolis. A better way is to drive from Baltimore, for just as you come to the Severn River bridge there is a beautiful panorama of water and distant buildings to welcome you. The most enjoyable route of all is to put your car on the ferry at Matapeake, Kent Island, on the Eastern Shore (pronounced "Eastern Sho"), and, sitting on the forward deck, enjoy the gradual lift of the town and Naval Academy buildings on the horizon as you approach from Chesapeake Bay. The old ferry boats used to be rather insignificant craft, but this present-day vessel is large, square-built and imposing, smoking violently and incessantly, altogether reminding one dimly of some terrifying lady partner in a bridge game. The boat comes up like thunder out of Matapeake 'cross the bay, and she is staunch and strong. During a recent severe winter, she alone of all the vessels was able to keep a path open through the ice.

Something should be said about the right time of year for a first visit to Annapolis. Of all the seasons, the best is that week which says good-bye to May and welcome to June. This is known locally as "June Week"; it is the Commencement season for the Naval Academy. Naturally, that is the year's gala occasion, and the old town sets her cap straight, brushes her curls, and puts on her best silk dress. It is true that two or three weeks earlier would show a more brilliant display in the gardens, for by this time the most vivid spring flowers have faded. The rambler roses and hollyhocks are only just beginning, but there are compensations.

The first morning of June Week would make one believe that some celestial flower cart had been unloaded overnight, sprinkling apple blossoms all over the town, and that each petal had sprung to life. For, in these days, Annapolis is a paradise for girls from everywhere in these United States. And since it would never do to wear anything but the smartest and the newest thing in finery, you see them go fluttering by in their pale summer frocks and picturesque hats. These maidens are pretty, too, for when a midshipman invites his "O. A. O." (One And Only) to see him get his diploma, he is apt to pick someone who is very gentle on the retina. Happily, at such a festive occasion, it would never do to wear the sort of garb they will later affect at a summer resort—no shorts, beach pajamas, culottes, or overalls, or any of the wretched, unbecoming bifurcated garments they like to put on. No, for this season, you can't tell the knock-kneed from the bow-legged, for, praise be, they are for once in long, graceful skirts.

At any rate, let us imagine it is a fine June morning and you are in Annapolis seeing it for the first time. Of course, if you do choose to come in June Week you will have to make your reservations far in advance, for the hotel is full to bursting and everybody who has a room, apartment, or house to rent is collecting a king's ransom therefrom. Girls cheerfully sleep six in a room, if necessary, and snatch the very slight allowance of slumber customary in June Week in a hammock or, if need be, on the floor. That, however, is just tossed out as a warning parenthesis.

Having stowed your car—for in June Week driving through Annapolis is a form of penance, if not purgatory—start on foot somewhere from the middle of the town and take a preliminary ramble to get the lay of the land. This settlement was laid out carefully when it became the capital of the province. Anne Arundel's Town was no group of houses growing up along an assortment of cow paths, like Boston, or out of a huddle of cabins in a stockade, like Pittsburgh. The highest part of the location was selected for the two "circles," one for Church and one for State. To this day, one is known as Church Circle and one as State Circle, containing, respectively, St. Anne's Church and the State House. From these circles the streets radiate in different directions. Washington, who visited Annapolis no less than eighteen times, was so impressed by the city plan that he sent thither Monsieur de l'Enfant, the architect of the city of Washington, to study it. And he himself made two visits for the purpose. But, admirable as it was for the eighteenth century, it does not cheer the heart of the motorist of today. In Washington the driver who runs round and round Dupont Circle like a squirrel in a cage, vainly trying to get out on Massachusetts

CORNHILL STREET

Avenue, may have Annapolis and George Washington to thank for his plight.

Even before the advent of the automobile—in the Good Old Days already referred to—strangers who depended on their feet sometimes became bewildered on the Annapolis Circles. I once met a man with a haunted look in his eye who stopped me to inquire, "How can I get out of here to reach the Naval Academy? I've been round this circle so often that if I do it again I know I'll meet myself coming the other way."

At any rate, the traveler should pause to take a look down these radiating streets and note some of their names, too. Here, for example, off State Circle, is one called Cornhill, in honor of a street in London which the early settlers remembered, perhaps with a homesick pang. And elsewhere there are Chancery Lane, Conduit, and Fleet Streets. Immediately one is struck by the fact that the dwellings are, in the English fashion, set directly on the sidewalk with their gardens in the rear, hidden from the gaze of the vulgar. Much that is ugly and modern has driven off the streets the beauty of the old, but there are still so many relics of the eighteenth century that one has the sensation of having slipped back, like the hero of the play, "Berkeley Square," right into the heart of an eighteenth-century English town.

To the west—that is, to the right of the traveler as he stands on the State House hill looking toward the bay—the early city planners apportioned the district for trade, and the quarter in which the tradespeople might live. Directly north, or back of the State House, just about where the Short Line station stands, now surrounded by Ethiopia, was "Bloomsbury Square," a place where the ordinary people were permitted to have their games and fun on stipulated occasions. In those days there was no talk about the Rights of Man; the shop-keeper or artisan had to know his place and be "content with the station to which God had called him."

But the end of Church (Main) Street was where the wharves and docks and warehouses stood for shipping the product on which the prosperity of Annapolis rested—tobacco. There were at that time tall square-riggers anchored in Spa Creek to take the hogsheads of tobacco to England and bring back in ex-

FLEET STREET, SOUTH END

change the treasures of London shops to grace the homes of the planters.

For these fine gentry, the water front to the east of the wharves was reserved. Here they built their mansions and laid out their gardens. The estate of Charles Carroll of Carrollton —distinguished now by the slender spire of St. Mary's Catholic Church—and "Acton," now buried in a suburban development, are the only two early estates that lay to the west of the commercial section of the town.

Let us turn east along Maryland Avenue toward the Naval Academy. You will not need to be told that this street leads to the Cradle of the Navy, for there is a procession of young men in white uniforms and brass buttons towing pretty girls alongside. This is the season when, as the astronomer might say, Venus and Mars are in conjunction—or perhaps here one should say Neptune. This is a time and place, also, when a civilian is a Mere Worm who should sneak humbly into the back alleys, for the Navy uniform is supreme.

To the stranger, unfamiliar with these scenes, especially one who doesn't know a gob from a vice-admiral, and still more especially if said stranger is of the feminine persuasion, there is no use calling attention to anything else for awhile. Yet even such a one might turn her eyes for a moment to the two magnificent specimens of Maryland colonial architecture that one comes upon, facing each other across the "Avenue." These are the Chase home, the large, square, three-story brick mansion on the left, and the Hammond, or Harwood, house opposite, with its two connecting wings. Either one of these houses would be a jewel in the crown of any city in our land. Perhaps it is a toss-up, or a matter of personal taste, between these two as to whether one or the other is not the finest example of colonial brick homes to be found anywhere. But we shall return to them later and the visitor may as well march straight ahead into the Naval Academy, through what is called the Main Gate. There one may obtain information about the drill program for the day, for certainly not even a dyed-in-the-wool pacifist would come to Annapolis without witnessing the dress parades.

The Naval Academy covers a wide territory and there is much to see even at other times of the year than June Week; but for the first glimpse it is enough to get the lay of the land, to know where the drills and other exercises are held, and to recognize by name the most important buildings. For example, the colossal mass of granite at the far end of the Yard, sprawled across so as to cut off the breeze from the bay, and also the view, is Bancroft Hall, the midshipmen's dormitory, probably the biggest dormitory on the planet. A dark, lugubrious dome near the gate marks the Chapel, and down in its crypt lies the body of John Paul Jones. Once this dome was gay with helmets and spears and standards in the decoration, which was white on a yellow background. The midshipmen referred to it then as the "wedding cake." But now, alas, the frosting has all been scraped off.

The winding walk under the trees in front of the Chapel is famous as "Lover's Lane." This is marked at one end by an obelisk (bearing the name "Herndon," after a departed hero) and by a band-stand at the other. As a place for love-making, this seems rather public, but they do say that in the Good Old Days there were more shrubs to give shelter, until some hard-hearted Superintendent cleared them all away. And for a great part of the year colored nurse-maids, who are so bulky that they prefer sitting to walking, tend to preempt the benches in the Lane. In June Week, however, the white-uniformed midshipmen and their girls like to drift back and forth along the walk and manage to give it some appearance of a lover's lane, after all. Here, by the way, is a fine place to listen to the morning or afternoon concert by the Naval Academy band, if the day is warm and you are not in the mood for any more sightseeing.

Out to the town again, by one of the other three gates, you may ramble at will by devious ways, turning back on your route wherever something looks attractive, cutting through little alleys and wandering along the water-front. In this way, you can get a picture of such a town as you have probably never seen before, and the distances are so short that even a product of the automobile age whose feet are in danger of dropping off from disuse will suffer no weariness in doing the town on foot. Indeed, a fat and lazy pedestrian, with hardening arteries, could manage to walk from one end of the city to another in fifteen minutes. It is much more fun for the stranger to pick his own course for this preliminary survey of Annapolis and make his own discoveries.

Here are some of the things he will notice. The ancient brick pavements that survive are all of a beautiful color but wave up and down like a heavy sea. Annapolitans navigate them without difficulty from long years of experience, but the newcomer, accustomed to modern, flat cement sidewalks, lurches and staggers in a suspicious way. The midshipmen acquire their sea legs on these sidewalks, they say, and it may well be.

Raising the eye aloft, one observes the telegraph poles and wires which have now all but disappeared from American towns. These poles were apparently set out about the time Morse clicked his first message, for they lean, many of them, with a weary air, and their wires are droopy and loopy, like the branches of a weeping willow tree.

The streets have mostly lost their fine old cobbles, alas! Once upon a time, anyone in a vehicle coming along an Annapolis street had his internal organs bounced together in painful confusion, and even the wheels of a buggy made enough noise to

ON THE WATERFRONT

wake all the babies on the block. In those days, the visitor drove from the station in one of a collection of famous hacks, described by the naval officers as "sea-going," doubtless from the heavy weather they made navigating the cobbled streets. The

"SEA-GOING HACK"

From the Annapolis Alphabet

constant shaking tended to make them dilapidated and their wheels revolved with eccentric wobbles, but they held together somehow. They were drawn by dejected and bony animals who were said to eat the straw from the cushions to eke out their insufficient rations. The drivers were young, very young, persons of color, who had the trick of dozing off as they sat on their perch, even while driving.

There is a cherished legend that once, about the turn of the century, a rear admiral arrived from Washington in special full dress, gold epaulets, cocked hat and everything, to officiate at some imposing affair in the quarters of the Superintendent of the Naval Academy. He stowed himself away in one of the sea-going hacks and drove off in state toward the Main Gate. Whether it was because he was especially heavy, or the hack was especially old, it happened that as the chariot rolled into Maryland Avenue, the bottom suddenly dropped out. The Senegambian in the driver's seat, serenely unconscious of the tragedy, clucked to encourage his Bucephalus to greater speed, and the innocent bystanders were electrified to see a hack clattering along, beneath which twinkled a pair of legs in gold-braided trousers, while ever and anon a red face under a cocked hat gasped curses from the window at the driver who could not hear.

Speaking of streets, be sure not to miss the names. Certain ones have already been mentioned that echo old London. There are four others that express the loyalty of the ancient citizens for their royal family. Just outside the Main Gate, lying athwart Maryland Avenue, is Hanover Street, in honor of a particularly dull family that had been imported from Germany to rule Britain. Next to it is King George Street, after the particularly dull representative of that family who was placed on the British throne. Next, to the west, is Prince George Street, after Prince George of Denmark, the husband of Queen Anne. Antedating these is the long street that runs from Church Circle straight across the creek, Duke of Gloucester Street. The poor little Duke was the only one of Queen Anne's flock of seventeen children who lived beyond infancy, but he succumbed also when he was only ten years old. Beyond, to the west, and parallel to this, lies Shipwright Street running down to the water, and still reminding us of the days when hammers were ringing all day in the shipyard at the foot of the street. There is some point in having street names like these, instead of such dull titles as "Second Boulevard," or meaningless ones like "Myrtle Street," where a myrtle never grew. In fact, the longer one lingers about a town like this the more sorry one feels for people who have to live in large cities, though probably most of them deserve and like their fate.

Returning to Duke of Gloucester Street, if one happens to be there about school-opening time in the morning, one is likely to see a little procession that seems taken right out of an old French provincial town, for the entire Carrollton estate is now the property of the Catholic Church, and one of the buildings is used as a parochial school. About nine o'clock a column of children comes out of the church, headed by Sisters, with others of the Order bringing up the stragglers in the rear. All the little girls are dressed in bright blue and they walk sedately two by two. The little boys have no uniform. For that reason, perhaps, they march on the side of the walk nearer the high brick wall, and they do not proceed so sedately as the girls. But it is a long, gay little parade, making what the English call a "crocodile," winding along the walk from the church to the door of the school. If you tarry a few minutes after the last urchin has scuffled in, you will hear a shrill burst of "Hail, Columbia," or "Maryland, My Maryland," with which the children greet the morn in lusty patriotism.

Supposing that the visitor does happen to be there at this hour of a bright June morning, he should certainly continue along

CHESAPEAKE BAY "BUGEYE" IN THE DOCK

the high wall of the church grounds to the bridge that leads over Spa Creek to the suburbs of Eastport (pronounced Eastpote). From the middle of the bridge, looking backward, one gets the most effective view of the towering Carrollton mansion and the graceful spire of St. Mary's. During June Week, the anchorage of the creek is filled with smart yachts and other glittering holiday craft. But in the channel there may be seen, from time to time, a sail boat of another type, one peculiar to Chesapeake Bay, the "bugeye." She is easily recognized by her raking masts and leg-of-mutton sails. She is apt to be dingy of hull and canvas, and if she passes through the open draw of the bridge you may get a potent whiff of very extinct crabs or oysters, but the "bugeye" represents an ancient and still mighty industry in the waters of Chesapeake Bay, and her skipper casts a contemptuous eye on the shiny pleasure craft on either hand.

It must be confessed that there are no special points of interest in Eastport for a tourist. The village occupies a low peninsula between two creeks, and its extremity, Horn Point, faces the bay. The location is beautiful; nevertheless, it always used to be an extremely shabby and unfragrant neighbor of Annapolis. Its roads were rough and untidy, and its houses slummy, especially the wretched shacks where the negroes lived. On one of its main thoroughfares lay a swampy pool, flanked by tattered and drunken billboards. Here, for sixty years, Eastportians cast their broken bricks, tin cans, and old stoves.

Today, however, the wayfarer finds none of these things, for Eastport, though still weak architecturally, now boasts of elegant roads. It has torn down its negro slums, banished the ancient odors, and even the old pool has been filled up at last, with grass growing over the lumpy graves of the stoves and the

ST. MARY'S

From an Eastport Shipyard

cans. The one charm of Eastport is still what it always used to be, the shipyards along Spa Creek, from which one can enjoy the most attractive view of Annapolis and the Naval Academy. Whoever loves the smell of fresh lumber and varnish and enjoys prowling around boats, will find Eastport a pleasant objective for a morning's walk.

To continue our preliminary stroll through Annapolis, we shall have to retrace our steps back across the bridge to the crest of Duke of Gloucester Street and then head toward the center of the town. Looking from Eastport, one saw, as the original city planners intended, that the State House dome dominates the whole picture, and thither we shall bend our steps. Here is the real heart of Annapolis, with the streets radiating away from it in every direction, through one of which at least may be caught a vista of Chesapeake Bay in a distant blue horizon.

Even during a first ramble about the Ancient City, one must pause at the Capitol and look inside, if only for a glimpse of the old Senate Chamber where Washington resigned his commission. At the time of that event, by the way, the dome of the State House had not been built; that feature belongs to the years immediately after the Revolutionary War. But the Senate Chamber itself, where the impressive scene took place, has been restored to look exactly as it did on that occasion, with its dais for the President of the Continental Congress, the desk for the Clerk of the Senate, the huge fireplace at one side, and the ladies' gallery over the entrance. On the floor beside the Clerk's desk is a plate indicating the spot where Washington stood when he read his speech.

Nor was that historic occasion the only one associated with

STATE HOUSE

From St. John's campus

this old Senate Chamber. These walls later vibrated to the eloquence of Henry Clay, Daniel Webster, and Kossuth, the Hungarian patriot. Yet, all of these were conscious of the fact that a far greater hero than they had first made that room memorable. It is Washington's address at the close of the Revolution that

ST. ANNE'S

has made the old Senate Chamber a national shrine. We shall return to that scene later in the story of the War of Independence.

Nearby is St. Anne's on Church Circle, standing like so many village churches in England, right in the heart of the town, with its dead sleeping at its feet. The present structure, the third church on this site, is not remarkable for either age or beauty, for it belongs to the era of the Civil War; but it has many features of the past, among them a communion service presented by King William the Third. There was a bell, too, the gift of Queen Anne, but that was destroyed in the fire of 1858, which consumed the predecessor of this edifice. And the little churchyard is rich in memorials of dim antiquity. Once this plot included all the ground now covered by the streets that encircle the church, but long ago many of the dead were removed to a quieter scene.

The few tombs that remain commemorate worthies of old Annapolis, men and women who lived in her Golden Age, and even earlier. Here lie fine ladies and gentlemen, people of "quality." Their flat tombstones expose to the view of heaven coats of arms embellished with ornate scrolls and flourishes. These are no common sinners lying here. Such memorials, dating as far back, in some instances, as the seventeenth century, surprise the visitor who is accustomed to the mean, slate headstones of an old New England cemetery, with their crude inscriptions and still cruder carving. Here, for example, lies the "Honourable Benjamin Tasker," a great citizen in his day, who was President of the Governor's Council for thirty-two years and Acting-Governor whenever His Excellency was absent. "No one was more respected, more loved," reads the inscription, "he was no one's enemy nor any his." Not a bad epitaph for any man.

Not far from him lies "Collin Nicholas Greenberry, Esquire," a great landowner and pioneer, after whom Greenberry Point was named in 1697. His gravestone bears a set of doleful devices, skull, bones, hour-glass, spade, and scythe. The last British Governor of Maryland is buried here, too, Sir Robert Eden, Baronet. Poor fellow, he tried so hard to keep the peace between

THE LIBERTY POPLAR

his colony and the homeland, but failed; and, then, when the fighting was over, chose to come back to end his days in Maryland. His remains, like those of several others lying here, were brought to St. Anne's from desolate little churchyards out in the country.

Wandering on up College Avenue from St. Anne's, one skirts the campus of St. John's College. There it is easy to distinguish one of the most famous landmarks of Annapolis, and probably the most famous tree in the whole United States, the old Tulip Poplar. It is said to be the largest tree east of the Rockies. According to tradition, this sheltered the conference between the Puritans and the Susquehannock Indians in 1652. It must have been a goodly tree even then. More than a century later, it became the Liberty Tree for Annapolis, because there the Sons of Liberty met to express their sentiments about the Tory Ministry. Later, in 1824, Lafayette was received by the citizens under its branches.

In another decade or two, it began to show symptoms of decay. The story is that some boys set off a charge of gunpowder inside its hollow trunk. They performed unwittingly a successful major operation on the old tree, for the blaze killed off the parasites that were working on its vitals. Relieved of its internal ailments, the old creature started all over again, and ever since has widened its girth and spread abroad its mighty branches. In later years it has had the benefit of modern science in tree surgery, and now it looks as if it were headed for its thousandth birthday. Some say that it must be from four to six hundred years old. At any rate, it is the last of the Liberty Trees of the Revolutionary War.

In this ramble you must have already noted an astonishing

number of magnificent old brick mansions, with exquisite white-painted doorways, all in the classical tradition, but no two just alike. You begin to feel the wealth and grandeur of the

TAYLOR STREET, NÉE CARROLL ALLEY

town in the days of its glory. In fact, no other city in America can compare with Annapolis in the wealth of its colonial houses. And, in addition, there are still many smaller, more modest brick dwellings, with gambrel roof and little dormer windows, which also date from the eighteenth century and are older than the grand mansions. These, no less, have an old-fashioned charm of their own.

In all these houses it is interesting to note the fidelity with which the builders followed the architecture of the mother country. Exactly the same homes were erected for the hot, tropical summers in Annapolis as were used in the raw and rainy climate of Dear Old England. But nobody seemed to mind, and the later attempts to provide verandahs were not happy from an artistic point of view.

Among all the houses, big and little, there is one striking feature in common—the chimneys. The style here was for end ones, two at each end of the house. In some, as in the Brice house, on East Street at the corner of Prince George, the end ones stand high above the roof tree, very wide and very thin. In other roofs the chimney sits large and four square. In old Fleet Street and Taylor Street (the latter, by the way, used to be Carroll Alley before it became socially ambitious)—which are now little negro alleys—stand houses with chimneys so huge in proportion to the buildings that they are positively comical. Anyway, it is interesting to see how these large chimneys which rise atop all the old dwellings give character to the whole, such as the spindly smoke-escapes of a modern house can never do. In some of these smaller dwellings, a chimney is very often actually muffled in a great mass of English ivy.

Of course, if one comes from the North or the West, the large number of negroes is evidence of the fact that Annapolis lies south of Mason and Dixon's line, and that here, befo' de wah, there was slavery. There are still ancient darkies who were born in slavery and remember the coming of the Yankees with their blue uniforms, which were known to conceal hoofs, horns, and forked tail. Probably one-quarter of the town's inhabitants are "colored people," but they are not restricted in residence to any special quarter. Instead, they seem to be run in, like chocolate layer cake, on streets and alleys between "white" streets. They are a quiet and orderly people, not given to exceeding the speed limit either in working or walking, but good-natured and polite to a stranger and his inquiries. Some of the colored men that you see are wearing the white uniform of the Navy. Here and there you notice small, brown Filipino mess-boys, also in uniform. All these are on shore leave from the squadron lying at anchor far out in the bay, waiting to take the midshipmen off for their summer cruise when June Week is over.

There was a time when the vessels of the old Navy came right up alongside the Naval Academy wharf to take the "cadets" aboard, ships like the ancient frigates *Constitution, Constellation,* and *Monongahela,* but the modern fifty-million-dollar floating fort has to anchor far out in the channel of Chesapeake Bay to keep from going aground. What is now only an open roadstead, as one looks out from the waterfront, was, in the days when Annapolis was young, a wide, landlocked harbor. The low line of Greenberry Point, visible to the left, marking the eastern boundary of the Severn's mouth, once extended southward, far out into the bay. Even in the memory of middle-aged Annapolitans, there was a lighthouse standing at least two hundred yards beyond where the water breaks today. Similarly, the promontory on the other side, Horn Point, reached far out toward the east, so that when George Washington looked from his window in Governor Eden's house, where he was a frequent guest, he could not see the line of Chesapeake Bay because of the intervening promontories.

FROM SLAVERY TO THE NEW DEAL

This is only one of the changes, though the most striking one, which has come over the scene. The old mansions still sit in massive dignity, even though jostled by tailors' shops or Ye Olde Tea Shoppes, or California bungalows, and they seem to say, "Ah, but you should have seen this town in *our* day." The

LIGHTHOUSE, GREENBERRY POINT, ABOUT 1880

After a photograph

fact is that Annapolis actually looks far better today than it has for a hundred years. But it is true that there was a day when she was a queen among the colonial cities. During the last years of the Revolution, the Continental Congress met here. Here, therefore, came General Washington to lay down the sword he had used with success and honor. And long before those stirring years of the struggle for independence, Annapolis was the center of wealth and fashion. Let's turn back the pages of her biography to the first chapter.

CHAPTER II

THE BEGINNINGS

NATURALLY the birth and early infancy of the city are a part of the origins of the colony. One spring day, in 1634, two squat little ships, high of stern and poop, called the *Ark* and the *Dove,* dropped anchor in the Potomac. They had arrived after a long, tedious voyage from England with the first consignment of two hundred settlers for a new domain in America. Sir George Calvert, the first Lord Baltimore, had applied to Charles I for a charter to lands lying north of the Virginia settlements, but he died before the royal seal was affixed. The grant, therefore, went to his eldest son instead, Cecilius Calvert. In the negotiations with the King, the elder Calvert had left the name of the new colony blank. When Charles asked him what the name was going to be, the diplomatic reply was that he had wanted to use the name of his sovereign, but that, unfortunately, Carolina had already preempted it. He was going on to suggest the name he had invented, "Crescentia," meaning Land of Increase, but Charles retorted promptly that the next best thing to his own name would be that of the Queen, Maria Henrietta, and so it became Terra Mariae, or Maryland in plain English. Thus the King preserved the commonwealth from having to labor to this day under the name "Crescentia."

The first settlers in the *Ark* and *Dove* went out under Cecilius Calvert's brother, Leonard. Most of the leading men in the passenger lists of these vessels were Catholics, for the Lords of Baltimore were of that faith, and the main inspiration of the colony seems to have been the desire to establish a refuge where English Catholics might escape persecution. And there were priests among them, also, in order that they might not lack the rites of the church in their wilderness home. But most of the yeomen —the artisans, farmers, and others—were Protestants. Of course, it would never do, with the temper of England as it was in those days, to establish a Catholic colony in the New World, and in order to protect their co-religionists the Calverts had the wisdom to found a commonwealth which should be distinguished by the toleration of all creeds. In fact, it was the first of the American colonies to establish this principle. Incidentally, the Calvert expedition marked the third permanent settlement on the coast, the other two being Virginia and Massachusetts.

After some preliminary exploration and peaceful dealing with the Indians, Leonard Calvert entered the "river," or inlet of the bay (still known by the name he gave it as a devout Catholic, "St. Mary's"), and laid the foundation of a settlement on the east bank, which he called "St. Mary's City." Perhaps, too, these names did graceful homage to the patron saint of the Queen for whom the new colony was officially Terra Mariae.

There is a striking contrast between the early history of Maryland and that of Virginia and Massachusetts. In this colony there was no such harrowing tale of suffering as clings to the story of Jamestown and of Plymouth. There were no Indian massacres, no famines, no epidemics. The aborigines seem to have given comparatively little trouble. The worst problem that Leonard Calvert had to face in organizing his brother's colony was stirred up by some of his English neighbors in Virginia.

One William Claiborne, an official of the Virginia government, had, before the arrival of the *Ark* and the *Dove,* started a trading post as his own private speculation on Kent Island in the upper Chesapeake, squarely inside the boundaries of the land granted to the Calvert family by Charles I. Despite the King's grant, he was for years a thorn in the flesh. For a while he was in open and armed rebellion against Leonard Calvert, who was not able to establish his brother's authority until after four years of bickering.

The turbulent state of England in the quarrel between King and Parliament naturally had its echoes in Maryland. The Lords Baltimore, as Catholics, had a dangerous course to steer with the rising tide of Roundhead power in England. In 1648 the Proprietor appointed a Protestant as Governor of the province, and in the following year, the same in which Charles was executed, the famous "Toleration Act" was promulgated. This offered protection to all of any faith who could claim to be "professing to believe in Jesus Christ." Under the kindly shelter of the Calverts all sorts of sects flocked into Maryland, including the Puritans. These latter were not characterized by gratitude for the hospitality they enjoyed under a Catholic Proprietor, for, encouraged by Parliamentary success against the Crown in England, they took up arms against the Calverts. And William Claiborne, who seems to have been a perennial nuisance, joined with them.

A number of these Puritans, driven by persecution out of Virginia, had settled on what is now called Greenberry Point, on the eastern boundary of the Severn, just opposite the site of Annapolis. They called their village "Providence." Scarcely had they planted their settlement when they defied the authority of the "papist" Proprietor by refusing to take the oath of fidelity, and held out for several years. In 1655, Governor Stone went after them with an armed force. The Puritans were in no mood to submit. As a certain contemporary, Samuel Butler, wrote of the sect, they

> Compound for sins they are inclined to
>   By damning those they have no mind to . . .
> And prove their doctrine orthodox
>   By Apostolic blows and knocks.

There was no doubt about their apostolic blows and knocks on this occasion. The two forces met on the south shore of Spa Creek in mortal combat and the Proprietor's forces were routed. Practically all of the little band was captured, including Governor Stone himself. The gentle leader of the Puritans planned to shoot all his prisoners—doubtless as enemies of the Almighty—but was finally dissuaded, after executing four. This, by the way, is the only battle on record in the immediate vicinity of Annapolis. All the other wars in American history surged around it without touching it.

Claiborne and his Puritan allies did succeed in upsetting the government of the colony for a while, but the neighboring Cavaliers of Virginia, unwilling to see Roundheads not only defy but actually overthrow the government of their neighbors who were loyal to the King, came to the rescue. Soon afterward, Cromwell's soul was wafted away somewhere in a great gale, and back to power came a Stuart king. This fact dampened the ardor of the cantankerous Puritans still further, and the province had a chance to quiet down.

Oddly enough, in later years, when King William set up the

Church of England as the established church for the colony, the Puritans made common cause with their old enemies, the Catholics, against the King's policy. Meanwhile, these godly settlers of Providence had been annoyed by the Susquehannock Indians, who were being pushed down on the bay by their enemies to the north. To straighten out this situation the whites negotiated a treaty with the tribe in 1652. This is the one which has already been mentioned as being signed and ratified under that Tulip Poplar tree which is now on St. John's campus, but at that time was doubtless in the heart of the forest.

Meanwhile, St. Mary's City was not thriving conspicuously. Apparently it was not as well located for a shipping center of tobacco as it needed to be. But in the thirty years following the accession of Charles II the colonists near the mouth of the Severn River were increasing. By 1650, the district was populous enough to be made a county, which was named after the recently deceased wife of the second Lord Baltimore, Anne Arundel, daughter of the Earl of Arundel. Gradually, the Puritan settlement of Providence disappeared in favor of a more convenient site on the western side of the mouth of the Severn. This was known by various names, "Severn," "Proctor's Landing," after an early inhabitant, and "Anne Arundel's Town," or "Anne Arundel Town upon the Severn." The foot of Duke of Gloucester Street where the bridge to Eastport begins, is still known as "Proctor's Point."

Because of its fine harbor, it steadily grew in importance as a shipping port. In 1683, the Maryland Assembly passed an act making Anne Arundel's Town the residence of various important officials connected with the export of tobacco, such as the "Naval Officer," who collected the duties exacted by Lord

Baltimore, and the "District Collector," and the "Deputies for the Dispatch of Shipping," or "King's Collector of Customs," who levied the taxes of the King. This was a great help to the little settlement. It may be noted that the complexion of Anne Arundel's Town was still distinctly Protestant, although the Puritan element had no longer the upper hand. The ancient Providence had disappeared.

When the "Glorious Revolution" of 1688 threw out of England James II, with his suspected Catholic leanings, the prospects again looked squally for the Calvert family and their domain. As early as 1674, the citizens of Anne Arundel's Town had offered their city as a site for the capital of the province and now there was a special reason for a transfer from St. Mary's City. The Dutch King William, who had his hands full with enemies at home and abroad, was glad to make a firm friend in the colonies wherever he could, and, of course, he allied himself with the Protestant element of the Maryland colony. He took the land away from the Calverts and made it a royal province like its neighbor, Virginia, and three years later appointed a governor of his own, Francis Nicholson.

The new Governor, in 1694, promptly moved the seat of government from Catholic St. Mary's to Protestant Anne Arundel's Town. Two years later, Princess Anne of Denmark—later Queen Anne—was waited on by the secretary of the province, "to request," on its behalf, "her gracious acceptance of the Governor's and Country's dutiful Respects in having denominated the Metropolis of the Province there but lately built from her Royal Highness' Name." Anne was very gracious about the compliment, and though she might have been surprised if she had seen what was "denominated the Metropolis of the Province," she showed it many kindnesses.

The new Governor, Francis Nicholson, was the real father and founder of this little capital. Under his hand, a new beginning was made by a city plan, the one whose vestiges still remain, as noted in the introductory walk about the town. There is a tradition cherished by the Davis clan in America that it was a Davis who drew up this plan for the Governor. A large circle, 538 feet in diameter, on the crest of the highest elevation, was selected for the seat of government. There the "Stad House" was to be erected, with other government buildings. Nicholson built the little brick edifice on the present State House grounds, which is known as the Treasury Building, and laid the foundation of a State House. This little Treasury Building served the early legislature until such time, in about 1697, as the State House was completed. The year following the moving of the capital to Annapolis, however, the provincial assembly was held in Major Dorsey's house, a large brick dwelling still to be seen on Prince George Street, and known nowadays as the "Marchand House." At the close of the seventeenth century Major Dorsey seems to have been the leading citizen of Annapolis.

Not only was each section of the town laid off for residence of gentry, of tradesfolk, shops, warehouses, and wharves, but special industries were told where they could operate, such as brewing, dyeing, tanning, and the like, in order that they might not offend the noses of the genteel. Indeed, Annapolis must have been one of the earliest examples in America of city planning with zoning ordinances.

It needed only the transfer of the capital from St. Mary's to start the town ahead on a rapid rise toward wealth and eminence, not merely in the province of Maryland, but also among all the colonies. The shipping of the Chesapeake naturally was centered at Annapolis, so that it became the chief place of export of the tobacco for all the Maryland plantations. The modest wooden dwellings that were typical of the town in its earlier day gave way to more pretentious ones of brick, though brick houses were by no means unknown before the town became the capital. Curiously enough, Governor Nicholson, in laying out the handsome estate for himself and future governors of Maryland, between State Circle and the harbor, built thereon a mansion of wood rather than of brick, a house that survived until 1870. But this did not set the fashion. Practically all the other important dwellings of the end of the seventeenth century, and throughout the eighteenth, were built of brick.

It is frequently said that the bricks used were "brought from England," but the opinion of the authorities seems to be that very little was imported. The term "English brick" meant a certain type of brick, a particular size and shape as distinguished from the "Dutch," rather than material brought from the Old Country. Indeed, the soil of Anne Arundel County contains excellent brick clay. By the way, it is pleasant to note that Mistress Anne Arundel, Lady Baltimore, though deposed from the title of Anne Arundel's Town, still has named in her honor the county in which it stands.

Besides his city planning, including a site for both Church and State House, Nicholson, in 1696, inaugurated a free school. This was called in honor of his liege lord, "King William's School," and the Governor headed the subscription list for founding the institution. This was the same Francis Nicholson who, as Lieutenant-Governor of Virginia two years before, had founded William and Mary College in Williamsburg and con-

THE WALTON HOUSE

From the Garden

tributed £300 out of his own pocket for the purpose. He seems to have had a genuine interest in colonial education.

According to tradition, the new school was first housed in the old brick building on Francis Street, once called "Kentish House," but now known as the "Walton House," from its present owner. Thence it moved to a new brick structure to the rear and west of State Circle. Apparently this was a compact affair, lodging the schoolmaster and his family upstairs and accommodating the classes on the ground floor. This school has long since vanished, but the little curvy lane on which it stood last still bears the name School Street. It started off with a great air, despite its humble surroundings, for its first Chancellor was no less a personage than the Archbishop of Canterbury.

King William's School for Boys later became chartered as St. John's College in 1784, after the Revolution had come to its end. During the Revolution it is said that the schoolhouse was used for a gun shop. Meanwhile, nearly all the famous Annapolitans who were leaders in Maryland affairs down to the Revolutionary War learned their "amo, amas, amat" in this little school.

This early temple of learning cannot be dismissed without the story of a certain William Workman, the son of a butcher in England, who came to Maryland as an indentured servant, and died one of the wealthiest men in the colony. On serving out his time, he received his fifty acres of free land, but instead of pinning his destiny to the tobacco leaf he established a neat smuggling business on Kent Island, and sold to his smugglers strong drink at a handsome profit. Governor Nicholson evidently had his suspicions of the chief source of Workman's fortune, and when he inaugurated King William's School he summoned the said Workman and extracted from him £150 for the same worthy cause. While it doubtless hurt to part with that sum, Workman did not dare refuse. It is a pity that more "malefactors of great wealth" were not drafted in later years to

THE SANDS HOUSE

help the daughter institution, St. John's College, which has desperately needed funds, "tainted" or otherwise, for the entire one hundred and forty years of its life.

Even in this brief summary, it is easy to realize that Governor Francis Nicholson was an official who regarded his post as no mere sinecure, but set his mark both on the new capital and the entire province by his wisdom and initiative.

Of the relics of Anne Arundel's Town, there are still a few surviving. What generally is regarded as one of the oldest dwellings is the Jonas Green house on Charles Street. Here was published the famous *Maryland Gazette,* the first newspaper in Maryland and a storehouse of contemporary history.

Another dwelling, said to have been built about 1680–1685, stands on lower Prince George Street, a quaintly shaped structure called the "Sands House." To the same year is credited the "Dorsey House," already mentioned; and the "Kentish" or "Walton House," noted above as the traditional starting place of King William's School, is given the date of 1696. Modest as this seems now, in its day it ranked among the most imposing edifices in Annapolis, being one of the very few built of brick.

Accordingly, aside from the old Treasury Building—whose date seems to be uncertain but which is commonly ascribed to 1696—Annapolis still boasts a few seventeenth-century houses which are used as dwellings to this day. Naturally, in a span of over two centuries, changes have been made both outside and in, but not enough to destroy their character as relics of their age.

Of the people who made up the population of Annapolis at the turn of the century, despite the fact that a Catholic English noble had been permitted to set up a proprietary colony as a refuge for English Catholics, probably by the year 1700 Catholics and Church of England communicants did not compose altogether more than a quarter of the population of the town. Of these inhabitants, practically all were associated in one way or another with the tobacco industry. Wages, salaries, and fees were for a long time paid in tobacco. When a ferry was started across the Severn River, the ferryman's annual salary was given in pounds of tobacco.

The town was not the important unit then, but the plantation.

The roads were primarily waterways. Down to the creek landings were rolled the hogsheads of tobacco along rough ways, called "rolling roads." There, at the water's edge, they went on board small vessels that conveyed them to the wharves of Annapolis for shipment overseas. The industry made work for

THE OLD TREASURY BUILDING

skilled artisans on the one hand, and unskilled black labor on the other.

Among the whites there was a special class, the indentured servants. These men and women contracted to work out their passage money by labor, without pay, for five or six years for some planter who had bought them from the shipmaster. It really was a form of slavery, except that the men and women entered into the bargain for the most part of their own free will, and the terms of servitude did not exceed five or six years. Ship captains were glad to sign up skilled and healthy specimens on which they made tremendous profits at the end of the voyage. When the term of service was worked out, each man and woman was allowed by law an outfit for beginning life on an independent basis. The men received fifty acres of land, an ox, gun, etc., and the women a "skirt and waist coat of penistone, a blue apron, a linen smock, two linen caps, shoes and stockings and three barrels of Indian corn." With these she was certain to get a husband, not a difficult thing to do in those days.

Among these bondsmen and women were some convicts whom it was cheaper to send out of England than to support in jail. Readers of Defoe's *Moll Flanders* will remember that Moll was sent to Virginia in commutation of a prison sentence, and crossed the bay to Maryland, but since in those days almost everyone whom we call a felon now was hanged on conviction, these unfortunate exiles were mostly victims of the debtor's laws, or brave and independent souls who stood up for their religious or political views at a time when it was dangerous to do so. Among the latter were Scotsmen who had followed Bonnie Prince Charlie, a considerable number of whom were shipped to Annapolis. Thus the *Maryland Gazette* advertised on July 28, 1747: "A number of rebels imported in the ship *Johnson* into Oxford (Maryland) are brought over here and are now for sale." The descendants of these men and women out of the prisons fought and died under Washington and DeKalb, and there is no disgrace in counting them among the first families. A tragic circumstance connected with the coming of these convicts was the fact that they brought "jail fever"—typhus—with them and spread death wherever they were sent. In that famous deportation of Acadians, known to mȯst people through Longfellow's "Evangeline," nine hundred of these unhappy people were dumped into Maryland. Many of them perished. It would be interesting to know how many of them made a footing in Annapolis.

The indentured servants included a considerable number of impecunious tutors. Even in those days the teaching profession was not one of gilded security, and many a younger son of a younger son who had had a good education found himself with nothing to eat. He, too, on some particularly hungry day, would sign up with a ship captain and take his chance of making a livelihood for himself in the New World.

Of course, the hard labor on the tobacco plantations was done by the black slaves, though it has been said that these negroes, as a rule, received better treatment than the bondservants or the convicts. In the seventeenth century these slaves must have been poor brutish savages, but lately kidnaped from their Congo jungles, unable to speak the language of their masters and a stranger to his tools. There were complaints in these days by the planters about the hopelessness of trying to make useful servants out of these newly imported negroes.

Of the white freemen there were some artisans, innkeepers, tradesmen, but mostly small farmers, clearing and cultivating their own tracts of wilderness. The planter class, with large holdings of land and slaves to work them, were rapidly advancing toward wealth, and even luxury, on the export of tobacco.

To return to Governor Nicholson. Among his public-spirited

acts was the foundation of the first church edifice on Church Circle in 1699. Thomas Bray, who arrived in Annapolis in 1694 —when it was still Anne Arundel's Town—as the representative of the Bishop of London, established the first public library in the American colonies. For this purpose he succeeded in obtaining from Princess Anne a subscription of four hundred pounds. This library was primarily for the education of the Maryland clergy. At the time it was the largest collection of books in the colonies. Some of these ancient tomes still survive in the college library at St. John's. Here are a few of the titles:

Dialogus Theologico—Astronomicus
Cogitationum Rationalum de Deo
Anatome Arminianismi
Opera by Gregory the Great
Comment on Epistles (Latin)
On Apocalypae (Latin)

These suggest that most of the reading matter was not light and popular, but happily there were also some volumes of the *Gentleman's Magazine*. Oddly enough, it was over two hundred years before Annapolis could boast another public library. Perhaps this first one was too much!

When the original charter was made out to Lord Baltimore by King Charles, the latter stipulated that the Proprietor was to "yield unto Us, our heirs and successors, Two Indian Arrows of those parts, to be delivered at said Castle of Windsor, every year, on Tuesday in Easter Week; and also the fifth part of all Gold and Silver Ore which shall happen from time to time to be found within the aforesaid limits." Those two arrows—one wonders where the collection is now—were doubtless regularly delivered to Windsor Castle, but not a grain of silver or gold ore ever arrived to enrich the royal treasury. In this respect, Terra Mariae was a great disappointment, as Virginia had been, but the tobacco plant in both colonies meant much more in wealth to colony and homeland alike than the silver and gold which Mexico and Peru had brought to Spain. And Annapolis, as the port from which most of this Maryland tobacco was shipped, thrived apace. By 1700, this "metropolis" boasted the staggering number of "forty dwellings." In 1708, the capital put on the dignity of a corporate charter, with all the pomp and regalia of a regularly organized town government. Unhappily, in 1704, Governor Nicholson's new State House went up in flames and very important early records went with it. But another was started at once. In 1715, George I of England gave back to the Calvert family the proprietary rights to the colony which King William had taken away, so that the fifth Lord Baltimore became once more the overlord of Maryland. By this time the family had diplomatically changed to the Protestant faith, a circumstance which made the restoration much easier.

This final date fairly launches the little town into the eighteenth century, and finds it well started on its way to the wealth and distinction that in another generation made it one of the most important cities in all the thirteen colonies.

CHAPTER III

THE GOLDEN AGE

IN 1708, one Ebenezer Cooke published in London a satirical poem, entitled the "Sot-Weed Factor." "Sot-Weed" was the current slang for tobacco, and "factor" was the word for the sales agent. This piece of verse was a take-off on the Maryland colony. Cooke knew the scene, for he was a resident there for a number of years, being no less than the "Deputy Receiver to the Right Honorable Charles, Fifth Lord Baltimore." He signed himself "Gent.," to be sure that there was no mistake on that score, and added frequently to his signature the title "Laureate." He claimed that Lord Baltimore had officially appointed him poet laureate for Maryland, and, if that is the case, Ebenezer is the only such official bard in American history. His father owned an estate on Eastern Shore, and a low, narrow promontory at the mouth of the Choptank still bears the name Cooke's Point. His description of Annapolis at the beginning of the eighteenth century is not beguiling. According to his poem, he found the houses few and leaky, and the citizens addicted to strong drink.

Governor Nicholson was, in a way, a professional colonial administrator, whose career from 1686 on took him to various parts of the Atlantic seaboard. Before coming to Maryland he had been Lieutenant-Governor of Virginia and had known what life was like in the little provincial capital of Williamsburg. But no doubt he had many a discouraging moment in the days when he was trying to establish his new capital for the Maryland colony. Perhaps it is just as well that he had no wife to suffer the discomforts of life in the early days of Annapolis. The dry weather of midsummer must have blown clouds of dust into the gubernatorial mansion, and wet days, especially during the winter and spring, meant red, sticky mud whenever one stirred from the doorstep. There was also the plague of flies, and another one of mosquitoes, from the marshes of the Chesapeake inlets. These were no respecter of persons and tormented people of quality as well as carpenters and brick-layers. And the intense heat of an Annapolis summer, though no worse perhaps than one in tidewater Virginia, must have made the Governor sigh for the cool weather of his home shire in England. No doubt his huge and elegant full-bottomed peruke, or "periwig," rested on a peg the goodly part of the summer months, and his long-skirted, brocaded coat must have been hung up, too, for these items of a gentleman's dress, which were tolerable in England, must have been unbearable in Annapolis from June to October.

The Governor was a forceful personality. His habits have been described by a censorious biographer as "profligate," but his two ruling passions were his devotion to the Church of England and his interest in education. He had a volcanic temper which blew off its crater every now and then, making his administrations stormy with quarrels, but, on the whole, his four-year term in Annapolis seems to have been the most peaceful and the most constructive of his career.

He seemed to like the work, in spite of the discomforts of living and the opposition of deputies and councillors. After Annapolis, he was sent back to Virginia, thence to Acadia where he saw military service as well, and back South again as Governor of South Carolina. On the whole, it may be said that Nicholson well earned the knighthood conferred on him in 1720.

No doubt Governor Nicholson's vigorous hand had much to do in that early period with the speedy growth of Annapolis. Also, for half a century there was peace in the land. The population and the volume of trade increased so rapidly that by the middle of the eighteenth century the village of forty dwellings had become one of the most important cities in all the thirteen colonies. The years between 1750 and 1775 may be called its Golden Age.

During this quarter-century Annapolis was not only important as a tobacco shipping port, together with its suburb, London-Town on the South River, but it was perhaps the very smartest. Here the nabobs of the tobacco plantations built their splendid town houses, in which they spent the winter months from early November to the beginning of warm weather. In those days there was no trouble about finding a market for their tobacco. No one had yet heard the word "overproduction." The merchants of London took all that the colonists could send. The profits were large and living was cheap. Game, fish, oysters, terrapin were apparently inexhaustible and easy to obtain, and not even the poorest, if he had a gun and fishing rod, needed to worry about feeding himself and his family. As for the wealthy, they lived on a plane of elegance that might have been envied by many of the British nobility. The "factors," as agents of the planters, did their shopping for them in London, and whether it was a pair of silver buckles or a table service costing a hundred guineas, it was all the same to the man whose wealth came so easily from his fields. Ship captains who brought furniture from London on speculation charged double the cost price in Annapolis, and advertised such a rate as a bargain for cash down.

There was no income tax in those days; nobody thought of rich men as "malefactors of great wealth"; nobody cursed them as "capitalists," for Karl Marx was still a century away. No wonder they walked the streets with their heads high and affected great anguish if their Madeira or port was not to their taste.

The connection between Annapolis and London in those years of the middle eighteenth century, and after, was very close; that is, as close as the bluff-bowed sailing ships could make it. The ladies and young gallants awaited eagerly the news of the latest fashion, together with the samples thereof, sent back by the faithful factor. It would never do to appear at an Assembly Ball in a dress without "panniers," when that was the proper costume for every lady of quality in London. And the "macaroni" hastened to have his sleeves cut down to the new mode and to change the shape of his wig for the same reason. Tailors and wig-makers and hair-dressers had plenty to do in eighteenth-century Annapolis.

Beside the constant exchange of tobacco for the luxuries and styles of London, there were arriving frequently the various officials connected with Lord Baltimore's government. These gentry came fresh from Vauxhall to impress what they were pleased to regard as the savages of the wilderness—"Colonials," a term of patronizing contempt, then as later. For their part, these colonials were determined that when a new governor and his lady, with secretaries and their ladies, landed in Annapolis, they should have their breath taken away by the elegance of their reception. "Colonials," indeed!

There was still another bond between homeland and colony in the fact that King William's School and William and Mary College in Virginia were not regarded as sufficient for the education of the tobacco aristocracy. After a brief space at the local school a boy was shipped to England to endure the miseries and brutalities of the Eton and Harrow of those days. After that, if he showed promise, he might be sent to Cambridge or Oxford. Then, when he returned, he would be quite the English gentleman and scholar, instead of a raw colonial.

Thus, the life of the town reflected in as many ways as possible all the aspects of life in an English city. Indeed, there was not a community in all Britain of the size of Annapolis which could have shown such splendor of living, with liveried servants, elegant coaches with four or six horses in clinking, silver-mounted harness, the sedan chairs painted with garlands and cupids and the owner's coat of arms where no one could miss it. The broad gardens, too, terraced, lined with box, and gay with flowers brought from English gardens—these, too, must have made the newly-arrived secretaries stare with amazement. Certainly Annapolis did not look like their preconceived picture of a town in the wilderness.

The winter season, beginning with the horse races in November, was one round of dinners, balls, and receptions. In addition to the festivities in the homes, there were fortnightly subscription dances in the Assembly Rooms. Probably not even Bath, in the days of Beau Nash, had a dizzier round of gayety. Indeed, Bernard, an Anglo-Irish actor, once referred to Annapolis as the "Bath of America." Not even the courtiers of

Louis XV had so little worry about their responsibility to society as these colonial aristocrats. Like the lilies of the field, they toiled not, neither did they spin. Often their origins harked back to ancient families in England. Thus they met all the requirements of a landed aristocracy and were supremely pleased with themselves.

For the amusement of the men, there were various clubs. The Tuesday Club was at one time the most famous, a weekly gathering of gentlemen who wrote burlesques about each other and their friends, and amused themselves hugely. Its membership was limited to twenty-five. This organization was founded by Dr. Alexander Hamilton, in 1745, and he wrote its history in highfalutin and wordy style, which was the sort of nonsense in vogue during the eighteenth century. For example, the handshake was referred to as "manuquassation." From these pages of his may be discovered the sort of fun that went on. Jonas Green, the publisher of the *Maryland Gazette,* proved so versatile that he was made the club's official "Poet, Printer, Purveyor, and Punch-Maker." The rules forbade anything more elaborate to be served than a "gammon of bacon," to which the members helped themselves, with no servant in attendance. No drinks might be served after eleven, which was the hour of departure.

As an example of the importance of the club, the following petition to its president, as duly spread upon the record, may suffice:

The humble petition and remonstrance of sundry of the single females of Annapolis showeth, That whereas it has been observed by sundry persons as well as your petitioners that a singular and surprising success has all along attended such happy females as your honor has been pleased to pitch upon as the toasts of the honorable chair, every one of whom in a short time after having been adopted by your honour has successfully and happily been provided with a much more eligible state; your Petitioners Therefore earnestly pray that your honour instead of conferring your favors in so partial a manner would in commiseration of our desperate situation include us *all* in the circle of favor that the benign influence of your honour's maritiferous notice may henceforth shine equally upon us all, which benevolent condescension in your honour will have a tendency to multiply the inhabitants of this city as well as better our present condition, and your petitioners shall ever pray.

To the honourable Charles Cole, Esq., President of the most worshipful and ancient Tuesday Club.

The Honourable President was pleased to declare that he would grant this petition as far as lay in his power.

The records contain many crude but amusing drawings, caricaturing the members. Among them is one of the "Honourable Charles Cole, Esq." showing him with a prodigious hooked nose somewhat askew.

The club met by turns at the homes of the members. On great occasions they wore a metal badge. They gave an annual ball to the ladies, and their gallantry required that the first toast of the evening should always be drunk "to the Ladies," even ahead of that to the King. It is an eloquent commentary on the habits of these fine gentlemen that they decided by a formal vote to carry their sand-boxes with them to the meetings in order that, as they spat tobacco, it might not sully the shining floors of their host's "withdrawing room."

Whenever a distinguished male visitor arrived from some

other part of America, or from overseas, he was likely to be entertained as a guest of the Tuesday Club. Such a one was the first citizen of Philadelphia, Benjamin Franklin. The club flourished for ten years, up to the death of its founder and chronicler, Dr. Hamilton. After his passing, the members did not have the heart to go on with it.

In 1770, another club was established. This was clearly inspired by its predecessor but was known as the "Homony Club." Unlike the other, it met regularly in a coffee house instead of the members' homes. Perhaps the simple fare indicated by the name, in its early spelling, was a sign of the greater democracy of the group, for it contained not only men of great wealth, like Paca and Dulany, and a King's official, Eddis, the Surveyor of Customs, but also Charles Willson Peale, the painter, and Jonathan Boucher, the rector of St. Anne's, who was elected the first president of the club.

They were evidently a jolly, congenial group of friends. Unhappily, events were soon to arise which parted them as enemies. Paca was a signer of the Declaration of Independence. Dulany lost his property and fled to England because, like Kentish Sir Byng, he "stood for his King." Boucher was such an outspoken Tory that he preached with loaded pistols on the cushion of his pulpit, defying the "Liberty Boys." Peale was an ardent rebel who painted his idol, George Washington, even more often than did Gilbert Stuart. On account of the bitter partisanship aroused by this quarrel between the King's ministers and the American colonists, the Homony Club expired in 1772.

Still later, there was a "Forensic" Club, whose home on Duke of Gloucester Street may still be seen. This was not devoted

HOME OF THE FORENSIC CLUB

entirely to debate. On the contrary, the wives of the members referred to it darkly as "that gambling den." For although the membership included very important personages of lofty titles connected with the government and the courts of law, tradition saith that these notables used to sit long hours over what was called, in those days of refined language, the "parti-colored gentry." This phrase did not mean, as might be supposed, mulattoes, but simply a pack of cards. In short, to use another genteel eighteenth-century phrase, it was a fashionable temple of the Goddess of Chance.

The most interesting club of the eighteenth-century days is one that still survives. Strictly speaking, it is not within the borders of Annapolis, but in the suburb between South River and Glebe Creek, near old London-Town. This is the South River Club. It remains a matter of debate as to whether this or the Fish House Club of Philadelphia is the oldest club in the country. Unfortunately, the early records of the South River Club were burned up, but the members have evidence to show, they claim, that their institution dates at least to 1722. If the historians accept this, then the South River Club may bear off the palm of antiquity.

At any rate, in 1746, the loyal members sent a congratulatory message to King George II, King of Great Britain and Ireland, Defender of the Faith, and so forth, on the victory of his army over the forces of the Pretender at Culloden. Here it is: "The gentlemen belonging to the 'Ancient South River Club,' to express their loyalty to his Majesty, on the success of the inimitable Duke of Cumberland's obtaining a complete victory over the pretender, and delivering us from persecution at home, and popery and invasion from abroad, have appointed a grand entertainment to be given at their club home on Thursday next." * Let us hope that the King was pleased and quite sober when this involved sentence was read to him. It has been a considerable time since an English King has had the honor of receiving congratulations from the South River Club, but maybe the Club will do so again after a fitting interval, so as not to make the event too ordinary.

The people who composed this group were planters who evidently liked a cozy little meeting-place nearer their homes than Annapolis. The sketch of the present frame structure does not suggest the grandeur of a Fifth Avenue club building, but the membership is far more exclusive. No nonsense about democracy here! For two hundred years the membership has been hereditary, open only to a select group of tobacco barons of Anne Arundel County and their descendants. You may have all the clubby qualifications in the world, you may be the Duke of Northumberland or the Prince of Wales, or His Serene Highness Something Else, but the little wooden door would remain closed to you forever, *unless* you can prove that you are descended from some one of the original members. Or, at least, that is the rule; members do say that on special occasions they have loosened up slightly in two hundred years, but they hate to admit it. A camel passing through the eye of a needle would have an easier gangway than an outsider trying to break into the South River Club. The Tuesday, Homony, and Forensic Clubs are gone with their members, but the South River Club flourishes still.

Out of compliment to their rivals of Philadelphia, the Fish House, a member of the latter was entertained at one time as a special guest. He taught his hosts how to brew the famous

* Quoted from Wilstach, *Tidewater Maryland,* p. 97.

Fish House punch, and that has been served regularly ever since at the South River Club dinners. They say this potion has the quality of seeming guilelessness as it slips down, but that it rises unexpectedly afterward to smite the tippler on the head.

Another perennial form of amusement and excitement was the horse race. The old race-track was a mile straightaway along what is now West Street extended. Probably it began just outside the city gates, which stood about at the corner of the present Cathedral Street. In the days of its glory it drew patrons from long distances. Even Colonel George Washington regularly made what must have been a fearfully uncomfortable journey in a coach from Mount Vernon to attend the Annapolis races and bet his money thereon. Not even Kentucky in her horsiest days ever exceeded the enthusiasm of Annapolitans for the track. Governor Ogle, for instance, was such a lover of horseflesh that he built his stables between his house and the street, and was probably happier in the company of his horses than in any other society. Governor Tasker also was a devotee of the turf, and when Governor Sharpe arrived he also turned his attention to importing and breeding race horses.

Annapolis was not the only place where these races were held. Nearby Chestertown and Marlborough had them as well. But, naturally, it was the Annapolis track which drew the greatest number of visitors, because the town was a gay rendezvous of fashion at that time of the year for the opening of the social season. In Washington's diaries for the years 1771, 1772, and 1773, he records his visits to the Annapolis races. In 1771, he put his stepson, John Parke Custis, to school in Annapolis, under the Reverend Jonathan Boucher, a member of the Homony Club, who apparently had some difficulty in persuading young

Custis to tread the path of learning.

In fact, there wasn't much atmosphere of the library and the university in old Annapolis. The boy's life was mostly outdoors with gun and horse and sailboat. Hunting with hounds was one of the amusements introduced from England as far back as 1650, when the first pack was brought over. There were not many books ordered from England along with the silver plate and the mahogany sideboards. It was a life of action and outdoors, with small encouragement to read or compose. Lord Chesterfield, at this time, defined a gentleman as one who was sure of his Latin quantities and any one who was shaky in that regard was to be shunned as a cad, but the Annapolis young gentlemen worried very little about whether a Latin A was long or short, and they regarded themselves as very fine gentlemen indeed.

Of course, the young ladies, after the current eighteenth-century fashion, learned to tinkle on the spinet and do needlepoint, and assist Mamma gracefully in the drawing-room, until such time as it pleased Providence to bring a suitor who was eligible. There was no sign of the blue-stocking element among the Annapolis ladies.

Nor was the Established Church any special help in the matter of learning, for although certain gentlemen in holy orders were glad enough to earn a little something as tutors to the boys in these grand mansions, they did not live an easy life, nor were they always shining ornaments of their profession. As evidence of what some of these eighteenth-century parsons were like, the following published notice of a Maryland court decision is eloquent: "9th July, 1749, A Mrs. S. C., of Patapsco, was fined the sum of one penny, for whipping the Rev. N——t W——r with a hickory switch; it being imagined by the court that he well deserved it." The Lords Baltimore were not too particular when some influential friend asked them to make a living for some scoundrelly parson who needed to be eased out of England. Some of the Annapolis clergy, therefore, were notorious drunken rogues, men who had to hold on to both sides of the pulpit while exhorting the faithful, and none too scrupulous about their debts. When the great Methodist preacher, Whitefield, visited these parts, he noted what he called a "distressing want of piety." It is quite possible, too, that the gentry looked down their noses at this Methodist revivalist and gave him scant encouragement.

One of the ungodly forms of entertainment that Mr. Whitefield must have frowned upon was the theater. There has been a claim that Annapolis boasted the first "temple of Thespis" in the colonies, but this is disputed by non-Annapolitans. Anyhow, as early as the middle of the century, there were professional companies of actors giving the fashionable plays of the period. These players held forth in Annapolis during the season for as long as the business was good, then moved on to neighboring towns. Just what building housed the earliest drama we do not know. In the smaller towns, such as Chestertown and Marlborough, it seems that an empty tobacco warehouse was adapted for the purpose. But, in 1771, there was a new theater erected in Annapolis, and its stalls regularly were filled with the notables of the town, like Governor Sharpe and his suite, the tobacco princes of the great mansions, and visiting persons of distinction, like Colonel Washington of Virginia. It must have been a curious little building, for even in the best London theaters the faces of the actors showed but dimly before a row of foot-lamps burning spermaceti oil. But, for the colonies, any theater at all was something to brag about. There was an old theater building that survived about a hundred years later, which was torn down to make room for the Presbyterian church on Duke of Gloucester Street. It is quite possible that this was the identical temple of Thespis of the Golden Age.

So far, mention has been made of the amusements of the people of fashion. But there was another stratum of society in Annapolis that did not have sedan chairs, decorated with a coat of arms, or a gilded coach and four when they went abroad. They footed it in heavy boots in all weathers, and their women folk tucked up their outer skirts and clumped along in the rain and mud with their "pattens." The elegance of the *haute monde* was not for these people. They had to work for a living. But they had their amusements and, like their betters, they copied the sports of their peers in London, or Winchester, or York. Bowling was a very popular game. Sometimes in lieu of a neat bowling green they used the dusty street in front of a tavern, much to the disgust of the neighbors and the people who wanted to drive through. Apparently bowls, as played by the yokels, was an hilarious and loud-spoken form of entertainment. Less pleasant to contemplate were the bull-baitings, where a powerful bull was set upon by fierce dogs, and the cock-fighting. The latter was specially popular among certain ones, for it invited no exertion except on the part of the feathered gladiators. It is said that in Annapolis some of the young men of quality from the handsome brick mansions might be seen at the ringside of a "cocking-main," just as in London.

Bloomsbury Square was doubtless the scene of other kinds of fun and jollification as well. Probably some of the village sports of Old England flourished there, like the folk dances, the wrestling matches, and heaving the stone or iron bar, as well as the prime favorite of bowls. But the one form of relaxation, common not only to the poor but to the rich as well, was getting drunk. There must have been an appalling amount of heavy drinking over both the mahogany table and the pine, and if the gentlemen were not ashamed of being carried home drunk by their servants any or every evening, the artisans could not be expected to be any more particular.

One curious sport which was enjoyed by every young man who was at home on his horse was the "tournament." People would gather from miles around on such an occasion to see the youths tilting at rings hung out on high poles. The one who caught the greatest number of rings on his lance had the privilege of choosing his favorite damsel as "Queen of Love and Beauty." All the other ancient sports have died out, but it is interesting to note, parenthetically, that the tournament, which is the oldest of all, flourishes still in rural Maryland. When August arrives each year, it ushers in the tournament season. Politicians make the welkin ring with exhortations to the young men to be Galahads and Launcelots. The perspiring knights charge at the rings, and by evening some freckled damsel is crowned Queen of Love and Beauty. But, alas, Annapolis itself has become too sophisticated and citified. The tournaments are here no more.

The inn or tavern of the eighteenth century was no place for a gentleman to lodge, for it was primarily a liquor shop with a few mean rooms, whose floor rushes were alive with fleas and whose beds were notorious for what the poet might call "the short and simple animals of the poor." The farmer who lodged at one of these caravansaries had no place to sit but in the tap room, and small wonder that when he woke from stupor to start home next morning the market money from his produce was all gone.

Of course, it is very pretty to picture the gorgeous side of the Golden Age, the gay liveries, the elegant costumes, the equipages, and so on, but there was another aspect not so attractive. One feature of it already mentioned was the tippling. And it must have been almost impossible to escape it, for at a formal dinner there was always a long string of toasts which it was obligatory to drink, and alcohol was the social bond for every occasion.

But there were other circumstances, also, not so romantic. If one were to return to the Annapolis of 1770 one would be unpleasantly impressed with the fact that the streets, walks, fences, door-steps were copiously bespattered with the juice of the "sot-weed." Unbelievable as it sounds now, the pews of St. Anne's Church were undoubtedly defiled in the same way. Even a hundred years afterward there were signs in some Southern churches begging the gentlemen not to spit in the sanctuary. Also, there would smite one from all sides most unpleasant smells, as slops and kitchen water were drained or emptied into the street. Sewers and garbage collection were still a long way ahead in the future. There were no sidewalks; only a row of posts to separate the pedestrians from vehicles.

As the gentlemen came along they would look very picturesque in cocked hat and scarlet coat, small sword, and silver buckles; still more, their ladies stepping out of their coaches in billowing satin and high-powdered head-dress with a beribboned hat perched on top. But, on close view, you would find that even most of these fine aristocrats had their faces deeply pitted with the ravages of smallpox. Inoculation was just making headway. For instance, Colonel Washington sent his stepson Custis up to Baltimore to get inoculated while he was going to school in Annapolis. But the older generation had known nothing even of that rough preventive against the smallpox. Washington himself bore pock marks on his face which Trumbull, Peale, and Gilbert Stuart always ignored, like true portrait painters. Practically everyone who did not die of the dread disease came out of it disfigured for life.

Nor was that the only blemish. There was no dental science. When a tooth ached unbearably, you went to the barber or the doctor who yanked out the tormentor with a pair of forceps to the accompaniment of shrieks of pain. Tooth-brushes were still a rarity even among gentlefolk, in 1800. So as one scanned the faces of the passersby one would have been struck by the dreadful teeth, or still more appalling absence of teeth. "Dentures" were yet to come into general use. Washington's set of artificial teeth were the first, or among the first, to be worn in America.

The most distressing fact about these Good Old Days was the state of medical science. A diarist in the last decade of the eighteenth century, who will be quoted in a later chapter, notes with dreadful regularity in one entry that Mistress So-and-So is sick of something. The next day's entry notes that she is dead. Apparently, they did not call the physician in until the patient was at death's door, and then, as the ancient quip has it, the doctor "pulled him through." In the quaint language of that day, it is easy to recognize "putrid sore throat" as diphtheria, and "mortification of the bowels" as appendicitis.

Nor was the treatment of the sick left entirely to physicians.

On one Annapolis shelf, at least, there reposes a book entitled *The Compleat Gentlewoman.* This, of a date two hundred years ago, is a guide for the young matron in all the matters of housekeeping on a grand scale. For instance, sample menus for formal dinners are given, involving sixteen or eighteen courses of fish, meat, and fowl with practically no vegetables. No wonder they suffered from gout! There are many recipes for preparing food and mixing drinks, but a specially interesting department of the book is the medical. Here is an assortment of remedies, most of which have been handed down from mother to daughter from the depths of the Middle Ages. Many of these reflect the medieval idea that diseases were caused by devils, and the best way to drive the devils out was to make their human habitation very unpleasant. It sounds romantic for a historical novelist to write about the "simples" of household medicine in the early days, but these simples are not so nice on close inspection. For example, in *The Compleat Gentlewoman* is a remedy for an inflamed eye, as follows: take the dry dung of a chicken, powder it, and blow it in the eye. For earache the treatment was to take an equally unpleasant substance, warm it in an oyster shell and pour it into the ear. This, mind you, was for gentlefolk. What the plain people did for medicine staggers the imagination. The persistence of these superstitions in the face of progress is illustrated by the fact that nearly two hundred years after *The Compleat Gentlewoman* was published, a dressmaker in Annapolis recommended exactly the same formula for an aching ear in the home of the person for whom she was sewing. She said it was an infallible remedy, handed down in her family.

We find also that Governor Sharpe sent to London a quantity

of dried rattlesnake skins as a valuable gift. Powder made from these skins was supposed to be the best remedy in the treatment of arthritis.

The state of medicine in any other important city of the colonies was probably no better, but those who sigh for the Golden Age, feeling sorry for themselves that they were born into this practical era of bustle and factories and general ugliness, may think twice about wanting to step back again into the eighteenth century. There is nothing to which romance lends such enchantment as a bygone period of history.

Yet it was really a Golden Age as compared with life in other small cities, either in the colonies or in Europe, during the third quarter of the eighteenth century. There had been peace for a half-century before the "French and Indian War," as we colonials called it, caused a slight flurry after the collapse of the Braddock campaign. A kindly Providence had "scattered plenty o'er a smiling land," plenty of food for all, plenty of work for the artisan, plenty of land for the pioneer, and plenty of money for the tobacco planters. No wonder the little capital grew apace. It is true, Annapolis never rivaled Philadelphia, Boston, or New York in population or volume of trade, but she preened herself on being called the "Bath of America," the home of fashion, of wit, of the art of living.

Having briefly sketched what the gay little stage looked like, we shall call up the ghosts of the interesting men who trod the boards both in the leading roles and in humbler parts. Up with the curtain!

CHAPTER IV

BIG WIGS AND SMALL

THE fact that Louis IV became bald early in his life and could not compete with his courtiers in the matter of long locks, which were the fashion in those days, led to his adopting a huge, curled wig. This not only set the style instanter, but condemned gentlemen to the custom of cutting off their own hair and wearing someone else's for the next one hundred and fifty years. During three generations, at least, a gentleman would almost as soon be discovered without his breeches as without his wig. An ancient explorer in North Africa in the late seventeenth century tells, as one of his harrowing experiences, that while being chased by natives he had lost a very expensive wig which fell off in the flight. Since these adornments came high, and only gentlemen who thought nothing of spending ten guineas on a hairy headpiece could wear them, the term "Bigwig" became a convenient word to describe the person of quality and influence as distinguished from poor, lowly wretches who had to wear their own hair.

In the Golden Age of Annapolis history the fashion of huge perukes had given way to smaller and lighter wigs, and by the time the outbreak of war between the colonies and the mother country brought that Golden Age to an end, there were radical young men who were starting the fashion of wearing their own hair, tied behind in a cue or eelskin, which, except for state occasions, they often neglected to powder.

Nevertheless, the term "Bigwig," meaning the man of importance, continued in use for another century and more, and it seems appropriate to use it here.

Naturally, the biggest of the Bigwigs would be the governors, and though many fine gentlemen of Annapolis would have denied them that supremacy, they may well be given precedence here. The first of these excessively important personages to whom the reader shall have the honor of being presented is Samuel Ogle. He was twice Governor of Maryland. The year 1731 found him a gentleman of noble lineage and large wealth but only a captain of cavalry in the British army. In that year the Lord Proprietor made him Governor of Maryland. He brought to his new duties an impressive pedigree, plenty of money, an ardent love of horses, and a pleasant personality. He struck up a close friendship with Benjamin Tasker, that citizen already mentioned in St. Anne's graveyard who was president of Lord Baltimore's Council for thirty-two years. Ogle and Tasker got along with each other splendidly, for the latter was as keen a horseman as Ogle. These two men are chiefly responsible for the fame of Annapolis as a racing center and, incidentally, for the importation and breeding of fine horses in the province.

Ogle was succeeded in 1742 by Thomas Bladen. This gentleman was born in Maryland, and married the sister of Lady Baltimore. He was also the uncle of Ogle's young wife. Bladen had grand ideas of what was due a governor, especially when that official was Thomas Bladen. He bought four acres of land in Annapolis, hired a Scottish architect named Duff, and started a gubernatorial mansion that would make the official homes of the other colonial governors look like mere shacks.

The work went on until the walls were completed and the roof nearly so. Then the Assembly, appalled at the bills coming in, refused to appropriate any more money. Governor Bladen gnashed his teeth, but was helpless. He had the mortification of seeing the work stopped altogether, and hearing people refer to the unfinished mansion as "Bladen's Folly." For forty years rain and snow beat into the ruin, and birds nested in the corners. Nothing was done until 1784. By that year the War of Independence had been won and the State Legislature gave the remains of the building to St. John's College. The work was completed by its trustees and it became "McDowell Hall," the administration building of the college.

Meanwhile, in 1747, Samuel Ogle returned to Annapolis for a second term as Governor. He did not attempt another mansion for a governor's residence. "Bladen's Folly" made that unwise, but he lived in the grand manner, for all that, and in the year of his return he bought a fine town house for himself, one that is still standing at the corner of King George Street and what was then "Tabernacle Street," now College Avenue. Here he had his stable of thoroughbreds, standing, one would think, unpleasantly near his residence. Of course, this house was only for the winter. In Prince George County nearby, he had a country seat, "Bel Air," consisting of no less than 3600 acres, with a deer park of 600 acres and his own private race-track and kennels. His park furnished deer for George Washington at Mount Vernon.

Ogle must have been a very impressive specimen of the British ruling class, especially when he drove up in state in his coach and four, with liveried postilions, outriders and footmen, to open the Assembly. In these latter years he had also the rank of lieutenant-general in the British army. When he stepped out of his coach in his scarlet coat, adorned with all the gold lace, epaulets and medals appropriate to his rank, he must have been an awesome and colorful spectacle for the common herd. Even a modern admiral in special full dress, such as occasionally sheds his effulgence on Annapolis in these days, is a drab and gloomy figure compared with a British general of the eighteenth century.

In 1752 Samuel Ogle died. His successor was a still more brilliant personage, Horatio Sharpe. Two years later, this young bachelor of thirty-four landed in Annapolis as the new Governor, and was welcomed with great ceremony by Benjamin Tasker, President of the Council, who had been filling in the interim as Acting-Governor. Sharpe, too, was an army man, and he also knew and loved good horse-flesh. He slipped easily into the place vacated by Governor Ogle's death, and made himself very popular, at least among the people of quality. (It seems as if the "vulgar herd" never took kindly to even the best of the governors.) At any rate, Sharpe seems to have had a singularly winning personality and also the gift of attracting to himself loyal and devoted friends.

He brought with him two of these in the persons of Dr. Upton Scott, an army physician who had resigned in order to accompany his friend to Annapolis, and John Ridout, his personal secretary. Both these young men rose to high distinction and great wealth, and their mansions are still standing in Annapolis. One of these, the Ridout house, is still in the possession of the Ridout family and occupied by one of his descendants. It was Governor Sharpe who built that superb country home still standing not far from Greenberry Point,

"Whitehall." In every direction, whether it was to check the persecution of Catholics, to improve the conditions in convict ships, or the treatment of the slaves, his hand went out to do good. This man was probably the most tactful, humane and enlightened governor Maryland ever had. But scarcely had he arrived when the difficulties with the French broke out into war, and later the quarrel with the mother country over the Stamp Act put him in the awkward position of trying to keep the peace with his Maryland friends and yet be representative of the home government.

In 1769 he was suddenly dismissed, and Governor Robert Eden, the son-in-law of Lord Baltimore, was sent in his stead. This gentleman seemed at first not to have the winning ways of his predecessor—it would have been hard for the best of men to succeed Governor Sharpe—and he found himself at odds with the Assembly immediately. But he had the best intentions and came to be popular anyway with many of the persons of quality. Like Sharpe, he wanted desperately to reconcile the colonists and the mother country, but to no avail. When the long-gathering storm finally broke, he had to leave Maryland, and one might think that he would never have cared to see the place again; but, oddly enough, he returned to the old scenes after the war was over, in order to spend the last of his days with "His Majesty's rebellious subjects," as Americans were then called. As a matter of fact, he had had close friendships with both loyalist and rebel in Annapolis, George Washington and Charles Carroll on one side, and the Dulanys and Ridouts on the other. Lady Edgar, in her life of Governor Sharpe, calls Robert Eden "the last and best beloved of the Royal Governors." He did not have long to live in his adopted land, for he died in the very year of his return, in the house of Dr. Scott. He was buried in St. Margaret's, across the Severn, and after one hundred and forty-two years, his remains were brought to St. Anne's Churchyard in Annapolis, where, we have already noted, his grave may still be seen.

So much for the governors. There was another Bigwig who flashed across the Annapolis scene for a brief moment like a comet, and made such a sensation that he cannot be overlooked. While Governor Sharpe was laying plans to organize the defense of his province against the advance of the French and their Indian allies, shortly after Major George Washington had been compelled to surrender to a superior French force, Sharpe was deposed from military command in favor of a real general, at the head of a force of regulars; to wit, General Braddock. Everybody agreed that such a man was what the situation on the western border needed. Major Washington meant well, but he was only a green colonial with no military ability, and the men he commanded had never pipe-clayed a belt in their lives.

It was a grand occasion, therefore, when General Braddock arrived at Annapolis early in the April of 1755, with his staff, for a conference. Here was the man who would teach those Frenchmen not to come poaching down the Alleghenies and seizing the Ohio River. Of course, Braddock paid his respects to Governor Sharpe, and there were long consultations between the two men over the coming campaign while the candles burned low and the Madeira in the decanter required replenishing. But, for a whole week, there was also great festivity in town while Braddock awaited the arrival of the other colonial governors. The streets of Annapolis were brilliant with the scarlet coats and white belts of the officers and men of the British regulars, and the young ladies were entranced. For the time being, the stock of the home-town boys fell very low. There were balls, dinners, and plays, and the Annapolis belles and the officers danced and flirted and had the time of their lives generally. Not much of the twenty-four hours was wasted in slumber during that gay week. Alas, most of those handsome young men, before many weeks had passed, were sleeping in narrow green beds beside the Monongahela, where they have lain ever since.

General Braddock called into consultation Major Washington, for he was to accompany the expedition as a sort of aide-de-camp because of his knowledge of the terrain. But he was such a big gawk of a colonial that the General felt rather impatient with him.

Among other items of business accomplished by General Braddock was the purchase from Governor Sharpe of a large coach in which he expected to make the journey toward Fort Duquesne. He was much disgusted on reaching the hill country to discover that the road was so bad that he could not use the coach any further. So he sent it back to Governor Sharpe, telling him to use it until the campaign was over.

While he was at Fort Frederick, Maryland, Braddock was met by Benjamin Franklin, then Postmaster-General of the colonies. Franklin ventured to suggest that the greatest danger to the expedition lay in its being flanked by Indians from ambush, but he was a mere civilian talking out of turn. Braddock wrote back to Sharpe saying that after taking Fort Duquesne, which would hardly detain him more than three or four days, he was going on to capture Niagara. That had the right sound.

In Annapolis, and Philadelphia for that matter, preparations were made for a great celebration just as soon as the post-rider should bring the news that Fort Duquesne had fallen. There would be salutes of cannon, dinners, toasts, a ball, and fireworks.

When the dreadful news leaked through of what actually did happen to that long line of redcoats stumbling through the forest, it caused a shock of amazement, horror, and fear. The entire expeditionary force had been shot to pieces. Braddock was killed. Two-thirds of the other officers also were killed or wounded, with half the soldiers, and practically all the artillery and supplies had been abandoned. What little had been saved from the disaster had been achieved by Washington and his Virginia riflemen who fought Indian fashion and covered the retreat. So these British regulars were not invincible after all!

The Sons of Liberty remembered that story when the regulars came again, brilliant with red coats and pipe clay, but this time not to Annapolis to be wined and dined and kissed.

* * * *

Other fine gentlemen of Annapolis were neither governors nor generals, but the leading citizens. Some of their names have already been mentioned, such as Benjamin Tasker, the right-hand man of every governor during an entire generation and one of two delegates sent by the province to the famous Albany Convention of 1754, which aimed for a closer union between the colonies. Still others have been named as members of the Tuesday Club and the Homony Club. But Annapolis had such unusually able citizens that we must pause, at least, to note a few of them.

The Daniel Dulanys, father and son, had a checkered career. The story goes that the elder Dulany quarreled with his stepmother while he was a student at Trinity College, Dublin, and indentured himself to a ship captain in order to get passage to the colonies. Arriving in Maryland, he was sold, luckily to Attorney-General Plater, a master who soon discovered that his bond-servant was an educated young gentleman. He then proceeded to treat the lad like a son and trained him for the law. Dulany was admitted to the bar, not only in Maryland but also at Gray's Inn, London. Then he married the daughter of his benefactor, in good storybook fashion, and became one of the most influential men in the colony. He was a member of the Council under three governors.

His eldest son, Daniel, did the proper thing for sons of Bigwigs; namely, he went first to Eton and thence to Cambridge. He returned to Annapolis and married the daughter of the biggest of the Bigwigs, Benjamin Tasker. He, too, became famous in the law. Charles Carroll of Carrollton did not like him very much. The two men were later on opposed to each other on political questions, but Carroll said of Dulany that he was "the best lawyer on this Continent." He held his head very high and rather patronized the colonial governor. He filled various official positions in the province, but his chief distinction came with a pamphlet he wrote defending the colonists' position against the Stamp Act. It is said that Pitt made that article the basis of his great attack on the Stamp Act in Parliament in 1766.

But, later on, Dulany stood out against Charles Carroll and the radicals, and when the break came ten years after the

Stamp Act pamphlet was published, he refused to turn rebel. For this stand the man was reviled and persecuted as a traitor. Practically all his vast estates were taken from him. He retired to live in obscurity at Hunting Ridge, near Baltimore, except for one brief visit to England in 1781, and died a proud, embittered old man. The *Dictionary of American Biography* says of him quaintly that "he suffered from ill health and haughtiness."

To this day it is not clear why Dulany should have been treated so badly, for other Tories in Annapolis were protected by special law from abuse during the war. In fact, there was perhaps no other place in the colonies where a Loyalist was respected for his unpopular convictions and let alone as in Annapolis. Perhaps his "haughtiness" deprived him of the friendliness felt toward other Tory neighbors by the Annapolis patriots.

The Dulanys were Catholics. So, too, were the members of another Annapolis family, the richest in all the thirteen colonies, the Carrolls. Charles Carroll, the first, had been granted a trifle of ten thousand acres with the title of "Lord of Doughoregan Manor" in Baltimore County. These old lords of the manor in Maryland and Virginia were disposed to feel that they were lords of creation, also, for they had not only great property but vast powers. They rather condescended to anybody short of the King himself, and many of them treated even that dignitary with scant respect later on.

The Charles Carroll, who signed himself "of Carrollton" on the Declaration of Independence, the son of the first Charles Carroll, was born in Annapolis. He was educated in Jesuit colleges in France, studied law also in Bourges, Paris, and

London, and returned to Maryland quite the traveled and polished man of the world. For a while, before settling in his native town, he took on a large tract of land his father had given him, Carrollton Manor, near the mouth of the Monocacy and took no part in politics until Mr. Dulany started a newspaper argument about a quarrel going on between Governor Eden and the Assembly on questions of fees and salaries for Episcopal clergymen. Carroll had kept out of politics because he was legally disbarred as a Catholic. Now he jumped into the argument in opposition to Dulany, supporting the popular cause against the Governor. From that time he advanced swiftly to his position as the first citizen in Maryland.

He was still in his thirties when his signature went down on the Declaration of Independence. The story that he added the "of Carrollton" to make sure that King George should not hang any one of the numerous other Charles Carrolls by mistake is not true. Ever since he had come back from Europe he had signed himself "Charles Carroll of Carrollton." During the war he served many important missions and it is typical of him that he threw all his influence against the persecution of the Maryland Loyalists, most of whom were cursing him bitterly. A remarkable man from any point of view, he lived to a great old age, always keeping a keen interest in life and the progress of the world. He, who was an ornament of the Golden Age when even stage coaches were rare, lived to be a member of the first board of directors of the Baltimore and Ohio Railroad in 1828. When he died at the age of ninety-five in 1832, he was the last survivor of the Signers, and the most beloved of them all.

There were other Annapolis citizens who signed with Charles

THE CARROLL HOUSE AND ST. MARY'S

Carroll of Carrollton on that famous day. Of the four Maryland signers, three hailed from Annapolis, and the fourth, Thomas Stone, studied law there before going to live and practice in Frederickton. It is something to boast about that three signers came from one small town, but it is only fair to admit that an even smaller one, Newcastle, Delaware, which still has much of its eighteenth-century charm, sent three, likewise.

One of the other Annapolis signers was William Paca. Having married a fine fortune, as so many Bigwigs contrived to do, he built himself a handsome town house in Prince George Street, now Carvel Hall Hotel, and there lived in state. In a very gentlemanly way he practised law. During the uproar of the Stamp Act, he and Daniel Dulany stood as champions together in the fight to have it abrogated. From that time he rose steadily into recognition as a leader of the popular party against the Proprietor, and was busy in public office continuously from 1768 on. He was a good citizen, if not brilliant. One of his less-known acts, but highly to his credit, was his service in behalf of returning soldiers after the war.

The third signer of the Declaration from Annapolis was Samuel Chase. Here was a picturesque, stormy petrel of a man. He was not born a Bigwig, for he was only the son of a Baltimore parson. Nor did he marry a fortune. But as he strode up and down on the streets of Annapolis you may be sure he took no condescending words or snubs from those who *were* Bigwigs. He was a Democrat with a "big, big D." Six feet and more in height, with a huge frame to match, one would think twice before picking a row with him. His face was so broad and red that his brothers in the legal profession referred to him

—doubtless only behind his back—as "Bacon Face."

When the Stamp Act was at its height, Samuel Chase openly rioted with the Sons of Liberty, much to the scandal of the mayor and aldermen of Annapolis, who voted that he was a "busy, restless incendiary, a ringleader of mobs, a foul-mouthed and inflaming son of discord." Not bad for one mouthful. But Sam came right back at these dignitaries by announcing his conviction that they were "despicable tools of power, emerged from obscurity and basking in proprietary sunshine." Not bad for another mouthful. In brief, this man was a born rebel.

After returning from a fruitless mission, together with Carroll and Franklin, to try to win over the Canadians, he campaigned to get the previous instructions to the Maryland delegation changed to a demand for independence. Then he hastened to Philadelphia, riding one hundred and fifty miles in two days, so that the Marylanders should be sure to vote for independence, and put his own name down on the famous document.

Later, during the war, he got mixed up in an alleged deal to corner the market on flour for his own personal advantage. The affair did not smell pleasant at all, and he sank out of sight for a while. But, after the war, Washington remembered that Chase had been faithful to him during the intrigues of the Continental Congress, and, on the earnest solicitation of Chase's friends, appointed him to the Supreme Court where he did admirably for a while. But under John Adams, still more under Jefferson, he made so much trouble with his high-handed ways that he was impeached, though finally acquitted.

Chase set his heart on having a house for himself in Annapolis as fine as any of the most aristocratic Annapolitans could boast, but planned it on so extravagant a scale that he could not finish it, and had to sell. That was typical of Sam Chase.

Two other notables have already been named in connection with Governor Sharpe—John Ridout and Dr. Upton Scott. These, like Dulany, stood out on the Tory side of the argument and stuck to their belief right through the long-drawn-out War of Independence.

Ridout was the devoted friend and secretary of the Governor. He married Mary Ogle, daughter of Governor Samuel Ogle, the young lady whom, it is said, Governor Sharpe himself had hoped to marry. If so, the arrangement did not ruffle the friendship between the two men. When Sharpe sold Whitehall, Ogle bought it for his daughter, and it became a Ridout home thereafter. John Ridout lies there now, by his request, in an unmarked grave.

Dr. Scott, like his friend Ridout, erected a fine mansion in Annapolis, and there Governor Eden died in 1784. Scott built up a fine practice and a high reputation, being called in consultation to everybody. Having married wealth besides, he was one of the exceptionally resplendent gentlemen of the Golden Age. Among his treasures was a brace of pistols, a farewell gift from his old commander, General Wolfe, at the time that Scott resigned to go to Maryland with Governor Sharpe. It is said that Wolfe wrote Dr. Scott to prescribe for his ailments during the Quebec campaign.

Both these men, Ridout and Scott, were born Englishmen, and it is not unnatural that when the break came they refused to turn against their native land. It is sad to reflect how that war broke up the close friendships between these men in Annapolis and such a neighbor as George Washington, who was a frequent visitor in the Ridout house and a close friend of Governor Eden and so many others of the Loyalist group. But it speaks much for the high principles of these Bigwigs that Ridout and Scott and Dulany risked everything they possessed because of their devotion to the King; and Charles Carroll of Carrollton, for example, knew that if the rebellion failed—and how often it came near just that!—he would not only lose all his property but would stand an excellent chance of being hanged as a traitor.

* * * *

To step apart from these fine gentlemen who practised law or medicine, or filled official positions, all in the grand manner, and lived (most of them, at least) like princes, we may meet other interesting figures on the Annapolis streets who may be considered Small-Wigs. They did not live like princes. In fact, to put the matter brutally, they had to make their living with their hands. One of these has been already mentioned as a member of the Homony Club. This was the portrait painter, Charles Willson Peale. His father was a schoolmaster, formerly in Annapolis, later in other parts of the colony, and on his death his widow came back there to live, bringing Charles with her, at that time a small boy. At thirteen, the youngster was apprenticed to a saddler, and for seven years he toiled at the work before he could be released to start on his own. When he became independent he set up his own saddlery shop with materials given him on credit by his former master, and an equally kind loan of money from Judge Tilghman.

But two years later came the Stamp Act excitement and Charles Peale joined the demonstrations of the Sons of Liberty with great gusto. This did not help his business, for all his patrons were Loyalists, and the result was that his trade was ruined. As it turned out, this was the happiest fortune he could have had, for he turned from saddles to painting portraits. He got Hesselius, a local painter, to give him lessons, they say in return for making him a saddle. He also met Copley on a trip to Boston and soon made a name for himself as a painter of portraits. Some friends in Annapolis—probably not the Tories—made up a purse to send him to study in London. There he toiled, like a whole flock of beavers, under Benjamin West, learning miniature work, the grand heroic style of painting, mezzotint engraving, sculpture, and yet finding time to do orders "on the side" to eke out his expenses. In fact, West generously helped him out in more than one tight financial situation.

He was back in Annapolis in 1769, shortly before the Revolution and found many portraits to do, not only in Maryland, but also in neighboring colonies.

Yet there must have been times, as almost all portrait painters can testify, when commissions ran out, and Peale had to turn to some other way of making a penny. Accordingly, in addition to his drawing and painting and modeling in clay, he made and repaired watches and clocks, stuffed birds and animals, and pulled teeth. Besides these accomplishments, he could always turn out a saddle or harness in professional style. But let us hope that he did not often have to resort to these other arts and sciences!

Mr. Wilstach, in his interesting narrative of *Tidewater Mary-*

land, tells of a blighted romance connected with the artist. He painted three portraits of the Tilghman family, still treasured by the descendants. One of them is of Mary Tilghman, and the story runs that while she was sitting for the portrait the two fell in love. Peale, it is true, was a widower with children, but that did not matter with Mary. He was a genius. The *affaire de cœur* did matter, however, to Mary's father. Whether he was the same Tilghman who lent Peale money to start out in trade as a saddle-maker is not told, but anyhow no daughter of the Tilghmans was to marry any mere dauber of paint, and an ex-saddler at that! So Mary was locked up in her room while the poor painter finished the picture from memory, took his money, and passed out of the door as fast as he could.

Peale comforted his heart with another damsel later on, a woman who bore him six of his eleven children—all, by the way, named after famous artists—but Mary never married and lived to an advanced age, always cherishing the romance of her painter lover. At "Cross Coate," the Tilghman ancestral home, you can hear the old lady's ghost, still moving about the house, tapping the floor with her cane, and still looking for her beloved.

Another version of the legend is that it was a stern brother who objected to the match, and that when Peale was sent away Mary ran off and married the county scapegrace to spite that brother. And, as for the ghost, not only does Mary still go tip-tapping over the floors at night, but an elegant, though ethereal, coach-and-four comes whirling up the drive. Perhaps there are other varieties of the story. The rule in such matters is to select the most romantic one and believe it. Anyway, some critics think that Peale's portrait of Mary Tilghman is the best he ever painted.

Peale left Annapolis for Philadelphia about the year 1776. When the fighting began he enlisted on the patriotic side as a private. He fought under Washington at Trenton and Princeton, and saw the rest of the Philadelphia campaign, including that miserable winter at Valley Forge. During this time in the field he made miniature studies of the officers, which later became an invaluable record of the Revolution. And he is most interesting to us today as the painter of Washington, who sat for him for seven different portraits, and many times again for the sake of replicas of these portraits which Peale had commissions for. Once his eighteen-year-old son, Rembrandt, had the honor of painting the Father of his Country, too, an occasion which inspired the Great Man to enter in his diary the quaint remark that he was, that day, "Pealed on all sides." As a grand total, Peale made sixty portraits of Washington, beginning with him as a colonel of Virginia militia in 1772. Gilbert Stuart did fairly well at this mass production, also, by turning out something around forty, but that makes him a rather poor second.

Peale, unhappily, tended to make the eyes of all his sitters too small, but at that it is believed that his portraits of Washington are more true to life than those of Stuart, who never saw the Father of his Country until four years before the great man died. He was then old and toothless, while Peale had known and painted him as a man of forty.

It must be admitted that the artist was afflicted with some of the stagy, heroic style that his master, Benjamin West, thought quite the proper thing, usually with classical vases or broken pillars in the background and a terrific thunder cloud coming up from behind. There is one of these gloomy canvases in the Annapolis State House now. It is a portrait of Lord Chatham, the friend of the colonies, looking extremely embarrassed in a short Roman garment, and reaching out in the gloom as if he were trying to find the rest of his clothes. This was considered the "grand style."

It is true, also, that Peale's horses are none too lifelike. Turfmen, like Ogle and Sharpe, would have laughed at them. His figure poses are often wooden, too, if one must be critical, but for all that he painted a large number of portraits which are a priceless historical record of the Golden Age. Above all, his portraits of the period of the Revolutionary War made him gain the title of "Painter of the Revolution," even over Jonathan Trumbull. He was certainly not a Bigwig himself, but his faithful brush shows what the Bigwigs were like, together with their wives and their offspring. They were so elegant, serene, so perfectly sure of themselves. They look out of the canvas at us poor drudges of this workaday age with ineffable superiority. We feel sure that if we arrived at their doors the butler would order us around to the "Tradesmen's Entrance."

There was another man clever with his fingers, who doubtless knew Peale well. This was John Shaw. In that latter eighteenth century there were born craftsmen who seemed to be able to turn their magic fingers to anything. Paul Revere was such a man in Boston, but John Shaw of Annapolis could have made Paul look like an amateur. At first he worked in partnership with Alexander Chisholm, but set up business on his own in 1776.

No matter what the material was—silver, pewter, mahogany, or steel—John Shaw could do wonders with it. He repaired clocks, he was a silversmith, and he was a cabinetmaker of exquisite taste and skill. Any one who owns a John Shaw desk or sideboard, or chest of drawers, has a museum piece priced in four figures. And Shaw had a sense of artistry about his work. After finishing some beautiful piece of furniture, he affixed, in an inconspicuous place therein, a little metal plate bearing his name. Why not? It was, in its way, quite as much a work of art as Peale's portrait of General Washington hanging in the State House today. The signature, or metal label, was made for him by an Annapolis goldsmith named Thomas Sparrow, who designed it and engraved on it the artist's name. In those days, before the Grand Rapids era, a table, a chest of drawers, or a bookcase was a finely conceived and executed work of art, a "masterpiece."

Probably at first he had difficulty in convincing the Bigwig patrons of Annapolis that his furniture was as good as what the ships brought over from London. But he was able to offer it at a so much lower figure that he could gain a foothold, and later the trouble between colonies and homeland cut off the trade in English furniture entirely. Besides, he was such a handy man! Perhaps you didn't need a new chair, but if your clock was out of order, or if you wanted to have a silver punch ladle mended after some hilarious evening when things in the dining-room got banged about, John Shaw would gladly oblige and do a perfect job. When the new State House was being built, it was he who was selected to make the furniture for the House of Delegates, a prodigious undertaking for one man, but a fine tribute to his reputation. Among other items, while he was on this job, he was paid for making a "Coffin for an Old Soldier," and "6 Spitting Boxes for the Senate."

160 PRINCE GEORGE STREET

Old House, said to have been "Aunt Lucy's Bakeshop"

He had a son, also named John Shaw, who was a close friend and classmate at St. John's College with Francis Scott Key. Father and son occupied the house, 21 State Circle, now the home of the Elks, and easily recognized, for it boasts a "walk," Nantucket fashion, atop the roof. This was once, as may be imagined, a charming gambrel-roofed cottage, but it has been ruined by a brick addition in the rear, a horrendous crime which should never have been permitted.

John Shaw, Junior, was a doctor, and a poet after a fashion. Perhaps it is because of his poetry that he gets a place in the *Dictionary of American Biography,* as his father does not. But if one were to lay a poem of John Shaw (the younger) alongside a secretary or sideboard of John Shaw (the elder), the poetry would look very feeble indeed.

A third master craftsman of the Golden Age, and the greatest of them all, was the architect, Matthew Buckland. It is a pity that architects did not establish the custom of signing their buildings, as painters put their names on a canvas. Unfortunately, we have to depend so much on circumstantial evidence to identify the architects of the Annapolis mansions. We do know for a certainty that Buckland designed the Hammond-Harwood house, but how much else he did is largely a matter of conjecture. Mr. R. T. H. Halsey,* who has made a special study of Annapolis houses, has expressed his belief that Buckland was the architect also of the six other great examples of Georgian architecture,—the Scott, Ridout, Chase, Paca, Brice houses and Whitehall. If the Brice house did come from his pencil, its date must be much later than that of 1740, which is commonly attributed to it, for Buckland was not born until 1734.

* *Great Georgian Houses of America,* p. 12.

At any rate, internal evidence makes that early date impossible because some of the decorations are copied from plates, some of which were not published in London until 1758.

Mr. Halsey's researches have brought to light Buckland's apprentice papers, showing that in 1748 he was apprenticed to his uncle, James Buckland, described as a "Citizen and Joiner" of London. This was followed by a four-year indentureship to one Thomas Mason, as a "Carpenter and Joiner." Mason, a Virginian, who had been studying law in London, returned home, bringing Buckland as a skilled craftsman to assist his brother, George, in building that famous country seat, "Gunston Hall," on the Potomac River. Thus, indentured as a mere carpenter and joiner, this brilliant young architect came to America.

Apparently George Mason was thoroughly pleased with what Buckland did at "Gunston Hall," as well he might have been, and gave him a warm letter of endorsement. The capital of the neighboring province was little over a day's journey away, and thither Buckland went to seek his fortune. His arrival was timed just right for the Golden Age of building as well as of social life in Annapolis, and evidently his gifts were soon given a chance to display themselves. If it is true, as Mr. Halsey believes, that those five patrician town houses and Governor Sharpe's matchless country seat of "Whitehall" all came from Buckland's drawing-board, he created not only the handsomest mansions in Annapolis but also the finest examples of Georgian architecture to be found in America.

His masterpiece is, by general consent, the Hammond-Harwood house on Maryland Avenue. It is said that Thomas Jefferson was so charmed with this dwelling that he sat down on the opposite side of the street and made a drawing of it. Most authorities agree that this house is the most perfect example of its type, and it marked the climax of Buckland's career. Unfortunately, he never lived to see his beautiful conception take form in brick and wood for he died that very year 1774, at the age of forty, shortly after the work was begun. With his passing, the Golden Age of Annapolis architecture came to its end.

The usual story, at least nowadays, is for owner and architect to wind up a job hardly on speaking terms, but in this instance Matthias Hammond, who paid the bills, and they were heavy, had the sense to appreciate the treasure that his architect had conceived. Indeed, he was so proud and so grateful that he commissioned that other craftsman of the pencil, Charles Willson Peale, to paint Buckland's portrait, which for many years hung in the house that he had created, and this portrait is so vigorous and lifelike as to place it among the best things that Peale ever did. It took about eight years to bring this house to completion, and it is likely that Hammond never lived in it himself, for shortly after it was finished he sold it to a cousin of Sam Chase, Jeremiah Townley Chase, Chief Justice of Maryland.

At that time an American architect did not make a design out of his own head. He owned, or had access to, portfolios and large volumes of engravings issued by English and Italian architects. From these engravings he would select—together with the owner—the type of dwelling best adapted to the site, and then modify it with his own ideas until the building became an original creation. This was the way Buckland worked. In this manner, all the finest of the Georgian tradition was transplanted from England, and yet changed for the colonial scene to assume an American character. In the following pages we shall wander about these grand old homes of the Bigwigs in their Golden Age.

Little is known about Buckland in Annapolis except the superb work that he left behind as his monument. Like John Shaw, Senior, he is an artist who was refused admission to the Valhalla of the *Dictionary of American Biography*. What a pity he didn't write some doggerel for the newspapers; then perhaps we should know something about him. For fame has been very kind to the quill-pushers as being contributors to "Early American Literature," but the early American architects seem, somehow, to have been regarded as such small-wigs that they have been ignored. And, no doubt, some of the great gentlemen in his day looked down on him as a mere tradesman of a sort, who had to make a living with his T-square. But we may salute him as a great artist, whose work is still a proud inheritance from a vanished age.

CHAPTER V

THE MANSIONS OF THE GOLDEN AGE

IN an earlier chapter the Irish actor, Bernard, was quoted as saying that Annapolis was the "Bath of America." He was probably thinking chiefly of the life of fashion and elegance which made the colonial city look so gay in comparison with Quaker Philadelphia or Puritan Boston. But Annapolis is like Bath in another sense; namely, that it was laid out consciously in the early eighteenth century and its buildings are all of the Georgian tradition. Of course, there are no such vast and imposing structures as the "Crescent" in Bath, but certainly nowhere else in America was such an array of splendid mansions both in town and country. And, happily for posterity, Annapolis was forgotten when the devouring monster of progress, and his mother, the Industrial Revolution, ravaged other beautiful colonial towns of America. No patrician residences were left to go to pieces in the slums, or torn down to make place for a factory. It is the great boast of Annapolis that more than any other town on this side of the world it preserves examples of eighteenth-century architecture, and among them the finest examples extant. These are also, incidentally, the noblest houses that were ever erected for Americans to live in. This chapter, therefore, is for readers who appreciate such things, those who know that every brick house with white trim, with a classical ornament tacked on here and there, is not "Georgian," and that large white pillars stuck out in front do not make a house "colonial."

There were not any architects in the early history of the colonies. You hear of none until about 1730. Carpenters and "joiners" put houses together out of books of working drawings. In the first third of the eighteenth century a building movement began in Maryland and men started to set up as architects; they went over to England and submitted themselves to a severe schooling. Not only did they learn by heart the classical "orders" and scan the designs of the masters of the Italian and English Renaissance, but they tied on their leather aprons, rolled up their sleeves and went to work as regular apprentices alongside the masons, the stonecutters, and the carpenters so that they

MC CANDLESS HOUSE

should know every practical detail of building, know it literally "from the ground up."

It must have been a gruelling discipline, especially as they had to eat tripe, drink small beer, and sleep with their fellow workmen, as well as toil the twelve to fourteen hours of an eighteenth-century laboring man's day. It wasn't any Beaux Arts course in architecture, you may be sure. But in this hard school they learned their business down to the last nail. An architect, trained as these men were, could fill the place of any workman on the job, and do it better, on a moment's notice. And no contractor could fool him on the quality of sand, cement or wood that went into the building.

The smaller old houses in Annapolis probably date from the period when an architect was practically unheard-of in Maryland. There are a large number of these scattered over town, pretty much of a type, a story-and-a-half cottage, sometimes with a gambrel roof, and usually of brick, with end chimneys. It is very hard to give any acceptable date to these earlier homes, especially as there is much confusion and contradiction among the references, and some claims to great antiquity are hard to substantiate. For example, the Jonas Green house has a tablet on its face set there by the Peggy Stewart Chapter of the D.A.R. to the effect that it belongs to "about 1680." This makes it one of the oldest buildings in Annapolis. In its present aspect the house suggests the dwellings built in town and country during the first third of the eighteenth century. Of course, the little porch over the entry is a very recent addition. It is only to be expected that the smaller buildings have undergone many changes in two hundred years. It would be tedious to catalogue here all of these charming small homes that Annapolitans built in the first forty

JONAS GREEN HOUSE

years of the eighteenth century, but they are a delight to the eye and some of them are sketched for these pages where they can speak for themselves. They were snug, homey dwellings, set, in old English fashion, on the pavement with their gardens and fruit trees in the rear.

Governor Ogle's house on King George Street, built in the seventeen-forties, was very elegant and imposing for its day and it represents the change from the simple homes of the first third of the century to the magnificence of the Golden Age. Possibly the handsome ballroom, with its fine doorway at the side, was attached later. With this should be grouped the Bordley-Randall house on Randall Place, to which is given the date 1737, but which certainly has undergone many changes in two hundred years. Once it had tall columns over its front entrance reaching to the eaves. This house, by the way, is unique among Annapolis mansions because it faces inward upon its own garden, while every other house faces the street, with spacious gardens in the rear. To this same period belongs another old dwelling of the seventeen-thirties, called the "Davis" or "Tydings" house, on the corner of Main (Church) and Conduit Streets, looking very much out of place now in that mart of trade, and rather discouraged, but once standing stately and impressive near the water-front of those days, looking out over the wharves to the anchored ships.

The grandest of all this earlier group is the home of the Charles Carrolls, facing Spa Creek. Here is one huge rectangular building, with gigantic chimneys and innumerable windows, severely plain, but of great dignity—a perfect castle of a house. This was built about 1735, though probably the original building has had additions since. In one of the rooms, Annapolis

DOORWAY, OGLE HOUSE

Catholics used to worship before they were free to have a church of their own. The entire estate is now the property of the Redemptorist Order.

These homes of the seventeen-thirties and forties were impressive when they were first built, but in another twenty years an entirely new style of mansion arose, which not only made the Annapolitan of that age stare with envy, but even in this sophisticated era fills the wayfarer with admiration. These were the homes of the Bigwigs of the Golden Age, and they are well worth our closer inspection. These grand ladies and gentlemen knew nothing about hygiene, or medicine, or plumbing, as has been hinted already, but what glorious homes they built for themselves to live in!

This new aristocrat among houses, with all its beautiful variations, became a type, frequently called "Maryland" or "Southern" colonial, because the Old Dominion built very similar manorial houses during the same period. The type did not change for a house in town or in the country. Briefly, there was one main portion, usually two and one-half stories high, and on either hand projecting wings connected with the main house by covered passageways, one of which led to the kitchen. Pantries were not provided for. The food had quite a long way to travel before it reached the table. The wing on the opposite side was usually the office. Most of these grandees practised law or held some official position in the government, and the office was where they conducted their business in a stately way. Sometimes these wings were flush with the front of the main house, sometimes they projected much farther, and they took a variety of shapes. Rarely, as in the Ridout house on Duke of Gloucester Street, are the wings entirely separate. Apparently there must have been some sort of kitchen in the basement at the rear. The Chase house has no connecting wings, although these were provided for in the original design. There is one small brick structure at one side of it, which may have had originally a covered passageway to the main house. The Upton Scott house seems never to have had any wings. But, in general, this plan of main part and side wings is followed by the whole group of brick mansions, beginning about 1750 and ending with the outbreak of the Revolutionary War.

This is just as true of the great country places, like "Tulip Hill" and "Whitehall" nearby, as it is of the Hammond and Brice houses in the heart of the town. Someone has called architecture frozen music. An architect like Buckland took this "theme" and worked it into many beautiful variations, exactly as a composer does, and it is a pleasant diversion to wander from one of these houses to another and observe what different aspects have been created out of this simple plan. For example, note the chimneys, and the different ways in which these humble necessities of a house are made to contribute to the design. Some, as in the Brice house, are at the gable ends, very high and thin, turning their edges to the street. By contrast, in the Hammond house they are subordinated quietly to the rest of the design and stand up well inside the main house. In "Acton" the chimneys are very important, and are built broadside to the street. Out at "Tulip Hill" they are hollowed out into slender open arches between the flues. And so one could go on calling attention to the varieties in the doorways also. Given the classical theme of pediment, pillars, and fan light, what good fun some of these architects had designing variations on that theme! Even far out in the country one may stray to some obscure old brick house set far back from the road, looking rather shabby perhaps, but surprising the stranger with a doorway of such exquisite design as to make a modern architect groan with envy.

In connection with Matthew Buckland, the observation was made that in his time architects did not worry about creating an utterly new and dazzlingly original design. They recognized, as their patrons did, that there were certain styles—strongly classical, to be sure—that were "in genteel taste." No one but a fool would try to do something better. They made no secret about their reliance on books of engravings imported from England, such as *British Architect and Builder's Treasury,* of 1708, by one Abraham Swan of London; the portfolio of engravings after drawings by Inigo Jones; a *Book of Architecture* by Joseph Gibbs, London, 1728; or those later books by another Swan, dated 1745 and 1758. And toward the end of the Golden Age no doubt there were copies of the designs published by those amazing Scots, the Adams brothers, for the Adams influence is seen in many places. After all, didn't Vergil consciously imitate his master Homer? And as no one thinks of the *Æneid* as a mere copy, so such a man as Buckland made his houses his own, in spite of his adherence to the styles and models of his masters.

Those who are especially interested in old houses and would enjoy studying them all for such details as architects like to note will find tucked away in the Appendix a list of these, with a brief notation about each; and on the town map, pasted on the inside cover, each of these old dwellings is located by a number. But for the general purpose of this chapter it will be enough to select a half dozen or so of the outstanding mansions of the Golden Age and mention some of the interesting facts about them.

W. O. Stevens

THE BRICE HOUSE

One of the finest of the town houses built in the grand style is known as the Brice house, standing on the corner of Prince George and East Streets. The Paca house (Carvel Hall), directly behind it, was built some years earlier. It resembles its neighbor in many ways, but the Brice mansion is a much finer achievement. It was set to face directly south, like the great Carroll mansion on The Creek. Probably there were lawns, terraces, and gardens extending directly to the water, which in those days reached as far up King George Street as the present corner of Martin Street.

Handsome as the Brice house is, it is unhappily now cramped in on all sides. A street cuts across it, on the other side of which stands a shapeless mass of brick, once a chapel and now a synagogue, and representing some of the most distressing features of the era of Grover Cleveland. But the mansion itself still rises with superb dignity over its shabby neighbors. Note the great chimneys, tall, wide and very thin, but flush with the end walls. Notice, too, the exquisite triple Palladian window under an elaborately carved cornice. This window is small but it is a thing of beauty. Until recently, the entire house was covered with a green mantle of ivy.

Inside, this building is noted for the beauty of its carving, plaster molding, elaborate marble fireplaces, a richness of ornamentation in keeping with the fine exterior. Some of this ornamentation is similar to that of Mount Vernon, as no doubt they both came out of the same book of engravings.

The drawing-room is considered especially beautiful on account of the mantelpiece and the cornice. In the library, there is a secret staircase leading to a bedroom above. Probably there were bores in the Annapolis of the Spacious Years, as there are now, and it must have been a great comfort for Colonel Brice, when he heard Mr. and Mrs. Clappertung announced at the front door, to make a quick escape by the secret stairway, doubtless leaving Mrs. Brice to stand the conversational gaff unless she reached this haven first! It is curious that modern houses are not thus equipped. (Will architects please note?)

It is said that William Paca, who built his own mansion in the rear of the Brice house, once lived here. Thomas Johnson, the first Governor of Maryland after the Revolution, and, by the way, a member of the Homony Club, also lived in the Brice house. Here, too, the Father of his Country was entertained as a guest.

Mr. Winston Churchill is supposed to have had in mind the home of the Pacas as the residence of Dorothy Manners, the heroine of his historical novel, *Richard Carvel,* still remembered with pleasure by people of middle age. It is a novel that belongs to that early day in fiction when there actually was a plot, when heroes were still brave and magnanimous, and heroines beautiful and high-born; before the day of hill-billy heroes, degenerate heroines, and no story interest whatever. The author had been a midshipman at the Naval Academy, and knew his scene first-hand. It is in honor of this well-nigh forgotten novel that the Paca house, now expanded in the rear to hotel proportions, is named "Carvel Hall."

The Brice house has a unique distinction among Annapolis mansions in possessing real ghosts. It is said that the last of the Brices was found dead on the floor of his library with a wound in his head. It was not clear whether this had been inflicted by a club or whether the old gentleman had suffered a stroke and struck his head in falling. However, since the negro valet had disappeared, it was believed that he had murdered his master. There is an old legend that from time to time the murder is re-enacted in the old house.

At any rate, it is true that ever since that time various occupants of the old house have reported hearing inexplicable sounds in the walls—as one described it to me, "a regular sort of knocking, something like the Morse code." A few have actually seen the ghosts. One young man, while occupying a top floor room, was astonished early one morning to see a negro walk through the open door of his chamber. He was so amazed that he sat up in bed and stared at the visitor. The negro turned and went out, and the young man sprang out of bed close on his heels. But, as he looked into the hall, there was no one there.

Another resident of an apartment on the ground floor, a professor at the Naval Academy, left his room about seven-thirty on a bright spring morning to go to an eight o'clock class. As he passed the library door he saw an old white-haired gentleman in a black stock and a black suit standing at the threshold. The professor gazed at the strange figure, speechless for a minute. Then, as he looked, the apparition gradually melted out of sight like a mist. "I'm not 'psychic,' " he said to me—and he is an old friend of mine—"I went to bed at ten-thirty the night before, and I don't drink. I can only tell you what I saw. Furthermore, it was in broad daylight." It may be added that my friend's head is as level as a billiard table and his word is unimpeachable. Further, two other recent residents, a naval officer's wife and her daughter, have testified to seeing the same old gentleman in the black stock, though they were reluctant to speak about it.

The skeptical may explain away these apparitions in any way they please. Personally, I here put it on record that though I

THE PACA HOUSE

Now "Carvel Hall," as it looked sixty years ago (after an old photograph)

have not seen them myself, I choose to believe that the Brice house ghosts are as real as its chimneys.

Nor is this the only creepy circumstance connected with this stately mansion. Not long ago the western wing was bought as a residence, and during the process of renovating the walls, a closet was discovered which had been plastered over. As the door was opened, it revealed a woman's skeleton within. The explanation finally arrived at was that once, long ago, it was whispered that there was an insane woman in the Brice family, who was kept in close confinement—for in those days insanity was a terrible disgrace. It is possible that when she died she was entombed inside the closet, so that no one should know of her existence, either in life or in death. But this may be nothing more than conjecture. At all events, the Brice house literally had its skeleton in the closet, and guarded the secret successfully for over a hundred years.

From the Brice house we may wander westward to Duke of Gloucester Street to look at another old mansion. On the way we pass a noble brick structure on Conduit Street which once spread its wings from Church Street to Duke of Gloucester Street. This was one of the homes of the Dulany family. It belonged to Lloyd Dulany, dating, it is believed, from before 1770. Lloyd was the youngest son of the elder Daniel Dulany, of the famous Tory clan, to whom the reader has already been introduced. Naturally, like his brothers, although American born, Lloyd stood by his King, and was so outspoken that he had to leave the country. His house was confiscated, like the rest of the Dulany property.

Lloyd went to London and while there one Reverend Bennett Allen, a drunken, scoundrelly parson who had once been sent by Lord Baltimore to St. Anne's Church as its rector, published a scandalous story about Daniel Dulany. In Annapolis, Lloyd's brother Walter had quarreled with the rascal and given him a richly-deserved caning in the street. Lloyd Dulany promptly challenged Allen on account of the libel on his father and was killed in the duel that followed.

The brother, Walter, led a force of American Loyalists during the war and he, too, lost his property; but in some mysterious way the family kept possession of the beautiful home he had bought from Simon Duff, the architect of "Bladen's Folly." This Dulany residence stood on the point of land at the mouth of the Severn. When this estate became an army post in 1808, the house was utilized as the quarters of the commanding officer, and later, when the property was turned over to the Naval Academy, it became the house of the Superintendent, serving in this capacity until as late as 1883, when it was torn down.

Meanwhile, in the good old days before the Revolution, Washington was entertained here at the Lloyd Dulany home on Conduit Street. The two men were good friends, dined together often, and went fox-hunting in the days when no one dreamed that they would soon be on the opposite sides of a bitter civil war.

For many years after the Revolution, the Dulany house was used as the famous old City Hotel. As late as 1872, an Annapolitan historian said of it that "the rooms are large and airy, and the table constantly supplied with all the delicacies of the season, and a corps of obliging and honest waiters are always in attendance." At any rate, as we pass by the old building, now a Masonic shrine and crowded in by plebeian surroundings, we shall take an admiring look at the handsome cornice and give a thought to the poor exile lying in a London graveyard with a bullet in his breast.

Turning left on Duke of Gloucester Street, and walking on until the wall of the Carroll estate appears on the right-hand side of the street, one comes to the residence of John Ridout, the secretary to Governor Sharpe, who married the beautiful Mary Ogle. This was built in 1755, and of all the homes of the Golden Age this may claim the greatest historic interest. Lord Baltimore came here to visit; Governor Sharpe was so frequent and welcome a guest that a room was built and set apart for him and known as "Colonel Sharpe's room," as it is to this day. To these hospitable walls came Colonel George Washington and his wife from Mount Vernon, and Martha Washington left here her nightcap in token of her intention to return soon and often. The last one she left there is a beautifully embroidered one, which she never called for. Probably after 1776 the Washingtons may have felt that the Ridouts, as Loyalists, might not feel as kindly toward their old friends as in the pleasant and peaceful years that went before. However, Mrs. Ridout was with all the other Annapolis ladies of quality who sat up in the little gallery at the back of the Senate Chamber in the State House and saw Washington resign his commission at the conclusion of the war. And she notes that the General was so deeply moved in making his address of farewell that everyone present was touched to the heart. So she couldn't have felt bitterly, even though Martha never did come again to use that nightcap.

Of this house it is interesting to know that it was seven years in building. Much material apparently was needed from England, and the voyages were very slow. But these were leisurely days. Better that years should pass and the building be done to perfection than that anything should be erected in haste. What would contractors think today of a house built on that principle? Finally, when John Ridout was twenty-eight years old, he walked through the doorway and took possession.

The separate wings of this home have been remarked earlier.

THE RIDOUT HOUSE

From the Garden

The bricks are all laid "head on," or endwise—what the architect calls "all-header bond"—a style seldom seen outside of Annapolis, though "Mt. Airy" in Prince George's county, built as early as 1650, has the same bond. Instead of having the Palladian window in front, the Ridout house has it in the rear, overlooking the garden and the harbor. The unusual feature here is tha instead of nestling under the eaves, as in the Brice house, thi window breaks the cornice to make a "jog" in the roof line.

The gardens of this estate never extended any farther thar they do now. It is a remarkable fact that from 1755 to this da not a foot of the original property has been sold. The owners as might be expected under these unique conditions, have many treasures of the past inside those dignified walls, relics that hark back to the time of the first John Ridout, some of them formerly belonging to Governor Sharpe. Incidentally, the block of three houses adjoining the mansion was erected by Ridout for hi three children, and the entire group may be considered as the Ridout estate.

Looking from the front steps toward the west, one sees over the brick wall of the property of the Redemptorist Fathers and St. Mary's Church, another square house with four tall chimneys. This lies on the next street parallel to the west, Shipwright Street, and may be approached for a closer survey from there. It is the house of Dr. Upton Scott, the physician whom we have met already, the friend of General Wolfe, and the man who came over with Governor Sharpe and John Ridout as the Governor's private physician. The house is now used as a convent for a Catholic Sisterhood, that of Notre Dame. It never was as handsome as the Ridout mansion and, unhappily, it has suffered in recent years. The beautiful old brick has been covered with thick grey paint, shutters have been added, and it is surmounted, like many another old house, with a red tin roof. A long, ancient garden wall has been removed. Inside, the graceful, arched doorways still stand, but it is said that the carved cornices in the rooms were taken down and the ceiling moulding replaced by modern metal. Someone thought he saw worm holes in these cornices and warned the occupants that everything might come crashing down on their heads!

The general plan is simple, though dignified, and foursquare. This is one of the houses that have no wings, whatever, a fact that seems curious, for an office set apart from the main house is just what a physician would need. This house has historic interest as the place where Governor Eden lived for some time after his arrival in 1769, and also where he died in 1784. Eden was patron of the architect, Robert Key, who finished "Bladen's Folly" for St. John's College, after the war; and his son, Francis Scott Key, stayed here during the years that he was a student at St. John's. This young man, author of a memorable poem in later years, was a grand-nephew of Dr. Upton Scott.

The house is pointed out as the original Richard Carvel home in the historical romance, but whether the author approves of that identification is very doubtful.

These great houses, the Carroll of Carrollton, now the home of the Redemptorist Order of priests; the Dulany house, now a Masonic Temple; the Ridout house, still a private home; and the Scott house, the residence of a Sisterhood, compel the wayfarer to do his gazing and admiring exclusively on the outside.

Retracing our steps to Duke of Gloucester Street and heading back to Main, we pass on the right what is left of the famous old Assembly Rooms, as a brass plate tells. Here is the scene of the subscription balls, where Washington often trod a stately measure and then retired to the rear room where the men who were not fond of dancing played cards and had their wine. Lafayette was an honored guest here, too. Owen Taylor, who wrote a History of Annapolis in 1872, and used the most genteel language, refers to these Assembly Rooms as a "spacious edifice." That isn't just the phrase one would think of in these days, es pecially as it houses a fire engine underneath, but for the selec society of the Bigwigs the room upstairs was spacious enough and one would give a good deal to be permitted to peep throug the windows at a subscription ball in the year 1770, at the reel minuet, Sir Roger de Coverley, Russian waltz, gavotte, and th Allemand, performed with stately elegance by the brilliantly costumed guests. The old walls still hum on occasion with th scuffle of dancing feet and the singing violins, but, above all there now rises the wail of the saxophone, and what passes a ballroom dancing might cause the ghosts of Mesdames Ridout Scott, and Ogle to rattle their fans and hoist their eyebrow with scorn. Perhaps, too, it might surprise these ghosts that th colored people have danced here, and a generation ago used t perform their cakewalks in this historic shrine.

The space underneath the old Assembly Rooms is sacred t the fire apparatus of the city. If the stranger walks back to th rear he will see a genuine relic of the Golden Age, the fire pum of 1775, a strange little contraption worked by hand.

Continuing past the attractive little house, once the home of the Forensic Club, we return to Conduit Street, locally pro-nounced "Con-dóo-it." Here we turn back to Maryland Avenue to visit the two most important houses, from the architect's point of view, to be found in Annapolis. Many critics regard them as the finest of their type in America, and, happily, they are open to the visitor.

These are the Chase and the Hammond-Harwood mansions, and there they sit like rival belles eyeing each other across the street and across a hundred and sixty years. The Chase home is he taller. This is the one that Sam Chase started to build in 769 and broke down trying to pay for it. He had to sell it to ;dward Lloyd but it came back into the Chase family again, nany years later, in 1847, and has borne the Chase name ever ince. Once its grounds extended all the way to Prince George treet, but it is now a bit cramped for a proper setting.

It is an impressive structure. Young Henry Randall, himself n architect, writing about it in the early nineties, calls it "as oble a dwelling as this country has produced." He thus turns is back on the rival belle across the street, whom many another over of fine houses would prefer. But, as between beauties, here is no accounting for tastes and infatuations; and since the oung architect mentioned attributed the Chase Home to the lesign of a certain other Randall, one may suspect a touch of amily pride in the selection. But there can be no disputing the act that it is a superbly massive structure. It rises to a full three tories, an unusual feature among Annapolis homes, matched nly by the Carroll mansion. In the original plan, which was ven more ambitious, wings were designed, but these were never uilt. The building follows closely the English manor house of he early eighteenth century. Indeed, architects have noted that ts façade is almost identical with that of Winslow Hall, Buckinghamshire, England.

On the left, as you face the house, you see a long mound. This narks the wine cellar. Sam Chase evidently was bound to have supply against any possible drought. This is arched over by wall made of brick.

The house is now used as a home for old ladies. But the visitor nay enter by dropping a quarter in the right receptacle. As you go into the central hall, you see directly in front of the entrance

PALLADIAN WINDOW, CHASE HOME

From the Garden

fine double stairway, and just above the landing is the most nagnificent Palladian window in Annapolis. The second floor s not for sightseers, but it is worth while to look about on the irst floor. All the doors here are of the finest mahogany, with ilver handles and latch rings. The mantel in the drawing-room s interesting, too, as an example of the ornamental mantels imorted from overseas in the Good Old Days. This particular one hows the Bard of Avon carrying on a flirtation with some atractive females, who, no doubt, are supposed to be Muses. The Brussels carpet of Victorian vintage is getting bald in spots, ut one's eye should rest on other details, such as the ceilings, nouldings, floor-boards, chair-boards, and shutters, especially n the dining-room, which are all carved wood. The astonishing mount of this work in the homes of this late eighteenth-century eriod makes one wonder where so many skilled craftsmen ould be found.

Among its treasures are a punch-bowl and sword belonging to Governor Sharpe, and a clock given by the Governor to John Ridout. In 1888, the building was willed to the Episcopal Church s a home for old ladies by Mrs. Hester Ann Chase Ridout. Her purpose, as she quaintly expressed it, was "to establish a ome for destitute, aged, and infirm women, where they may ind a retreat from the vicissitudes of life."

There are two melancholy incidents connected with the ineteenth-century history of this old house. Originally there vas a large fireplace in the hall, and the story runs that a daugher of the house, Miss Matilda Chase, fell asleep in a chair beore the blaze. A spark leaped over the fender and set her dress n fire. Before she could be rescued, she was burned to death.

The other tragedy was associated with financing the Chase

Home. After Mrs. Hester Ann Chase Ridout had deeded th property for the purpose of an old ladies' home, she came t realize that it needed an endowment. Accordingly, she sent fo her lawyer to come and draw up a codicil to her will, provic ing $200,000. But at the same moment that he arrived ther breezed in a chatty neighbor, and Mrs. Ridout had to ask hin to return the next morning to transact the business. Alas, a seven the next morning, Mrs. Ridout passed to her reward, an thus the Chase Home was deprived of its greatly needed endow ment.

On leaving the old mansion one turns to notice once mor the beautifully designed doorway, unlike any other in An napolis—observe the unique side windows—which is reache high above the street level by a flight of steps. Samuel Chase, a a self-made man, probably liked the idea of being able to loo down on the Bigwigs, especially those stiff-necked Tories, a they passed under his windows.

Shortly after this building was finished, Mr. Matthias Ham mond, as rebellious a Son of Liberty as Sam Chase himsel started his own home across the street. Being a gentleman an a good neighbor besides, Mr. Hammond determined that hi house should not obstruct the view of the bay which meant s much to Mr. Lloyd, then the owner of the Chase house. Ac cordingly, he requested Mr. Buckland, his architect, to devis a long, low type of dwelling. It is said that Mr. Lloyd offere to pay for the wings on the new house so as to avoid makin the house three stories high. So runs the tradition. And Buck land, after first looking over his volume of plates, picked out house of the general type suitable for the site and agreeable t Mr. Hammond's taste. Then he went ahead to modify an

DOORWAY, CHASE HOME

change the original type for the sake of greater beauty. The result is the finest, or one of the finest, of Georgian homes in America.

Some few years ago, Mr. R. T. H. Halsey, formerly of the staff of the Metropolitan Museum of Art in New York City, came to Annapolis as a member of the faculty of St. John's College and was most active in the work of restoring this house as a museum of the Golden Age, for which purpose the College had purchased it. For a while, thanks to the friends whom Mr. Halsey was able to interest, the old mansion was resplendent again with priceless furniture, and in the place of honor hung once more Peale's portrait of the architect, Matthew Buckland. But evil days came upon the project. All the beautiful antiques are gone, the walls and floors are bare as a barn, and a treasure has been lost to Annapolis and all visitors thereto. But still one may enter by means of getting the key from a neighbor. As I was risking my neck to get a view of the house through the great clumps of box in the rear, I was accosted by a colored domestic in the adjoining yard with the welcome query, "Does you want to git inside de house?"

"I does," was my prompt reply, and thus at the cost of two bits was enabled to wander upstairs and down through the old mansion. The "office" wing is now most appropriately the headquarters of the Company for the Restoration of Colonial Annapolis, and perhaps the time may return when the main residence will again be utilized as a treasure house of Colonial and Revolutionary antiquities. Or, as has happened in the country seats, such as "Whitehall" and "Tulip Hill," perhaps someone with funds and a reverence for the past may buy and occupy it again as a home.

DOORWAY, HAMMOND-HARWOOD HOUSE

The front of the house speaks for itself with grace and charm, rather than the austere dignity of the Chase Home opposite. The interest is centered in the beautiful doorway. Over it is a fine window, and in the pediment above is an ornate round window. On either hand are the wings. The one on your right, as you face the house, is the kitchen, which has been restored to its original appearance, with its ancient ovens. The wing on the left, oddly enough, never did connect with the main house, in spite of the covered passage between. On entering the front door, you will notice the unconventional way the hall is designed, with a stairway leading off to one side. The grand dining-room is the place where the architect lavished the most elaborate ornament. In fact, it is chiefly the carved woodwork of the interior that makes this house noted among architects and antiquarians. This one room is a monument to the taste of the designer and the skill of the wood-carvers of that late Georgian era. The room above this was the grand ballroom. Here in the mantelpiece are the garlands and urns that suggest the influence of Robert Adams. Hammond built this house from 1774–1782. He was a bachelor and the story is that he built it for a prospective bride, who, alas, never led him to the altar, for he remained single. Perhaps that is why he sold it soon after it was finished. There is a legend to the effect that the girl he loved jilted him because, she declared, he cared more about his new house than he did about her.

For years the interior of the house was totally inaccessible. It was occupied by two old ladies, the Misses Harwood, to whom we shall be introduced later, who were as fiercely proud as they were desperately poor. Few other feet than theirs stepped across the threshold for half a century, and one of the trials of these ladies was the inquisitiveness of architects, who every now and then would be caught hanging on the wall outside the back windows trying desperately, with a pencil in their teeth, to get a look at the carved cornice and chair-board and mantel of the dining-room. Just as they started to make a notation one of the Miss Harwoods would sweep them off like flies, to drop ignominiously to the ground and scamper off the premises. The fact that the house came into the possession of the Harwood family gave it the name "Harwood House" by which it is still more popularly known than by the name of its original owner and builder.

In the rear is all that remains of what was once a beautiful garden going down probably to meet the wall of the Paca estate. Some huge masses of box are left, and that is all. The view of the house from the garden, as well as from the street, is most impressive. Naturally, the back entrance is not as sumptuous as the front door, but one gets an equally fine sense of the noble proportions of the building from the rear. A unique feature is the use of four tall brick pilasters that break the horizontal lines and support the pediment.

But no list of details can give the sense of the whole. The longer one studies the house the more its beauty reveals itself. Among all the mansions of the Golden Age, this one is the queen.

CHAPTER VI

THE COUNTRY HOME

ANY visit to Annapolis should include a glimpse of the countryside. Many of those eighteenth-century grandees in their fine town houses looked forward at the coming of spring and the drying up of the mud to the return to their country estates for the major part of the year. And these rural places were, if anything, more handsome and more imposing than their town residences. Governor Ogle's home on King George Street, for example, looks very modest compared with his country place, "Bel Air," with its vast acres. Especially in these days, some of the Annapolis mansions lose effect by being crowded in. Their fine gardens of the eighteenth century have been for the most part cut up into building lots on which ugly little modern shops and dwellings have sprouted. These town houses, like the Chase Home, need more room to show to the best advantage. But out in the country there still is the fine sweep of lawns, groves, and long vistas to the sea, which give even a simple house dignity, and to the grand manor house an air of distinction that is almost regal.

Naturally, the years and changing styles and fortunes took their toll of these old country homes. In the mid-Victorian era some of the owners unhappily "improved" their houses by adding porches, bay-windows, and even towers. Pictures taken at the end of the nineteenth century show some of the finest of these country seats in decay, their pillars disfigured with brown paint, and their doorsteps deep in rank shrubbery and weeds. But, fortunately, in recent years people have come to appreciate these old homes, and such treasures as "Tulip Hill" and "Whitehall" have at last come into the hands of those who delighted in bringing them back to their old-time beauty. By the same token, these are private homes, and as such they are not open to tripper, souvenir hunter, or snap-shooter, any more than they were in the eighteenth century.

Still, one may turn his car out on the highway and see something of the countryside around Annapolis and find other relics of the past. A short drive out to the South River bridge gives one a view of a wide, placid waterway that once was bristling with tall-masted ships, but that now has scarcely a fishing boat to break the reflections on its surface. On the farther bank, long ago, lay London-Town, where these ships took on cargoes of tobacco for another London Town on the Thames.

A short way up the road from the bridge one comes upon the little church of All Hallows surrounded by its ancient gravestones and shadowed by tall oaks. This has been restored, from time to time, but it probably still looks very much as it did in the days when the citizens of London-Town drove up in their chaises for Sunday morning service, and where also they laid themselves down when their life story was done. It is typical of the parish churches planted at ten-mile intervals throughout the county, neatly built of brick, but having no spire, hanging its bell under a little wooden shelter outside. The trim slate roof and fresh-colored brick give the church a spruce, new look that belies its age.

All Hallows was erected in 1690. In that year Annapolis was still "Anne Arundel's Town," a straggling settlement, not yet the capital of the province. The grass grows tall in the old churchyard, but most of the tombstones stand high, with their inscriptions clear. They are handsomely incised, like those in St. Anne's. Here and there, also, as in St. Anne's, may be found a grand flourish of scrolls surrounding a coat of arms, to indicate where a gentleman and his lady are interred. No doubt at the last trump these fine people, accustomed to sleeping late, will be permitted by the archangel to slumber a bit longer than the common herd.

But most of the people who lie here were engaged in trade, and one at least, James Dick by name, is not ashamed to admit the fact. He does it in Latin, in the inscription to his wife, Margaret. He had the education of a gentleman, anyway:

In Memoriam Margeritae
Uxoris suae monumentum hoc posuit Jacobus Dick maritus Londinopoli mercator.

Next to her lies his thirteen-year-old daughter. Death came early to those families. And there is the grave of poor "Anne, Wife of Thomas Sparrow," who died in 1697, only sixteen years old, having been married a little over two weeks. A bitter honeymoon that!

There is one tombstone much later than these on whose crumbling surface can be deciphered just the words, "My Louisa," and that is all. The story is that a young clergyman in South Carolina was engaged to be married to a girl who, it was discovered, had contracted tuberculosis. In the effort to find health for her in the open air, he set forth on a journey in his carriage, accompanied by the girl's aunt as chaperon. But when their travels had reached as far as Anne Arundel County in Mary-

SOUTH RIVER NEAR THE SITE OF LONDON-TOWN

land, the girl died. The broken-hearted lover buried her in All Hallows churchyard, and "My Louisa" was all he could find it in his heart to put on the stone.

There's another historical fact about All Hallows worth mentioning. Parson Weems came here for his first and only pastorate

ALL HALLOWS CHURCH

and preached from 1784 to 1789. This is the man who attained fame as the first biographer of George Washington, and the veracious historian who gave to the world the story of young George, his trusty hatchet, and the unhappy cherry tree. "I cannot tell a lie, father, I did it with my little hatchet." Well, the parson did it with his little quill pen, and let us hope he could not tell a lie either. It's a good story still.

From in front of the churchyard gate a road turns east, and by following this, and making judicious inquiry, one may drive past the clubhouse of the famous organization mentioned already, the South River Club. The traveler may wander freely about the yard and scan this clubhouse as closely as he likes. There is really not a great deal to see. It looks so much like an old-time

THE SOUTH RIVER CLUB

country schoolhouse that one is likely to pass without a second look. There is a little front porch with benches, but otherwise the house is a square, white, clapboard cabin with an end chimney and nothing more.

It is hard to imagine at first glance why this distinguished and most exclusive club ever pitched its tent in such a spot, but the building stands on high land between Glebe Creek on South

River and Rhode River next beyond. This site evidently made it easy to reach when gentlemen did most of their traveling by water.

The deed to the half-acre on which the clubhouse stands was executed in 1742. The *Maryland Gazette* of 1746 describes the dinner held to celebrate the downfall of the Pretender, that occasion, already mentioned, on which the Club sent its formal congratulations to the King.

In this little meeting-place, the planters of the neighborhood came every Thursday until the Civil War. The ceremonies and the menu were as simple as the clubhouse itself. It was a rule that punch must not be served till afternoon, but the sessions lasted all day and there was no closing hour. Another rule was that each member in turn was the host for a meeting and he was required to furnish the food, the liquor, and the tobacco. It still is the rule that whoever is newly elected to membership puts up the dinner on the next occasion.

After Appomattox, meetings were resumed until 1874. Then they were dropped until 1895. On the Fourth of July of that year, the custom was revived, some new members were elected, and the club got its second wind. But the meetings do not come so often now. There are just four during the year: the third Thursday in May; the Fourth of July; the third Thursday in September; and the Thursday before Thanksgiving. The membership is limited to twenty-five, and the building is constructed to hold no more than thirty for dinner. This larger number is a concession to possible guests.

Not far from this clubhouse stands a comfortable gambrel-roofed house, identical in style with so many in Annapolis. This is now owned by Mr. Clayton Brewer, of Annapolis, who has made a delightful summer home of it. This, too, is a relic of great age. However much the original house may have been altered, it goes back, they say, to about 1660. It was known as "Folly Farm," because apparently the builder picked a site that gave him a beautiful view over the countryside but was not lo-

"FOLLY FARM"

cated with a practical eye for business. For this was originally a tavern. Here, it is said, the Maryland Provincial Assembly met once, at least, the lower House meeting in the tap room below on the ground floor, and the Council, together with his Excellency, the Governor, gathering on the floor above. In a word, this little house was once, for all its nickname, the capital of Maryland.

Continuing eastward by devious routes for a few miles—we must depend on the gas station attendants to point the way—

we traverse the site of London-Town. This dead city was once a hustling little port when the Puritans were still laboring to make a settlement of "Providence" on Greenberry Point. In 1683, London Town was made a "port of entry." Its leading citizen then was one William Burgess, who died three years later, and whose gravestone may be seen in All Hallows churchyard. He and his brother-in-law owned and operated a fleet of ships trading between the various Maryland landings on the Chesapeake and England. Naturally, Burgess made London-Town the home port for these ships. He laid out streets and started to develop a real boom town, but he died before much was done.

When Annapolis became the capital, most of the glory of the older settlement faded, along with the "cage, whipping post, pillory, and stone," which were moved in 1695 to the new center, in order to discourage sinners. But it still continued to do a good shipping business as late as the Revolution. The success of that rebellion broke all the trade contacts with the mother country, and London-Town rapidly vanished.

One of the things that Burgess did to make a success of London-Town was to erect a fine brick building on a point of land overlooking South River, which was to be the Town Hall and Court House. At least that is the story, though its present appearance suggests a gentleman's country house in a beautiful setting. It stands there today, disconsolate and threadbare, for it is only an almshouse now. It is the only building left.

As for the rest of London-Town, there rises one tall, gaunt chimney, with yawning fireplaces, in a tuft of trees. This is all that remains of some fine residence, and that is every trace of old London-Town today. The ground is now covered in all directions by depressing little vacation shacks of the Coolidge and

THE OLD COURT HOUSE, LONDON-TOWN

Now an Alms House

Hoover eras, set out amid scrubby woods or in rough clearings. Probably it has been two hundred years since the ghost of William Burgess enjoyed haunting the scene where he once dreamed of establishing a great city.

In this section of the countryside, where those beautiful long arms of Chesapeake Bay—South River, West River and Rhode River—reach far inland, are some fine old houses that belong to the same Golden Age as the mansions of Annapolis. One, indeed, Cedar Park, goes back much farther, proudly dating from the last decade of the seventeenth century. It stands in the neighborhood of West River in the midst of groves and pastures and fields. For a long time it was famous for its deer park—

CEDAR PARK, GABLE END

which, by the way, has never yet been plowed—but, as the accompanying sketch shows, it was no grand mansion but a simple little farmhouse, with huge end chimneys and long slanting roofs. It is a child of the seventeenth century, when even the residence of a fine gentleman in the colonies, North or South, was a small, primitive affair as compared with the homes of the generation that followed. The architectural glory of the eighteenth century passed by Cedar Park without touching it. Evidently, the owners felt it was good enough to live in just as it was.

Then came the drab nineteenth century, during which it became a school for young ladies. To accommodate these, the school principal added on at right angles an "L," sticking back into the old garden like a sore thumb, but from the windows of which the girls could see the blue waters of the bay. It must have been pleasant to learn geography, needlework, and painting on velvet in such surroundings. The school is gone, but the "L" still remains. In the sketch, branches of the tree at the left have been made to grow out far enough to conceal it.

In contrast with this little seventeenth-century type of farmhouse, which belonged to the Murray family, is a neighboring one, reached also by a narrow, winding green lane and standing on an upland overlooking West River. This is "Ivy Neck," an example of an eighteenth-century country house representing a great advance in comfort and spaciousness over Cedar Park. This house is still occupied by descendants of the same Murrays. It has suffered from nineteenth-century additions in its outward appearance, but inside it is all of a piece, dignified and beautiful. In the rear, there is a sort of ground porch of stone flagging, where one may sit and look at the bay and feel a fresh June breeze rippling over the water. How pleasant it must have been in a former age to rest there in a cane rocker, with a glass of something fragrant and cool at one's elbow, and watch the slaves toiling in the sun. Yes, suh, Ah should give the institution of slavery mah unqualified approval!

If one is curious about such matters, directly across West River from "Ivy Neck" there is a lonely tomb in a field. The man who lies there was Thomas A. Francis, who perished on his way to a party by being drowned when his boat capsized. His wife, wearing the billowy skirts of the day, was kept afloat by the air in them until rescued. The inscription on the gentleman's grave is an acrostic spelling his name, beginning "Though now in silence I am lowly laid."

All around and about "Ivy Neck" stand immemorial trees.

OLD SLAVE CABIN, CEDAR PARK

That is one of the specially fine features about the Maryland landscape, where the settlements have been standing for centuries. And that is the first thing that appeals to the eye in approaching the most beautiful of all the country manor houses in this section, "Tulip Hill." This old mansion stands not far

TULIP HILL

back from a main highway, but a grove of splendid, great trees makes a dark green curtain that shuts away the outside world.

This stately house with its spreading wings belonged to the Galloway family. Samuel Galloway built it about 1755–56 as a gift for his bride, Anne Chew. Here George Washington was a guest on more than one occasion when he came from Mount Vernon to attend the Annapolis races.

The legend runs that a certain scion of the house, feeling exhilarated on some occasion—perhaps just having his blue blood boil in his veins—entered the house on horseback and rode up the stairs. It is said that the scars of the hoofs may still be seen. This house has what the architects call a "pediment porch" over its front door, and up in the center of the pediment, under its peak, there is a charming little cupid, showing the Adams influence, and a unique ornament in these parts. Both indoors and out, this dwelling is rich in carved woodwork and paneling.

Handsome as "Tulip Hill" is from the front, the most impressive view is in the rear. On the back door hangs a "canopy," smothered in climbing roses, and from here one looks down a series of terraces through the gardens and away across golden grain fields—a glorious expanse of at least a mile—to where Chesapeake Bay lies like a deep blue ribbon, and beyond rises the pale azure shape of Kent Island. It doesn't seem like present-day America in such a setting, but as if one were standing in some ancestral estate in England.

There is one more country place near Annapolis which is even more impressive than "Tulip Hill." It lies on the other side of the town; in fact, one can only see it from the deck of a boat after rounding Greenberry Point. This is the famous "Whitehall," the country seat built by Governor Sharpe.

He had not been long in Maryland before he bought from Nicholas Greenberry a tract of one thousand acres, seven or

ANNE ARUNDEL FARM HOUSE

Old Style

eight miles from Annapolis, on which he set up a lumber mill and a brickyard by which most of the rough work for the building materials could be done on the spot. The house was erected about 1760, and although it is only five years younger than

"Tulip Hill," the front has the new style of high portico with tall, white, fluted pillars, topped with elaborate ornate capitals, which makes it rare, if not unique, among mansions built a decade before the Revolutionary War. In a way, it suggests Monticello, the home of Thomas Jefferson. Years ago, I once had a glimpse of "Whitehall" through a long vista lined on either hand with huge lilac bushes all in bloom, and it would be hard to surpass anywhere among the homes of men that vision of serene beauty and dignity. From the lofty portico I looked back through that same avenue of lilacs and lawn to where Chesapeake Bay lay shimmering as far as the eye could reach. No wonder Horatio Sharpe delighted in the place, spent here all the time he could spare from official duties, and when, in 1769, he was suddenly deposed to make a place for Governor Eden, retired with a smile to take his ease in "Whitehall."

According to the opinion of Mr. R. T. H. Halsey, the antiquarian, this masterpiece was one of those designed by the architect, Matthew Buckland. If this is true, it is interesting to notice the many differences in style between "Whitehall" and another of his houses; for example, the Hammond house, built only about five years later. And, yet, both are faithful to the same theme of main house, "curtains," and wings.

Although "Whitehall" gives such an impression of grandeur from a distance, it really is not so spacious as many another home in the country that appears smaller, for, despite its wide façade, it is only one room deep. Such an arrangement was appropriate for a country house in Maryland that needed, for at least four months in the year, rooms with uninterrupted ventilation, especially to give full play to the prevailing summer breeze off the bay, which all the front windows faced. The central hall

WHITEHALL

has the same airy treatment, and here again it suggests Monticello, for it is two stories high and without a staircase.

Inside the house, as one would expect, there is a wealth of superb carving, but the ornamentation does not adhere to the same patterns as in the other Buckland houses. For example, the window casings by the doors have a flourish at the bottom quite different from the severer lines of the earlier styles.

About this wood-carving there is a story that has been told before but which will stand retelling. It is said that among Governor Sharpe's indentured servants was a young man whose appearance and manner attracted his master's interest immediately. The youth was proud and bitter over his fate, and would not talk about himself. On the books he was listed as a criminal, but the Governor respected his secret and treated him with special kindness. When he discovered that the man could handle tools as a wood-carver, he turned over the entire task of decoration in "Whitehall" to him, telling him that as soon as the work was done he should be a free man. Eagerly, the poor fellow accepted the bargain, nor did he stint on his share. Cornices, mantels, window and door casings, chair and base boards, came under his chisel, as he deftly copied the designs furnished probably by the architect himself from his own portfolios. As long as daylight lasted he toiled, each day bringing him nearer to his promised freedom. Meanwhile, the youth contracted consumption, and scarcely had the last acanthus leaf been completed when he had to lay down his own frail body, together with his mallet and chisel, for a long, long rest. Not the least tragic feature in the story is that while the carving was in progress Governor Sharpe had been investigating the reasons for his servant's conviction as a felon, and hardly had the young man been laid n his grave when the evidence arrived from London to prove his innocence.

There are many other stories about "Whitehall." One is that during a festive evening there, such as Sharpe delighted in, George Washington trod a measure while Benjamin Franklin played the musical glasses. Another is that the house itself was destined as a home for Mary Ogle, whom Governor Sharpe had hoped to marry, the same pretty Mary who married his secretary, John Ridout; but there is nothing to suggest that the legend has much foundation. In fact, Mary was very much younger than the Governor, and certainly he showed no signs of an aching heart or of the green-eyed monster in his dealings with the Ridouts afterwards. It delighted him during his last years in London to know that Mr. Ogle, who bought "Whitehall" in the stormy years, had immediately presented it to his daughter, so that John and Mary Ridout were living in the old place where they had been entertained so often, not merely as guests but as intimate friends. Here, beneath the apple blossoms, John Ridout was buried, and, by his own request, with no memorial stone.

If there is one special tradition that still lingers about "Whitehall," it is the lavish hospitality for which Horatio Sharpe made it famous. Probably, in those days of rough roads, most of his guests from Annapolis preferred a staunch and roomy sailboat that would make the long detour round the end of Greenberry Point to the Sharpe landing on Whitehall Creek. And these boatloads of guests included not only the bigwigs and the government officials with their fat dowagers, but also the gay young girls, all a-giggle with excitement and bursting with their tight stays, together with their beaux who were trying to look like seasoned men of the world at eighteen, in their first dress wigs.

Let us hope they encountered no rain squalls on their return trip around Greenberry Point, but perhaps they had such a good time that they wouldn't have minded such a trifle as a wetting.

And so we may leave "Whitehall." Happily, it stands today as fair as ever, with its pinkish brick and snow-white pillars. Much as it appeals to the eye of the architect, it may stand even more significantly as the monument of Horatio Sharpe. The King of England had then, as he has now, many able and conscientious servants in the colonies, but in the whole roster it would be hard to find one who combined more fine qualities than the master of "Whitehall." His generosity, kindliness, tact, and dignity in a pioneer land, under the most trying circumstances, have made his administration a fragrant memory still in the history of Maryland.

The Revolutionary War made it necessary for him to remain in London until his death, but like his successor, Eden, his heart seems to have been still in Annapolis. Once after the war, when Sam Chase was on a government errand in London, Sharpe waived ceremony and called on him, much to the latter's surprise and embarrassment. But Sharpe soon put his old acquaintance at ease and talked freely about the old scenes, just as if there never had been any war. When he asked how his Annapolis friends were, he was careful to inquire, not only after the Scotts and Ridouts and other Tory families, but also to express the same interest in the welfare of that arch rebel, Charles Carroll of Carrollton, still his "old friend." For such a man as Horatio Sharpe, "Whitehall" is a fitting memorial.

CHAPTER VII

"BREAKING HOME TIES"

ON the twenty-seventh of January, 1761, there were grand doings on Stad House Hill. For that was the day Annapolis learned of the accession of their new King, George III, "The Most High and Mighty Prince, by the Grace of God King of Great Britain, Scotland and Ireland, Defender of the Faith, etc." Thirty-four minute guns boomed, to the great delight of the small boys and the intense annoyance of their mothers. A procession wound solemnly round the Circle and through the streets. The multitude shouted huzzas and "Long live King George!" until they were hoarse, but punch was to be had for the asking to soothe the roughened throats. The day closed with a banquet amid interminable toasts, and many citizens made their way home with difficulty. If there was any spot on the planet more loyal to King George III than Annapolis in 1761, it would have been hard to find.

But a war between Britain and France had been going on several years before this new King George mounted the throne, and the conflict had carried the drums, banners, tramplings, and volleys into the American wilderness. When peace was signed in 1763, and the British ministers did some figuring on the cost of this war, they found that the American campaigns alone had aggregated a figure of thirty-two million pounds. It seemed only fair and decent for the American colonists to show their gratitude to the mother country by paying a trifling little tax in the form of stamped paper to be used for various leg documents, and for the newspapers.

Accordingly, the Stamp Act was passed in March of 176 Promptly there was a roar of protest. It was all very well to sho loyalty by shouting for the King and drinking his health in fre punch, but this did not extend to paying a tax laid on them b the King's ministers with never a by-your-leave. As for the cos of the war, wasn't it the business of the home government t defend the colonies? Who made the war in the first place? An let the ministry remember that the Americans had gone to n small expense to fit out their own military expeditions in tha war. In brief, there was a tremendous commotion. The *Mary land Gazette* came out with black mourning bands and a skul and cross-bones where the stamp was supposed to be. The edito did not like the prospect of having to buy stamped paper, either

A certain Mr. Hood, who was at the time on a journey t London, was appointed receiver and distributor of the stamp in Annapolis. As soon as that appointment was known, a pro cession of citizens paraded through the streets with an effig of their fellow townsman, Zachariah Hood, sitting in a cart lik a condemned felon on his way to execution, and in its hand were sheets of the accursed stamped paper. The procession wen to the gallows, where Mr. Hood's counterfeit presentment wa duly hanged. Then, to make a thorough job of it, the danglin figure was consumed over a burning tar barrel.

Later, when Mr. Hood in person tried to land on his retur from London, he was met by such a threatening mob that, afte sending his resignation to Governor Sharpe, he fled in terror t Long Island, where some New York Sons of Liberty hunted him down and made him recant in humble terms.

Such was the uproar throughout the colonies that the minis-y backed down and the Act was repealed. News of this came Annapolis on May 22, 1766. Then there was another demon-ration of loyalty. Both houses of the Assembly adjourned to the ouncil Chamber in joint session. Again guns were fired and any toasts were drunk. All was joy once more. A fortnight ter the King's birthday was the occasion for still another cele-ration to demonstrate the loyalty of His Majesty's subjects in nnapolis. On that great day more cannon boomed down at the ocks, more speeches were made, more punch poured down yal throats, and more headaches next day. In November of at year the House of Delegates voted that a marble statue of ord Chatham, the friend of the colonies, should be erected in nnapolis, and a portrait of Lord Camden should be hung in he court room. The tourist to Annapolis, however, will find either today. In fact, they never came to pass, for the Council uietly voted this noble resolution down, doubtless on account f the expense involved.

At the time, the sky seemed peaceful and blue, but the ques-ion was not settled. The Exchequer needed money and it would ever do to yield to the claim of the colonists that they should not e taxed. Whoever heard of such a principle? If the Stamp Act vas unpopular, something else might be tried, and so came the Tea Tax. Again an uproar. In November, 1773, the Bostonians ad their little demonstration on some of the ships in their har-or, and the action was loudly cheered in Annapolis, at least by he "People's Party." Almost a year later, there occurred a more pen and spectacular tea party in Annapolis.

Despite the known position of the citizens of the town and province generally, Mr. Anthony Stewart allowed his brig, the

Peggy Stewart, to be loaded with over a ton of the "detestabl plant" and paid the duty thereon. She arrived on October 1 1774, and dropped anchor in Annapolis harbor. Since this wa open defiance of the non-importation agreement, Stewart's ac tion aroused hot feeling. A committee of citizens refused to al low the vessel to discharge her cargo until the mature sense c the community had been expressed.

A general meeting of citizens was called for in Annapoli on the nineteenth. It was a grim assembly. The belated apolog offered by the merchants concerned, and that of Stewart him self, were not accepted. The radical minority was shouting fo tar and feathers. The majority counseled quieter measures, bu Stewart became frightened. Some of the Liberty Boys hac erected a gallows in front of his windows as a gentle hint o their sentiments. So at the suggestion, it is said, of Charles Car roll, he offered to burn his ship, cargo of tea and all. That offe was accepted and a committee of the minority went on boarc with him to see that he carried the matter through. Stewar sailed the brig until she grounded near Windmill Point, a spo now covered by the wide level space between Bancroft Hall, ir the Naval Academy, and the present harbor. There he set fire tc her and she burned until she sank. About a hundred and forty years afterward, when the dredging and filling were going on for the enlarged Naval Academy, charred timbers of the vessel were brought up, some pieces of which are still treasured in Annapolis homes.

There is a painting in the State House depicting the scene of the burning. Mr. Stewart stands in a heroic and graceful pose, waving his hat with one hand and holding aloft the blazing torch with the other. But there was nothing very heroic about he performance. Stewart had been bold and defiant at first, and hen caved in from sheer terror of his life. He signed an abject pology as well, and probably would have eaten a peck of dirt he had been required to do so. Shortly after this incident he

PEGGY STEWART HOUSE IN ITS ORIGINAL FORM

After a photograph

fled the country and Annapolis saw him no more. His house, now greatly changed in its exterior, still stands on Hanover Street; and the local chapter of the American Revolution have taken the name of the ill-fated brig as their own.

Of course, a cynic might observe of the Sons of Liberty in this incident that their stern attitude toward Mr. Stewart did not cost them a penny, but made a fine bonfire. It was somebody else's boat and somebody else's tea that went up in smoke. And it is true that there were citizens of Annapolis who though that this was carrying things too far. Once I happened to me tion the burning of the *Peggy Stewart* to Miss Hester Harwoo the last personal owner and occupant of the Hammond-Ha wood house on Maryland Avenue.

"The thing was done," she sniffed disgustedly, "by som rough young men out in the next county." I received the im pression that Miss Hester thought them very plebeian indee "At any rate," she went on, "I know that Great-Grandpap always said that *he* thought it a very unneighborly thing to d to Mr. Stewart." That, of course, is not the official point of view but perhaps Miss Hester did not belong to the D.A.R. And i must be admitted that Sam Galloway, of "Tulip Hill," th friend of Washington, denounced the performance as "in famous," and his neighbors, the Murrays, thought so, too, a did a good many other leading citizens.

After this incident of the *Peggy Stewart,* as every America schoolboy knows, things went from bad to worse, and in an other six months the shooting had begun. But in the spring o 1776, when the colonists had an army in the field, the hope wa still cherished that very soon the British government would se the light and give in; then all would be happy again, as before Few men in Annapolis in January of 1776 even breathed th idea of independence. Like Washington himself, they wer gradually pushed into that position by the force of events, much against their will.

Poor Governor Eden came back from England in 1775, jus at the wrong time, and soon found himself powerless, a mer figurehead at best, and at worst something like a prisoner. He, too, was anxious to have the home government see matters in a different light, but he could do nothing. The finest thing about this unhappy and awkward situation was the courtesy and dignity with which Eden, on the one hand, and the patriot leaders of Annapolis, on the other, behaved toward each other. They all liked him personally, and they had all been among his friends. Once the Governor tried to have them come to dine with him just to thrash things out over the table in open and friendly discussion. Since they felt they could not accept without compromising their position, Charles Carroll of Carrollton invited the entire party, including Governor Eden, to his own house for dinner, and they talked freely and honestly. The patriots admitted that there were overtures being made to France, as Eden declared, and he, in turn, admitted that the British government was hiring Hessians to shoot the American rebels down. But, to the very last, when Eden finally departed, the delicate situation was handled with a tact which speaks well for the character and breeding of all the men involved.

Thereafter, the war dragged its way through seven dreary years until the Yorktown surrender brought an end. During all those years, not a battle was fought on Maryland soil. Though many Maryland boys left their bones on battlefields from Long Island to Guilford Court House, Annapolis suffered no attack, heard not even a shot fired in anger.

For the young ladies this war was thrilling, because all they saw of it was the arrival of troops, especially the French armies with their gay and elegant officers. Lafayette came in March, 1781, and entranced all female hearts—though, alas, he had a wife back there in France—and the following September Rochambeau arrived with his army of four thousand Frenchmen on the way to the Yorktown campaign. There is a marker in the

Naval Academy grounds and a monument in the rear of St. John's campus commemorating the place where the army was encamped and especially those who died and were buried here.

It must have seemed strange that dinners and balls and plays should be given in honor of these officers in white uniforms (speaking, as a rule, no English), in the same theater, Assembly Rooms, and homes where only twenty-five years before Braddock and the British redcoats had been the sensation of the hour. Perhaps not all the homes that welcomed Braddock and his staff were thrown open again to Rochambeau and Lafayette, for, of course, there were some Tories who probably could not bear the sight of the French. And yet it appears that most of the Tory ladies, at any rate, enjoyed the society of the French very much, for they wrote sprightly letters about the gay times they were enjoying. Mrs. Benjamin Ogle, for example, who was on the Tory side of the fence, wrote that Annapolis, in March, 1781, "would be intolerable were it not for the officers. . . . It's all marquises, counts, etc. . . . I like the French better every hour. The divine Marquis de la Fayette is in town, and is quite the thing."

A year later Ann Dulany, a member of the Toriest family of them all, writes that she finds the Frenchmen agreeable. "They say the Tories are the people of fashion at least and they love and pity them for their sufferings. This is French flattery, some may think. But I beg leave to differ from all such." Ann, in another year, married a Frenchman and left her native town forever.

In the spring of 1783, Mrs. Walter Dulany wrote to her exiled son in London about the "infinity of French beaux, all of whom are very gallant."

It is quite probable that the handsome aristocrats in white uniforms who came over with Rochambeau found the Loyalist families more to their liking than people like Sam Chase, as Ann Dulany says. No doubt as these French officers talked things over at their wine there was some shaking of heads about what their King was doing for these American rebels. Of course, it was a way of getting revanche for the humiliating treaty that the sacré Monsieur Pitt had forced on France, but it was a dangerous thing to encourage all these notions about a government by the canaille. Suppose such ideas ever got into France!

Perhaps, ten or a dozen years later, some of these same officers thought bitterly of those days when the time came for them to beg their bread at the courts of Berlin or Vienna, or when they sat in the tumbril jolting over the cobbles to bow their proud heads to Madame Guillotine. But life was so gay in Annapolis that the officers seldom bothered their brains as to what the fighting was all about, rejoicing that their duty led them to such an agreeable spot, where wine was good, the ladies beautiful, and the hospitality lavish. What more could a French officer ask?

It was not only the French General who came to Annapolis. In November, 1781, Washington also passed through on his way back from Yorktown, and the whole town was agog to see him. Once a familiar figure on the streets, and the friend of many Annapolitans, as a Virginia planter, he was now the one leader of the patriot cause. He came first, and there was no second. And so everyone shut up shop and ran out into the streets to take a look at him.

Then, finally, when the fighting was all over, and the last redcoat had left New York, it was here at Annapolis that the chieftain returned to give back his military commission to those who represented the new nation, the Continental Congress. In those days this body was meeting alternately at Trenton and Annapolis, and it happened to be at the Maryland capital in 1783. The event took place on December 23, 1783. Facing the General, as he stood to read his brief speech, were some twenty members of the Congress, seated in armchairs and all wearing their hats. Also, both Houses of the Maryland Assembly were present as guests. Above, in the gallery, were seated all the Annapolitan ladies who could crowd in, grouped around the central figure of Martha Washington, who had come up from Mount Vernon to welcome her husband home after eight years of campaigning.

The occasion was very formal indeed, and every item of the program had been prescribed beforehand. In fact, the Father of our country had been instructed to bow to Congress as he rose to speak, and also when he had finished. The members of Congress, for their part, were to return this salute by "uncovering without bowing."

It was not merely formal, but deeply impressive. Washington began, "Mr. President, the great events on which my resignation depended having at length taken place, I have now the honor of offering my sincere congratulations to Congress, and by presenting myself before them to surrender into their hands the trust committed to me and to claim the indulgence of retiring from the service of my country." And he concluded, "Having finished the work assigned me, I retire from the great theater of action, and bidding an affectionate farewell to this august body under whose orders I have so long acted, I here offer my commission and take my leave of all the employments of public life." Stately words, but sincere.

Up in that ladies' gallery sat Mrs. John Ridout. The fact that she belonged to the Tory faction could not keep her away. And there, doubtless, she met her old friend, Martha Washington, whose nightcap still lay in the guest-room upstairs in the Ridout house. Lady Edgar, in her biography of Horatio Sharpe, quotes a letter written by Mary to her mother, Mrs. Ogle, just after witnessing this scene.

"The General," she wrote, "seemed so much affected himself that everyone felt for him. He addressed Congress in a short speech, but very affecting. Many tears were shed. He has retired from all active business and designs to spend the rest of his days at his own seat. I think the world never produced a greater man, and very few so good. . . ." That last sentence is not a bad tribute from a Tory!

For this visit, however, Washington was not a guest of the Ridouts. He stayed at the Mann Tavern, which stood just at the corner of Main and Conduit Streets under the shadow of the Dulany mansion. A regal dinner was given there in his honor, with interminable laudatory speeches and enough wine to float a frigate. No doubt he went through the ordeal with great dignity and patience. But, thereafter, with a sigh of relief, he started away with his wife for his beloved Mount Vernon, and his departure was undisturbed. In those quaint and backward days, there were no microphones to be compelled to talk into, no news-reel photographers flashing lights in the face, no swarms of reporters demanding copy, no autograph hunters, no women trying to kiss him. Even a great national hero like Washington was allowed to receive his honors with dignity and to enjoy his privacy. Sometimes the phrase, "Good Old Days," does seem exactly right!

Another event of importance in Annapolis was the formal signing of the treaty of peace with Great Britain on January 14, 1784. Congress at that time was still meeting in the Maryland capital. Two years later, a gathering of representatives of the new-born nation was called at Annapolis to try to straighten out the hopeless muddle of trade between the states. Only twelve delegates from five states appeared for the meeting, and after some discussion it was voted to call another convention at Philadelphia, in order to go to the root of the trouble and draft a constitution for the United States.

This "Annapolis Convention" closed the episode of the Revolution and led to the forming of "a more perfect union." It marks also the beginning of the long, slow decline of Annapolis. Shortly afterwards, a French traveler called it "The Finished City." Possibly he meant the phrase in a complimentary fashion, but, on the other hand, he might have given off a sly *double entendre*. More than one cause contributed to this decay. Baltimore proved to be a better port than Annapolis, for many reasons, and grew rapidly at the expense of the ancient capital. The winning of the war for independence severed many of the commercial ties on which the city's trading prosperity had rested. Whatever the reason, the old-time glory faded with the Revolutionary War, and for the next century Annapolis existed in a long, deepening twilight. For a while, its citizens dreamed that it might be selected as the capital of the new nation. When hope of that failed, it had for some years the cold comfort of being merely a convenient place for officials to land from their ships en route to Washington.

The town's decline and fall were like that of Rome, so gradual that no generation—at least not the one at the close of the eighteenth century—felt any alarm. The magnificent homes surrounded by their luxuriant gardens were still there. Entertaining went on, though not quite with the old extravagance. The theater still gave its winter performances and the Jockey Club had its races. But society was no longer so brilliant as in the Golden Age, because the leaders of the old set had been mostly Tories. Some of these had left during the war and others had been impoverished.

For a picture of what life in Annapolis was like during the post-war period, we are indebted to the Maryland Historical Society for a reprint of a journal kept during the years 1792 to 1804, when the last entry was made just a week before the death of the diarist. This man was one Mr. Faris (born in London), described as a "silversmith, watch and clock-maker, designer, portrait painter, tulip grower, tavern keeper, dentist, gossip, and diarist." Apparently he did everything but preach. He must have been a rival of John Shaw in several of his trades, though he left behind no special repute for skill at any of them.

This diary of seven hundred closely-written pages gives a full picture of life in Annapolis during the closing years of the eighteenth century, and the beginning of the nineteenth. And some of it is racy reading. Mr. Faris had a sense of humor, not always sanctified or benevolent, but still something to be thankful for in a diarist. He is nothing if not a gossip, but as long as all the people he talks about have been dead much more than a hundred years we might allow ourselves a somewhat reprehensible curiosity in that, too. In fact, some of his gossip is so scandalous that the Maryland Historical Society did a little judicious deleting, here and there. What was left out must have been pretty bad, for some of the items left in are rather startling. Evidently people, even of those far-away times, tended to the same errors as their descendants of the present day.

Here are a few bits:

March 9. Blew very hard. Upset Miss Kittey Fleming on the Stad House Hill, carryed away all her top rigging and bruised her face, made her nose bleed.

Miss Betsey Wright is married this day to a French officer whose name is —— he has been in town 8 or 10 days. He courted her or rather was in her company 6 or 8 Times and cannot speak a word of English nor she one word of French.

That may stand as a record for fast work under difficult conditions. The French officers must have been still visiting Annapolis or passing through, for Faris speaks of having

Dined on Board the French Ship, a 3 Decker had a Very Ellegant Diner.

A great many of his entries run to a formula: "Mrs. So and So was brought to Bed of a fine Boy"—or Girl, as the case might be—and similarly of the deaths, with the funeral the following day. A large proportion of the entries have to do with births and deaths. As, for example, Jan. 15, 1795,

James Shaws death, he died yesterday of a mortification of the Bowels.

Faris also makes frequent mention of the Jockey Club races and the purses won. On Nov. 4, 1794, he notes that

Messrs. Washington, Ridgeley, Taylor, and Williams horses ran for the Jockey Club purs and was won by Mr. Taylors horse.

Of his own work there isn't much said, except that he mentions starting to build a "forty-Piano" on July 22, 1795, and on Dec. 16, notes that he "this Day finished the Stand of my Forty Pio Anio all but painting it."

Now for some society notes: One entry gives a long list of guests at tea followed by this item.

Drank tea and after Tea they had the Fiddles and Danced till after 9 o'clock Miss Gassaway [one of the guests] had a Fitt.

So the thé-dansant is not a modern invention after all.

Here's this about poor Mrs. Quynn.

Yesterday evening Mrs. Quynn went in to the Cow pen to milk, and one of the Cows poked her and broke her thigh.

Now for some real gossip:

June 18 (1794) There is a report—and Mr. Joseph Mogg says he Realy believes its true that Mrs. West the Wife of James West Cruelly killed a negro boy by stamping and beating it—was buryed this evening.

May 9. In the Evening Capt —— marryed —— and the Town talked that he should have marryed her sooner as she is with child . . .

On the subsequent August 12 appears the following:

Either las night or this morning —— [the same bride] was Delivered of a Daughter. I think they have not been idel being only marryed the 9th of May last.

Once in a while, after some such entry, he takes it all back the next day by admitting that what he had heard was "a false and mallishous Storey." But he leaves that one as it stands.

This morning Miss Nancy Quynn [related perhaps to the woman who had an encounter with her cow] went in the Stage with her Brother Allen for Baltimore from there to Frederick where's she to stay, the Town says she is with child and not of her own couler.

When he has something outrageous to report he prefaces it by "The Town says." Incidentally, the Quynn house is still standing on Northeast Street.

In these records it is appalling to see how swiftly death follows a mention of illness. For instance, on June 21, 1794,

Miss Eliz Gassoway's young Daughter Kittey was taken unwell. June 22, Mrs. Gassoway's Daughter Died about 1 o'clock. June 23. Mrs. Gassoway's Daughter was Buried.

Here, too, one sees the approach of the dread plague of the seventeen-nineties, yellow fever, raging first in New York and Philadelphia, then coming to Baltimore, and finally creeping into Annapolis. One entry of the diary reports news of yellow fever in Philadelphia and adds that the pestilence "carries off 40 or 50 of a Day, they are well and dead in 6 hours." Of the visitation of 1800, he makes this tragic note,

Sept. 1. About 2 o'clock this morning my son Charles Faris Died of the Yellow Fever in 36 year of his age.

Faris must have been something of an oddity in his character. Outside of this diary the only other record of his life is his last will and testament. This was formally and legally indorsed as follows:

W. Faris, watchmaker at Annapolis, Maryland, his will,—composed by Miss Charlotte Heselius, first wife of Thomas

Jennings Johnson Esq., and daughter of Heselius, the portrait limner.

Evidently he had called upon Miss Charlotte to write his will for him in rime, so that it should be different from other people's wills. We are indebted to an artist of Annapolis, Mr. Frank B. Mayer, for the printing of this document in the course of an article he published in *Scribner's Monthly* for January, 1879. "Heselius, the portrait limner," by the way, is the man who is said to have given Peale his first lessons in painting.

At the time Faris made his will, he had, besides his wife, three sons and two daughters, who are remembered in his will by various items and sometimes frank comments. The following excerpts will serve to give an idea of how sprightly a will can be if one has sense enough to dispense with lawyers and employ a charming girl-poet instead.

. . . Then I give and bequeath to my dear loving wife,
  In case she's a widow the rest of her life,
The plates, spoons, and dishes, pots, kettles, and tables
  With the red and white cow that inhabits the stables.
The landscape, and "Judith" that hangs on the wall,
  And the musical clock 'hind the door in the hall.
My buckles and cane to son William I give
  And no more, because he's got substance to live.
His road I took care in his youth to instruct him.
  Though I say it myself a Princess might trust him.
The dog grew ungrateful, set up for himself,
  And at Norfolk, they say, he has plenty of pelf.
Since he's gone away 'twill be best for his brother,
  I give Hyam his portion to comfort his mother.
My coat, which I turned is a very good brown
  And may serve many years to parade in the town.

He admits that the coat is soiled where the "club" of his queue has rubbed it, but gives directions for his son to clean it. To his son, Charles (the one who died of yellow fever as noted in the diary), he wills his watch, bird organ, and a collection of all the teeth he had ever pulled, "rather curiously strung."

This will is original also in the fact that it not only specifies his benefactions—which, by the way, include not a penny in cash—but also mentions his pet aversions.

Thank God! I've but two that I hate from my heart,
  And, as ill luck would have it, they're not far apart,
In the greatest dislike—God forgive me the sin—
  But indeed there's no bearing that old Allan Quinn.
There's another I hate bad as Quinn for the fraud
  That his heart is so full of, that is Jonathan Todd.
This sin as I die, I hope will be forgiven:
  Or else I am sure I shall ne'er get to heaven. . . .

(It will be remembered that the Quynn family figured in his diary.)

He bequeathed the spinet to his daughter, Nancy, even though she had disappointed his hope that she would learn to play. For this purpose he says,

But I soon found 'twas money and time thrown away.

The music master in the case was one Harry Woodcock, and of him Faris says,

All the town knows that Harry's a very great liar
  And music from him she could never acquire . . .
But I still like old Woodcock I vow and declare;
  As a proof I shall leave him a lock of my hair.

Finally, he remembers the old sexton, Solomon Mogg, who was himself a famous character.

I leave to Sol Mogg for tolling the bell,
  My old hat and pipe which he knows very well.
To my nephews and nieces my blessing I give
  And entreat that they will mind and learn how to live.
My thanks to the public I cannot express;
  Their goodness to me has been quite to excess.
My feelings are many but words are too few
  To tell how it pains me to bid them adieu.

* * * *

There is a rare little book called "Personal Recollections of the Stage, embracing Notices of Actors, Authors, and Auditors During a Period of Forty Years, by William B. Wood, Late Director of the Philadelphia, Baltimore, Washington and Alexandria Theatres." It was published in 1855, but the earlier part of the narrative goes back to the closing years of the previous century. He tells how as a boy of nineteen he went to Annapolis to meet Mr. Wignell, an old friend of his father. Wignell had taken his company of actors out of New York on account of the yellow fever and brought them to Annapolis, which was considered far enough away to be comparatively safe.

Young Wood made his debut in the Annapolis theater with Mr. Wignell's company, and thus began his lifetime of acting.

Chief Justice Taney, whose gloomy statue broods on the Stad House Hill today, is said to have referred to his home town as the "Athens of America." It is not quite clear what Annapolitans corresponded to Pericles, Sophocles, Plato, and the rest, but when a Southern gentleman warms up about his home town one should not be too literal. At any rate, when Mr. Wignell gave his young protégé a chance, he said, "You shall have an opportunity to try your ability here at once in this place, although you will have to face as intelligent an audience for its number as can be found in America."

Mr. Wood fell ill in Annapolis of what he calls "Southern fever." Mrs. Lloyd, widow of the former governor and the mother of a future governor of Maryland, took the young stranger into her own house, now the Chase Home, and there nursed him back to health as if he were of her own family. It must have been a severe illness, perhaps typhoid, for he notes that he was "unconscious and delirious." And his parting comment in writing of the event, sixty years after, is, "What hospitable, what charitable beings are these Annapolitans!" Their fortunes were beginning to decay, but evidently not the traditions of kindness to the stranger within their gates, for which the town had always been famous.

About the time the young actor was recovering from his illness, another stranger appeared in town, an émigré from France. On the walls of many of the old homes in Annapolis hang portraits in pastel by this man who, at the beginning of the nineteenth century, became a familiar figure on the streets and in the homes of the "Athens of America." Although the years that knew him in this section of the country were from 1803 to 1807, he distinctly belongs to the eighteenth century and the *ancien régime*. It was that very fact that brought him from his native land to find refuge and make a living in the new republic. For he belonged to the French aristocracy. When the year 1793 came round he fled to America, and not any too soon to escape the guillotine. His name was Charles Balthazzer Julien Fevret de Saint Memin, by no means a name of the Sansculottes, and since he had to make a living he decided on portraiture, which in those days, before that other Frenchman, Daguerre, invented photography, was a resource for anybody who could draw at all. In the time of Charles Willson Peale, and earlier, there had been itinerant portrait painters who, like scissors-grinders, went from house to house, in town and country, with their paraphernalia and made portraits, or at least paintings that were intended to be portraits. Sometimes these painters carried with them canvases with full lengths and busts already painted in elegant attire and aristocratic pose, so that all that was necessary was to paint in the head.

Saint Memin also was an itinerant portraitist, though his work was far better than that of these early men. The Baltimore newspapers of 1803 carried his first advertisements, and from then until 1807 he divided his time between Baltimore, Annapolis, and the new capital, Washington.

Not having any training as a professional artist, he depended on a curious mechanical contrivance, called a physionotrace, invented a few years before by another French artist. This was a machine four feet high which, when nicely adjusted, cast an accurate profile of the subject on the paper. This profile would be carefully traced, and then all that was necessary was to lay in the modeling and the color. If a miniature was required, or a small portrait, he would again rely on a contrivance still familiar to commercial artists, the pantograph. If all this sounds too mechanical, it is only fair to remember that many another artist, ancient and modern, has leaned on similar gadgets to make sure of a likeness. Naturally, as he depended on this physionotrace, his work was limited to profiles.

It must be admitted that Saint Memin's terms were reasonable. For a single portrait his fee was only eight dollars. If h went further and engraved a plate from the portrait, his charg for that, together with a dozen prints, would be twenty-fiv dollars for men, but thirty-five dollars for women. Apparentl the ladies always gave him ten dollars' worth more trouble i the engraving.

From the purely artistic point of view, this work of Sain Memin's isn't what we would call priceless, and for some reaso he used to do many of his portraits on paper of a poisonou magenta or strawberry pink. But because his work was so muc cheaper than a painting in oil, he did many heads, and thes make an interesting historical collection of the worthies of tha time, together with their prim-looking wives. Among the no tables of Annapolis who sat for his physionotrace was Charle Carroll of Carrollton.

Finally, the time came when he could return safely to France Whereupon, with great joy, he smashed his physionotrace int many pieces, for, he said, it "symbolized the chains that ha fettered his aristocratic pride." In brief, as a French gentle man, he wanted no reminder of the fact that he had once bee compelled to work for a living.

There are a few events of this post-war period which ar worthy of remark. The capitol, which was uncompleted whe Washington resigned his commission, was given the additio of the dome, the same that is the familiar landmark of the cit today. This was finished in 1793. The preceding year a new church was erected for St. Anne's congregation, which durin the war had to worship in the theater. In 1784 the legislatur chartered "St. John's College." (Apparently, though this is a debatable point, the name comes from St. John's College, Cambridge, through the grateful memory of an alumnus of the English University.) Two years before, it had founded "Washington College" in Chestertown, and the idea seems to have been to establish a college at Annapolis for the boys of the western shore of Maryland. Some of the distinguished citizens gave their names to the enterprise, such as William Paca, Samuel Chase, and Charles Carroll of Carrollton. The following year the trustees of the old King William's School combined their property with that of the new college, and in 1789 Dr. John McDowell, as the first president, launched the institution. Unhappily, the college that seemed born to a bright future was hampered from the first by lack of funds, and to this day has had a bitter struggle against poverty.

"Bladen's Folly" had been completed and transformed into a building where the college was inaugurated. In later years, this was named "McDowell Hall," after the first president. Washington sent G. W. Parke Custis here in the spring of 1798, but the young gentleman made heavy weather of his Latin and Greek. Indeed, his studies were disturbed by the familiar but upsetting experience of falling in love. The Father of his Country, the stepfather of this young man, had to write to Mr. McDowell to try to keep the lad from falling in love again. Fortunately, for the peace of mind of those in Mount Vernon, the young lady refused the hand of the enamored student. By September it was deemed best to withdraw Mr. Custis to his own fireside.

The most distinguished of the St. John's alumni was Francis Scott Key, who graduated in 1796. It is an interesting commentary on the way the Loyalists of Annapolis became adjusted to the new republic that Francis lived as a student in the home of his great-aunt, Mrs. Upton Scott, a name which he bore himself, and in a few years, during another war with Great Britain, had written the poem that has become our national anthem.

One final commentary might be made on this episode of the Revolutionary War in Annapolis. It is true that most of the big-

MC DOWELL HALL

From the athletic field

wigs, the social leaders, tended to uphold the Crown, as they did everywhere in the colonies, and as they naturally would do. For the rebel is usually the man with nothing to lose and everything to gain. The man of property has little use for uprisings, for he has everything to lose. But this rule did not work well in Annapolis. Here, men seem to have taken their stand in the quarrel on the matter of principle, either way. Charles Carroll was the richest man in the colonies; William Paca and Matthias Hammond lived like princes, and yet none were more ardent in the rebel cause than they. And the Tories, for their part, stuck to their convictions when they were in the hopeless minority, when all they had was likely to be confiscated and they might even suffer physical violence, as brother Loyalists did elsewhere.

These men are only names and shadows today—the Ridouts, Scotts, Pacas, Carrolls, Dulanys, and the rest. But they deserve from this generation, which has never had to face such a test of principle, a respectful salute. One way or another they took their stand, and either way they were Americans of whom we may well be proud.

CHAPTER VIII

"THE ATHENS OF AMERICA" AND THE COMING OF THE NAVY

IT is true that our national anthem, the Star-Spangled Banner, was composed in the Patapsco River harbor, and by a man born in Frederick County, but Annapolis has always felt a special claim on Francis Scott Key. This rests on his connection with the Upton Scott family, whose house was his home for a number of years, his education at St. John's College, and, finally, his marriage to an Annapolis girl in the drawing-room of the Lloyd mansion—now the Chase Home.

Key, to tell the truth, lives in history solely by that poem, and there is another anecdote that connects it with Annapolis. The verses that were scratched roughly on the back of a letter, which Key had in his pocket during the night he spent on the *Minden* watching the British bombardment of Fort McHenry, were rewritten the next day in a clean copy as soon as he had landed again in Baltimore. Then he took it to the home of Judge Joseph Hopper Nicholson, whose wife was the sister of Mrs. Key. Judge Nicholson was a resident of Annapolis, but he had taken command of a volunteer company at the time of the British invasion and was, in fact, second in command at Fort McHenry.

The Judge was immensely taken with the poem and declared that it must be printed at once. Mrs. Nicholson promptly marched off with it to the printer, and soon the newsboys were hawking it about the streets on hand bills. The poem immediately caught the popular fancy, as well it might, the day following the bombardment. Judge Nicholson, after feeling about in his mind for some tune that would fit, set the words to the music of a popular drinking song, "To Anacreon in Heaven." This had been composed some fifty years earlier but it was still popular and everybody knew the air. That night it was sung in the theaters of Baltimore amid great enthusiasm. Finally, in recent years, the Star-Spangled Banner, with this music, was selected officially as the national anthem for Army and Navy.

With due deference to the good Judge Nicholson, his choice of that particular air has doomed the Star-Spangled Banner to be the most unsingable national anthem in the world. Of course, Judge Nicholson did not know that he and his brother-in-law had created a national anthem between them, and perhaps it is better to have a distinctive tune rather than an air like the one for "My Country 'Tis of Thee," which is shared by the British, the Swiss, and the Germans.

After the first excitement, Key gave his copy of the poem as a keepsake to his sister, who took it home to Annapolis with her and locked it up in the back of her writing desk in the Nicholson home. This was one of the old mansions of Annapolis that has been sacrificed to make the Naval Academy of today. There used to be a street called Scott Street, running parallel to Maryland Avenue down to the Severn River. This street ran east from about where the present Naval Academy Chapel stands, and on the south side of that street was the Nicholson home, just about where the bandstand is today.

The manuscript lay there in that writing desk, forgotten, from 1814 till 1845. In that year, Mrs. Rebecca Lloyd Shippen, Judge Nicholson's daughter, who had inherited the desk, rummaged about in the pigeonholes and brought to light the historic document. Thereafter, you may be sure, it was treasured by the family, for they held a relic of national interest. Mr. J. Pierpont Morgan once offered $25,000 for it, but the family declined. Instead, they sold it for a trifling fraction of that sum to the Walters Art Gallery in Baltimore, on the condition that the manuscript remain always in Maryland. Accordingly, it is in the Walters Art Gallery that the curious will find this historic sheet of paper, but it is interesting to remember that it slept for thirty years in the back of a desk in an Annapolis home on land long since dedicated to the task of training young men to serve that same Star-Spangled Banner upon the seas.

The War of 1812, like the Revolutionary War, passed by Annapolis without so much as a pistol shot. When Admiral Cockburn's squadron went up the bay in August, 1814, to attack Baltimore, after burning Washington, he passed the ancient town on the Severn without so much as a glance. It is lucky that Annapolis did not succeed in becoming the capital of the United States, for Cockburn would then have laid in ashes not a raw little settlement of new government buildings and rickety boarding houses, as Washington was at the time, but the most beautiful eighteenth-century city in America. At the mouth of the Severn there had been erected a little fort, in the shape of a pill box, put up in 1808, when the outrage perpetrated upon the U.S.S. *Chesapeake* by the British ship *Leopard* made it look as if there would be another war. But whether that little fort would have discouraged any British squadron from entering the Severn River in 1814 is doubtful. The Battle of Bladensburg, known ironically as the "Bladensburg races," took place not far from

Annapolis. Some citizens may have taken part as volunteers in that farce, but they never cared to discuss it afterwards, for at the first volley of the British the entire body of militia took to their heels, led by the Secretary of War in a chaise, frantically whipping his horse to get away. Captain Joshua Barney and his sailors were left to cover the rout as best they could.

So that is as near as the smell of battle came to Annapolis during "Mr. Madison's War." But, by this time, most of the old Loyalists had gone to their beds in the churchyard, and many of their sons were active in the service of their country. Such a one was William Pinkney, the most outstanding native son of the city in the generation following the Declaration of Independence. In that notorious battle of Bladensburg there was one Annapolitan, at least, who had no reason to be ashamed of saying he was there. This was Pinkney, who though Attorney-General in Madison's cabinet, became a major of Maryland militia for this occasion and was sufficiently in the front of action to be badly wounded in the arm.

William Pinkney was born in Annapolis, the son of an Englishman who had emigrated to America, settled down and married in Annapolis as might be expected. The father was a staunch Tory, and as such lost all his goods by confiscation, like the Dulanys. Young William at the age of thirteen had to be removed from King William's School on account of the stormy times, and ended then and there his formal education. The story was that the boy's sentiments were as enthusiastic for the rebels as his father's were for the King, and that William would run away to the nearest camp of the Continentals to fraternize with the soldiers.

On reaching young manhood, he began to study medicine in

Baltimore. One evening while he was pouring out his oratory in a debate held by some medical students, Sam Chase happened in and was so much impressed by the young man that he offered him the free run of his own law library if the lad should choose to desert medicine for law. Whatever the elder Pinkney may have thought about his boy's associating with such a notorious rebel as Chase, the young man eagerly accepted the offer and read law. Three years later, 1786, he was admitted to the bar and from that time his rise to distinction was swift and spectacular. Washington, Jefferson, and Madison sent him on various diplomatic missions or gave him cabinet posts, and he became known as a great constitutional lawyer. At least the slave states thought so, because he was one of their ablest champions. He was extraordinarily well read, had a real gift of oratory and was up in the forefront of statesmen in a day of political giants. But the great man, alas, had no sense of humor and was vain as a peacock. Having deep lines under his eyes, he applied paint to conceal them, and finding his equatorial region getting expansive he laced himself into a corset. He posed theatrically for the ladies' gallery when he spoke, and walked the earth like an archangel among the mortals. He was really one of the Bigwigs, born out of his time.

Incidentally, this haughtiness seems to have been a trait of the Pinkney clan. The last descendant of the line was a terrifying old lady who, even after free pews were ordained in St. Anne's Church, insisted on a proprietary right to her own. Years ago, I slipped innocently enough into her pew one Sunday morning. Shortly afterwards, a stern finger tapped my shoulder and as I looked up it pointed the way out. She made it clear that in worshiping among "us miserable offenders" she preferred her pew and wanted all of it for herself.

The Pinkney house is a modest brick structure on St. John's Street, but it once stood where the Court of Appeals building is now, on a fine location near the State House. It must grieve the shades of all those proud Pinkneys to see where it has now been moved, tucked away on a side street with an ugly porch on one side and the Baptist Church almost leaning against it on the other.

Annapolis can boast of another statesman of the front rank in the first half of the nineteenth century. This was Reverdy Johnson, who first drew breath of life in the Bordley-Randall house in 1796, the very year in which President Washington sent young William Pinkney to England as one of the commissioners to adjust war claims under the Jay Treaty. He graduated from St. John's College in 1811, and about the time of the battle of Waterloo was admitted to the Maryland bar.

Johnson, like Pinkney, made himself famous as a constitutional lawyer, and he, too, was an effective speaker, being blessed with a rich, deep voice. He was the major defense counsel in that famous Dred Scott case, which was argued before another Marylander, Chief Justice Taney of the Supreme Court. Johnson believed that slavery was wrong, but strove to be fair to the slaveholder's rights, and to keep the peace between the two sections. When, at last, the quarrel blazed into war he worked mightily to keep Maryland loyal to the Union, and, though a Democrat, supported Lincoln in the crisis. After the war he fought in the Senate to give decent treatment to the conquered South.

He served in various capacities in the national government, as Attorney-General under Taylor, as Senator at different times, and finally as minister to Great Britain in 1868, where his negotiations paved the way for the later settlement of the *Alabama* claims and other disputes. Perhaps he was not so haughty and impressive an actor as Pinkney. He probably was not so fascinating to the ladies in the gallery. But he certainly had a warm good humor and kindly heart. He never took himself too seriously. Half his life he was handicapped by partial blindness, but he carried on with no slackening in his stride. When he died in 1876, he was the last survivor of that succession of statesmen which the "Athens of America" had given to her country's service.

Judge Taney, who bestowed this resounding title upon the capital of Maryland, was almost a native of Annapolis, for he was born only a little south of the line of Anne Arundel County. In spite of the steady decay of Annapolis in importance and wealth during the early nineteenth century, there seems to have been no corresponding decay in local pride. A commission of naval officers solemnly reported: "A polar expedition is useless to determine the earth's axis; go to Annapolis rather. It should be called the pivot city. It is the center of the universe, for while all the world around it revolves, it remains stationary."

Far to the north, there was another state capital; to wit, Boston, which also claimed for itself the title of the "Athens of America." And the irreverent Dr. Holmes, who was practically a native son, went still further and called Boston the "Hub of the Universe." It is true that Annapolis cannot boast of any such group of writers as flourished in Boston and vicinity during the nineteenth century. No Emerson, Longfellow, Thoreau, Hawthorne, Lowell, or Holmes lived on the Severn. Little St. John's College had such a desperate struggle for existence that it cannot be said to have been a serious rival of Harvard at any time.

But those decades from the twenties to the sixties saw emanating from the Boston area the most extraordinary epidemics of moral and intellectual crusades, which swept the country. Foreign missions, abolition, total abstinence, women's rights, Utopian settlements, transcendentalism, vegetarianism, blue glasses, bloomer skirts, phrenology, hypnotism, Buddhism,—these hardly do more than begin the Catalogue of Causes to which Bostonese devoted their lives. The famous New England conscience seems to have gone on a prolonged rampage like a Vermont spring freshet. And culture was such a passion that a Boston girl, as she wiped the dishes, propped up on the shelf before her a copy of Emerson's essays, where now her descendant tacks a picture of Clark Gable.

Apparently none of this flood of moral and intellectual fervor sent so much as a trickle into Annapolis. The old town in those years was a synonym for conservatism. There was not even a public library during the whole nineteenth century, or, for that matter, for a score of years in the twentieth. As for religion, the Catholics were content with their Pater Noster and the Protestants were satisfied with the Book of Common Prayer. Why change? And if the Annapolitans do seem to have been a bit stodgy during those years, be it remembered that they did not go crazy and make themselves ridiculous, tilting at windmills. Like those people in the graveyard of Stoke Pogis,

> Along the cool, sequestered vale of life
> They kept the noiseless tenor of their way.

Perhaps it is not so ridiculous that in an era of howling fanaticisms some Americans did prefer the noiseless tenor of their way to a shrieking soprano. In other words, if there had been more Reverdy Johnsons and fewer Charles Sumners there might never have been a Civil War. Still it must be admitted that by the middle of the nineteenth century the "Finished City" had also become the "Forgotten City."

But just about that point of time an event occurred that was to have a profound and beneficent influence on the future of the town. This was the founding here of a school for the training of young men to become commissioned officers in the Navy. So important has that school become that the very name of Annapolis is synonymous with the naval institution, just as West Point means the national military academy.

It is curious that although the town lay on what was considered a fine harbor, and there was a brisk trade with London during at least two generations before the Revolutionary War, Annapolitans did not enter the Royal Navy, as some other colonials did from Virginia to Massachusetts. Even when the war began, the navy men of Maryland in the Continental forces hailed from elsewhere, such as Commodore James Nicholson of Chestertown, or young Joshua Barney of Baltimore.

Naturally, the American Navy tended to copy the ways and traditions of the British service, despite the hatred felt for the British nation in the wars. When, in 1798, the new-born American Navy served in the Caribbean with the British in suppressing the French commerce-destroyers, the ranking American officers seem to have borrowed the British regulation book, and swallowed it whole. It was a good thing for the future of the service that this was done, instead of taking over the republican features of the French Navy, where Citizen Ordinary-Seaman was just as important as Citizen Captain. There was a decided monotony about the way the French ships either sank or surendered during the Revolutionary and Napoleonic wars which id not appeal to the tough old Yankee martinets who commanded our first frigates.

This English tradition governed not only the regulation book nd the cut of the uniforms, but extended also to the manner f taking young officers into the service. The boys admitted as midshipmen were expected to pick up all they needed to know bout life aboard ship, punctuated by the kick of a boot on the tern sheets, or a wallop of the speaking trumpet on the skull. The system tended to develop ignorant bullies who, when the ime came, might prove to be excellent fighters; but in the long ntervals between wars they were no shining ornaments to the profession or their nation.

Life aboard ship was very simple. The captain insulted and browbeat the First Lieutenant. The "First Luff," in turn, bullied he junior officers and everybody below him; each in turn kicked he men lower in rank, down to the wretched negro mess boys, who had nothing to kick but the galley cat. It is hard to realize n these days the miserable existence which was considered appropriate for the "young gentlemen" who were destined to be officers of the United States Navy. The youthful aspirant, all aglow with his dream of treading the quarter deck, shiny in gold lace and brass buttons, was catapulted into the midshipmen's "steerage," a tiny space which would have accommodated two comfortably, but would actually be inhabited by a dozen. Other inhabitants were taken for granted, rats scuttling about in a friendly way and armies of cockroaches. Some of these boys were too young to be thrown into the hurly-burly of the midshipmen's quarters. Farragut was only nine when he reported for duty with his midshipman's warrant, and Rear Admiral

Goldsborough received his appointment at the age of seven, though he did not go aboard ship till four years after. The bullying suffered by those little fellows at the hands of the older ones can only be compared to what was the rule in the English public schools of the same period, and probably the English Navy also.

For food, these midshipmen, on the long cruises of those days, lived on a monotonous fare composed chiefly of salt beef, salt pork, and "ship's bread," with a modicum of molasses, bean or pea soup, and rice and oatmeal. The ship's bread or hard-tack soon became inhabited with weevils; and when it became actually restless as it lay upon the platter, it was consigned to the galley to be baked, bugs and all; that being, in fact, the only fresh meat the boys had from one port to another. There were villainous, greasy concoctions made of hard-tack (with or without weevils) and salt pork which appeared in the midshipmen's mess, not to mention choice viands copied from the forecastle, known as "burgoo," "dunderfunk," "skilligallee," "doughboys," and "dog's body," all about as appetizing as the names suggest. Sundays and holidays, there was the weekly treat of plum duff, a pudding containing raisins, made into a sphere of about the size, shape, specific gravity, and digestibility of a 24-lb. shot. The table appurtenances were plain, also. The tin plates were dented and bent from being used as missiles, and one admiral says that in his mess they had to take their soup from a cigar box.

Midshipmen had their grog ration in the old days, too, some of which they gave to the seaman who was their "hammock man." And it is not surprising that many a lad became a confirmed drunkard in his teens. Shore leave was the signal for a spree to the steerage as well as to the forecastle. It was a rare young man who could stand fast against the life into which he was thrown, master languages as a hobby, as Farragut did, or teach himself advanced mathematics, like Maury.

Besides dissipation, shore leave was the occasion for settling "affairs of honor." In that crowded steerage many a quarrel broke out, and the more the midshipman felt his oats as a gentleman, the more he insisted on settling his personal difficulty by the method of mutual assassination, called the duel, which held fast in the Navy long after it had been frowned out of existence in most sections of the country. Many boys, who were the hope of their parents, were left permanently ashore in various ports all over the world—"dead on the field of honor."

The most notorious American duellist of the nineteenth century, Alexander McClung, who strutted under the title of the "Black Knight of the South," began his career in the Navy, and in 1828 fought his first affair of honor as a midshipman. Oddly enough, this was the only time in which he was wounded. In all his subsequent fourteen duels he killed each adversary, seven of them being men of one family. He yearned to shoot Jefferson Davis, his superior officer in the Mexican War, but never succeeded in calling him out. Finally, he turned his fatal pistol on himself, after writing a poem to death. McClung represents the *reductio ad nauseam* of the duelling code as it flourished in both Army and Navy up to the era of the Civil War.

In all this life aboard ship, every influence tended to coarsen and brutalize the boy sent into the Navy, and to deprive him of anything that might be called a decent education. A book on one of these old frigates was as rare as a hen's tooth. It probably would have been considered "sissy" to show any interest in a printed page, except before the examination for promotion, when every midshipman laboriously memorized his Bowditc for the great ordeal.

To meet the charge that the young naval officer was almos illiterate, Congress provided schoolmasters immediately afte the War of 1812, to be distributed at least among the large ships. If there was any wretch on board who suffered wors than the galley cat it was the schoolmaster. Not only was he pai miserably, but he had to be berthed right among his pupils i the crowded steerage, with as much privacy as a traffic police man on Broadway, but without one shred of his authority. I the schoolmaster was holding a class in mathematics, one or al of the boys might suddenly be ordered on deck. Since the school master was only a "damned civilian," he had no authority ove his pupils. In a word, the conditions were so unspeakable tha very few self-respecting men could endure them.

Then Congress, in its infinite wisdom, decided to remedy th situation by calling these unfortunate pedagogs not "school masters" but "professors of mathematics." Strange to say, th midshipmen did not seem impressed, and continued to learn a little as possible, even with the changing of title.

This kind of training may have been tolerable during th years when practically all an officer needed to know was sea manship and a little navigation. But, with the coming of steam it was another story. The principles of the steam engine wer not so easy to pick up as the orders for going about or coming to anchor. The invention of the rifled gun and the immense in crease in range of even the smoothbores meant, also, that the naval battle of the future might be settled by something differ ent from Nelson's maxim that you should get so close to the enemy that your guns cannot miss. There was a new science in gunnery, too. In short, the Navy was rapidly coming to be a profession, not a mere means of getting a living at sea with a prospect of war only once in a generation.

Lieutenant Matthew Fontaine Maury, the most brilliant intellect the American Navy ever boasted, grew up in the old tradition, and was so utterly disgusted with the condition of things that he wrote a series of letters to the *Southern Literary Messenger* concerning the abuses of the Navy. He particularly urged the establishment of a naval school, corresponding to West Point. There had been some loosely organized schools ashore at the navy yards of Norfolk, Boston, and New York, but a more important beginning was made at the Naval Asylum in Philadelphia in 1839. That is the real forefather of the Naval Academy at Annapolis, because when the time came for the birth of the new institution, four of the ablest men who had been teaching in the Philadelphia school, Professors Chauvenet and Lockwood, Lieutenant Ward, and Passed Midshipman Maury, were selected to start things going in Annapolis.

A special impetus to the creation of a training school for the Navy came in 1842, with the tragedy of Midshipman Philip Spencer. He was the son of the Secretary of War, but apparently a trouble-maker wherever he went. While on the little brig *Somers* he was convicted of attempting to organize a mutiny to kill all the officers and inaugurate a career of piracy on his own. Being found guilty, he was hanged at the yard arm. On account of the political importance of his father, the newspapers were filled with the story and one of its morals was clear—that the Navy was getting to be regarded too much as a reform school for incorrigible boys. By this time there was a strong sentiment, both in the Navy and out, for establishing something that should do for the Navy what West Point had long been doing for the Army. And when the historian, George Bancroft, accepted the post of Secretary of the Navy, he did so with the full intention of bringing this to pass.

It is interesting now to observe how cleverly he went about the task. He was too wise to go before Congress and ask them to agree to his plan. In the first place, there would have been a howl about an appropriation that would bring nobody any votes. Again, since West Point was in the North, every member of the Southern delegation would demand the site of the Naval Academy for their own territory. Of course, with a fight going on between all the Southern ports, the Northern congressmen would enjoy blocking every move to take the Academy south of the Mason and Dixon line.

Bancroft himself had selected Annapolis. It happened, luckily, that the Army was ready to quit its useless little post on the Severn, the fort there having long since become obsolete. And since the Secretary of War, Marcy, the father of Passed Midshipman Marcy, the professor at the naval school in Philadelphia, was entirely in sympathy with Bancroft's idea, he readily transferred the Army post to the Navy. President Polk also heartily concurred in this plan. Meanwhile, Bancroft had obtained a full assent to his plan of a naval school at Annapolis from two boards of naval officers, one representing the older men and the other the younger.

Having gone so far he needed money, but again he was careful not to ask Congress. Instead, he took the $28,200 which was annually appropriated for the professors in the Navy but designated in the act simply for "instruction." Bancroft, by degrees, let out most of the Navy professors on "waiting orders"—that is, without pay, and thus had something with which to carry on. He took over from Philadelphia the four men already named, and selected Commander Franklin Buchanan, a Marylander, as the first Superintendent. Buchanan had the task of adapting the Army buildings to the needs of a school, as well as organizing the curriculum and the staff. Lockwood, who had graduated from West Point, was sent back to visit his old alma mater in order to pick up useful ideas for an academy for the Navy.

On October 10, 1845, the new institution was formally inaugurated. Superintendent Buchanan mustered all hands in one of the classrooms, told the midshipmen that he was going to exact obedience of the regulations, and urged upon them the shining virtues of "obedience, moral character, and temperance." In front of Mahan Hall is set the tablet commemorating this occasion, and stating that the "Naval School" was founded on the date mentioned, under "James K. Polk, President of the U. States, George Bancroft, Secretary of the Navy." This tablet was originally set up in the old Recreation Hall. It is one of the very few things left to keep alive the fact that such a man as Polk ever lived, and whatever share he had in the project, it should be chalked up to his credit. The term "Naval School" became "Naval Academy" years later.

Thus, Secretary Bancroft managed to have his school well under way in the fall of 1845, so that when the next spring brought the need of fresh appropriation, Congress was shown a thriving institution, and there was nothing to do but to accept it.

The staff of men assembled as the first faculty consisted of Commander Franklin Buchanan, Superintendent; Lieutenant

J. H. Ward, Executive and Instructor in Gunnery and Steam; Professor William Chauvenet, Instructor in Mathematics and Navigation; Professor H. H. Lockwood, Instructor in Natural Philosophy; Professor A. N. Girault, Instructor in French; Chaplain George Jones, Instructor in English; Surgeon J. A. Lockwood, Instructor in Chemistry; and Passed Midshipman S. Marcy, Assistant Instructor in Mathematics. Four of them deserve special comment. Commander Buchanan was selected for his known abilities, especially as an organizer. He later had distinguished service, especially in the Confederate Navy as captain of the *Virginia* (*Merrimac*) in her duel with the *Monitor,* and still later as admiral commanding the *Tennessee* in the fighting against the Union fleet at Mobile Bay. His firm and wise handling of the new institution was of great importance to its future. Lieutenant Ward was noted, in a day when naval officers were ignorant and did not care who knew it, for his keen interest in the scientific side of his profession, especially in gunnery and the new field of steam engineering. He was the author of lectures and text-books, a really fine intellect. One of his first requests to the Superintendent was to establish a library, and in particular to have an allowance for books on ordnance and gunnery. This Buchanan granted, "provided that the whole cost does not exceed one hundred dollars." Ward was a very important member of this first faculty group. Unhappily, he was the first Union naval officer killed in the Civil War.

Chauvenet was a brilliant young mathematician, the son of a soldier of Napoleon. He graduated from Yale with high honors in mathematics, and was only twenty-five when he reported for duty at Annapolis. He brought from Yale the system of marking on a 4.0 basis, with 2.5 as the passing grade. His influence was very important on the early academic policies of the school, and he made a reputation for excellent teaching. He wrote numerous text-books, some of which were still used in high schools when the present middle-aged generation was studying its algebra and plane geometry. His reputation spread to Europe, he was active in learned societies, and came to be recognized as one of the brilliant mathematicians of America.

Lockwood was one of the old "professors" in the Navy who had managed to make a success of teaching aboard ship by sheer force of personality and will, and had been selected for the corps of teachers at the Naval Asylum School in Philadelphia. There he helped Lieutenant Ward with the gunnery courses and Chauvenet with his mathematics. At Annapolis he was responsible for introducing the infantry drills, which he had learned at West Point, and which have been a part of the Annapolis routine ever since. When the Civil War broke out he got leave to command a regiment of volunteers. He was promoted to brigadier-general in the same year and served with distinction. For example, he commanded a brigade at Gettysburg. Refusing a permanent commission in the Army, he returned to Annapolis to take up his teaching again at the close of the war.

Lockwood had his trials with the young gentlemen of the Navy, for from the first they resented the idea of playing soldier, and they made things difficult until, backed by the Superintendent, Lockwood made them take their infantry manual and like it.

Park Benjamin, in his story of the Naval Academy, tells an

anecdote which was cherished and retold in midshipmen's quarters for more than a generation. Lockwood stuttered. One day he had the midshipmen marching toward the Severn River. He tried to call the order, "Halt!" but his tongue betrayed him. What he shouted was not the word "halt," whatever else it sounded like, and the midshipmen, with great gusto, kept on over the bank down into the river, field pieces and all, determined to swim, if need be, to Greenberry Point. Finally, Lockwood managed to emit the right word, and his charges stood meekly in the water up to their waists. "Theirs not to reason why."

As the visitor sees the modern Naval Academy grounds, it would be hard to picture the smallness and primitive character of the first setting. The entire lot of land, now comfortably covered by Bancroft Hall, amounted only to nine or ten acres. One of the virtues of this army post for a naval school was that it was enclosed on the land sides with an eleven-foot wall. For the rest there was the little stone fort, fourteen feet high, with its eight old-time guns resting their muzzles on the parapet. Above the level of the guns, the parapet was covered with sod. Within the enclosure was a small brick magazine. In addition, there was an assortment of ten or a dozen small buildings, which had to be adapted as best they could to the purposes of education. The one outstanding dwelling in this group was the Superintendent's house, that former colonial home of Walter Dulany, mentioned in an earlier chapter. In 1845 the water came far inside of the present shore line all round. The grounds were ragged and unattractive. On the Severn side there was a steep bank; between that and the river was a marsh. There was no sea wall. The outstanding landmark, which survived until 1895, was the famous old mulberry tree. This stood near the shore, about half way between Fort Severn and the wall that separated the Navy Yard from the town.

But the Superintendent's difficulties were more with the personnel under his command than with the material. In that very first year, among the fifty midshipmen sent to Annapolis there was a surprising number of cases of drunkenness, eloquent of the demoralized condition of most midshipmen ashore in those days. And there were clashes of personalities in the staff, also. But the launching was far more successful than many people in and out of the Navy were ready to believe.

Secretary Bancroft, in his first "plan" as sent to Commander Buchanan, outlined a system which has set the tone and character of the school to this day. He provided that the teachers be selected, as far as possible, from the Naval officers, and he created the "Academic Board," consisting of Heads of Departments, to manage the school business, especially the standings in scholarship. The original age limits were set from thirteen to sixteen, which have been raised in the course of time. Bancroft was careful in his requirements for admission to stick to the Three R's, with a modicum of geography. This was so that no Congressional opposition could kill off the school on the ground that requirements were so high that only the sons of the rich could get in.

From the first, there was a "weighting" of the different subjects. That is, a mark in seamanship was worth five times as much as a mark in English or chemistry. This idea has survived in the present Academy.

At first there were three distinct groups of students. Out of that original fifty who reported for duty in October, 1845, thirty-six were "oldsters" looking for promotion, having already taken studies at the Naval Asylum School and served six years in the Navy. Their ages ranged from eighteen to twenty-seven. Then there were thirteen "youngsters," who had entered the Navy four years before. Finally, there were seven young greenhorns, who had just been admitted. One of the problems of discipline had to do with what these young gentlemen regarded as their rights and perquisites. The "oldsters" were indignant at being treated like schoolboys. The "youngsters" were outraged at not having the free run of the town, as they would have had if they had been sent to the Philadelphia school. The seven poor little novices, however, learned very quickly that they had no rights or privileges whatever.

Just how the townspeople viewed this new institution is not recorded. Probably it seemed too trifling a matter, to exchange an army post for a naval school, to deserve any special comment. No one then could foresee that the school of fifty would some day expand to 2500, that it would be the one resource that would give the "Finished City" a new lease on life, and identify its name with that of the "Cradle of the Navy."

CHAPTER IX

THE MID-CENTURY AND THE "WAR BETWEEN THE STATES"

THE new educational institution, in spite of its fair start in 1845, had great difficulties almost from its birth. Scarcely had the recitations begun when the Mexican War broke out and, naturally, the midshipmen were wild to get to sea. Some of the "oldsters" did so, but the youngsters were held behind to keep on with their algebra and drills, much to their indignation. Buchanan himself looked for and obtained his sea orders in 1847. He was not the sort of person who would stay on a school assignment if there was fighting going on anywhere. But it was a pity that he did not see his duty otherwise, for he was needed at Annapolis. He was succeeded by an officer, Captain Upshur, who proved so weak that the midshipmen ran riot over the school and the town. Only when some of them hanged Professor Lockwood in effigy, on account of his infantry and artillery drills, did Upshur finally wake up and call a court-martial on the ringleaders. Since these young sea-lawyers argued that they had not been "disrespectful to a superior officer," because Lockwood was not an officer, the faculty members in civilian dress went to Congress and succeeded in creating for themselves a special corps in the Navy called "Professors of Mathematics," with rank corresponding to commissioned ratings, which made them "superior officers" from that time on. The old professors of mathematics on the ships had no uniform or rank.

The boys who had to stay behind during the Mexican War made up as best they could for their enforced detention at Annapolis by subscribing to the erection of that little marble monument standing alongside the walk leading to Bancroft Hall, dedicated to those other midshipmen who had been killed in the performance of duty. That monument, and the Herndon obelisk on Lover's Lane, are the only two memorials which have never been moved from their original location. At the time, the bank on which the Mexican War monument stands was the shore of the Severn. All the present area, now covered by tennis courts, is "made" land of a far later date.

In 1850 the name of the school was changed to "United States Naval Academy," and an important advance was achieved the next year when the present four-year course was established. Thereafter, the confusion of oldsters and youngsters and plebes studying mainly to pass promotion examinations was gradually ended, and it became a real educational institution. But the bad effect of a superintendent leaving in two years, as Buchanan did, to be succeeded by an utterly different personality has remained with the school ever since. It has always been hard to have any consistent policy at the Naval Academy when one superintendent is succeeded by another every two or three years, and most of the officers under him, every two years. It is remarkable that there has been, on the whole, so little upset in all its history.

In the *Illustrated News* (London) for March 26, 1853, there is an article on "The American Naval Academy." It is embellished by some quaint woodcuts which make the Academy of that day appear as a rather dismal and shabby assortment of little buildings. Most of the article, however, is about Maryland statistics. Evidently the writer did not know much to say about the institution, but he did get off this flourish: "In this school is formed from the rough material the highly educated and most polished gentleman, to be put forth as a sample of his countrymen in every port and under any flag of Christendom."

Buchanan had small chance for distinction in Mexican waters. His most important duty, between the founding of the Naval Academy and the command of the *Virginia,* was as flag captain for Commander Matthew Calbraith Perry on the famous expedition that resulted in opening up Japan to the rest of the world. The long-suffering Japanese, for the last eighty years and more, have had to listen to visiting Congressmen and others informing them how an American squadron "opened the door of Japan to civilization." A special reason for this benevolent act was to obtain some kind of a commercial treaty with the Nipponese, because at that time American whalers were operating in large numbers off the islands and they had no port of refuge in distress. If shipwrecked off the Japanese coast the whale men were promptly thrown into prison.

After endless delays, the start was made in the fall of 1852. Commodore Perry, brother of the more famous Oliver Hazard Perry of Lake Erie fame, had been selected to command the expedition. Perry was as cold, forbidding and over-awing as the Bunker Hill monument. Officers who served under him in their youth still quaked inwardly at his very name when they themselves had become rear admirals. The bravest thing Farragut ever did was to report this terrifying dignitary to the Navy Department during the Mexican War, and all he got for it was to be sent off to blockade the port of Tuxpan, where he was almost certain to die of yellow fever. In fact, he nearly did so. Anyway, it was thought that such an Olympian as Perry was just the man to impress the Orientals.

Yet, perhaps, there were a dozen others who might have done as well, for Matthew Calbraith Perry was not the only Pooh-Bah of the Navy. In that period of peace between 1815 and 1861, it was a generally accepted fact that captains were above laws, orders, and regulations. Whatever they said *was* law, order, and regulation. Captain was the highest rank in the Navy, though the older captains enjoyed the courtesy title of commodore. And these old fellows held on to their rank like grim death because there was no retirement scheme whatever until 1855. They never resigned and seldom died; at least so the younger officers thought. For example, Captain Charles Stewart was captain in 1814 and was still a captain when he died in 1860. Another captain had been bedridden for ten years, but he was not only still carried on the active list, but even promoted. But the great virtue of the grade was that, by having that rank, one could do almost anything and get away with it. No court-martial had any terrors for a man of the grade of captain after 1815. One who was tried for leaving his station off the African coast without orders and coming home was sentenced "to present this court with a bottle of good whiskey."

An amusing example of this independence deals with two captains. One of them was a lordly resident of Annapolis, and the other's home was not far distant. They were great cronies. Once, as the story goes, two vessels were ordered out of the Chesapeake to Europe. They were commanded by these two men. Before starting from Annapolis they primed themselves vell at the old City Hotel. Then they were rowed out to their hips. As they sailed down the bay, the happy thought occurred o one of them that this was watermelon time. He passed the uggestion to the other captain by signals that they heave o and send the men ashore to look for watermelons. The other, being in an equally benevolent mood, readily agreed. In a short while the Eastern Shore farms of that neighborhood were raided by sailors, who confiscated any watermelon n sight as contraband of war. Returning to the ship, they were permitted by their captains, who were now feeling even more amiable, to have a watermelon feast on deck. When this was over, one of the captains decided that it was an intolerable shame to go on a long cruise across the Atlantic and leave behind all that fine old French brandy in the City Hotel to be imbibed by mere land-lubbers. His friend subscribed to this sentiment heartily. Whereupon, to the astonishment of the ship's company, orders were given for the two frigates to come about, and soon they dropped anchor again in Annapolis Roads. And the Annapolitans who had just bade their naval friends a long farewell, were taken aback to see these two captains, arm in arm, laying a course west by south for the City Hotel. They made heavy weather of it, but eventually they reached their destination and ordered their cognac. When at last they recovered from their respective headaches, they embarked again for Europe, but in their own good time.

Since both these captains were great moguls in the Service, and one of them a particularly distinguished officer about whom a solemn biography has been written, this ancient bit of gossip shall not be adorned with real names. And perhaps it is high time that we return from this digression to

Commodore Perry's mission in Japan.

The story of the expedition to Japan touches Annapolis because the formal start was made from this port. On account of interminable delays and breakdowns it was only the side-wheeler, *Mississippi,* that actually got going down the Chesapeake, and after touching at Norfolk made out to sea where, by various rendezvous, she met other vessels of the squadron. It was in Annapolis that Buchanan reported for duty, and there, probably, that the various presents for the Emperor of Japan and his official family were taken aboard.

The story of that expedition is well-known and has nothing further to do with Annapolis, but the presents Perry selected to take on this mission, with which he expected to impress the Japanese, are interesting in what they reveal of the education and the mentality of an American commodore brought up under the old tradition in the first half of the nineteenth century.

His selection included a miniature railway, a model telegraph, clocks, life-boats, and other mechanical contraptions. There his ingenuity failed him, and he fell back on huge quantities of perfumery. The Emperor and Empress, for example, drew six dozen bottles apiece. For the latter, he included a "chinaware tea set," which, considering the high state of porcelain art in Japan, must have been amusing. To go with this, he added some minute quantities of tea, one a "fine ten-cent variety," and some that was "even finer." It is just possible that tea in Japan might have been available of quite as good quality as the tea "even finer" than ten cents a pound. But Perry never suspected it.

Art was represented by lithographs, or "chromos," distributed o all persons of note. These included "A View of San Francisco," a lithograph of Georgetown, D.C., a "View of New Orleans," and for other subjects there was a picture of "A Steamer," and of "An Elephant." Just why the elephant was selected is a mystery. Perhaps Perry rather fancied pachyderms. But no doubt the countrymen of Hokusai and Hiroshigi went into raptures over these examples of American art.

As for literature, Perry announced that what he took would be of a "statistical nature," so as to impress the heathen with the "greatness of our institutions." He picked out as being suitable for the Mikado, "The Natural History of New York" in sixteen volumes; Morris's "Engineering"; Bancroft's "History of the United States"; and the "Farmer's Guide." To bolster up this light literature with something substantial, Perry selected "Annals of Congress," four volumes; "Laws and Documents of the State of New York"; "Catalogue of the New York State Library and Post Office"; "Journal of the Senate and Assembly of New York"; and two volumes of "Lighthouse Reports." There's a damnable iteration of New York public documents here, but perhaps they were handy and to be had for the asking.

But the great bulk of the gifts to the Mikado and the rest was in liquor. Here was something that could readily be measured according to rank. Of course, one Samurai might get angry because he had drawn the lithograph of "An Elephant," while a brother official of lower rank drew the "View of San Francisco," but liquor could be measured in quantities, and therefore carefully graded by gallons from the Emperor down. Only the Empress was spared a gift of wine or spirits; a lady in 1850 did not "drink." When the expedition came to its climax, at the Treaty House in Japan, over a hundred barrels of whiskey alone were rolled up from the beach.

At the formal dinner on board the flagship, the unsuspecting Japanese were all made roaring drunk, and thus they had their first experience of the "gift of civilization," which Perry handed them with such appalling solemnity.

Of course, it isn't fair to blame Perry alone for such faith in alcohol. There was little sentiment against hard drinking in those days. A Whig President had recently been washed into the White House by a freshet of hard cider.

The interpreter of Perry's expedition was an American missionary in China, Dr. Samuel Wells Williams, and Perry put him in charge of these presents. Dr. Williams says in his journal that he is very much disturbed by the fact that Perry did not have religious worship on the ship every day, and showed a callous indifference to the Sabbath, but the Reverend Doctor saw nothing improper in presenting the Japanese with this huge amount of wines and liquors as an introduction to a Christian civilization.

Only a few years stand between the Perry expedition and the outbreak of the greatest of civil wars, wherein again Christian civilization was not shown up to any shining advantage. In 1858, the midshipmen at the Naval Academy witnessed the great comet of that year, the tail of which spanned a quarter of the firmament and whose light was described as that of a full moon. The old superstition was that a comet presaged war. Three years later that superstition was confirmed.

How the question of secession came to the boys in the Naval Academy of 1860–61 has been described by more than one naval officer in his memoirs. After the initial act of South

Carolina and the other states of the deep South, scarcely anything else came up for discussion at the midshipmen's mess. It is curious nowadays to see the confused and bewildered points of view among these young men of 1860 in the face of political ideas which they did not understand. Popularly, the impression was that State's Rights meant that in the future every state would be sovereign and have her own navy. Those from New York preened themselves on the size and wealth of their home state and the kind of navy *they* would have. The most woebegone midshipman was a fellow from the District of Columbia who was gleefully informed by his classmates that the District had for a navy only one small steamer on the Potomac and that *she* was rotten! Cushing, later famous for his exploit in sinking the ram *Albemarle,* wrote in his diary, "If it comes to blows between the North and South, I will shed the last drop of my blood for the State of New York." Even he, as a Northerner, thought first of his state as an object of loyalty and patriotism.

As the states seceded, the orders came from home to resign, and one by one the Southern boys left the Academy gate with their carpet bag in hand, some puzzled by the new turn of affairs and wondering what it was all about; others, confident of a future career in the new nation. Often the Southerners were escorted to the Gate by their classmates, walking arm in arm—sometimes singing—to bid their friends good-bye. It never occurred to the Academy authorities to put any obstacle in the way of these lads going South, despite the imminence of war. It was assumed that they had the right to go home freely, even if it meant that they would be taking up arms against the government of the United States. Lieutenant

C. P. R. Rodgers, the Commandant, urged them to "stand by the old flag," but that was all.

Some midshipmen, indeed, like Robley Evans, disobeyed the orders from home and stayed with that "old flag," but for the most part the Southerners filed away in little groups to seek their homes in the seceded states. The graduating class of that tragic year met and pledged each other everlasting friendship, come what may, but it was not long before these classmates were firing at each other across a chasm not of their own making or desire. Practically all of the one hundred plebes berthed on the *Constitution* saw service on both sides during the war.

It is very much to the credit of the Navy of that time, with its high morale, that although the large majority of Southern officers resigned their commissions and went South, none betrayed the trust committed to him. One such captain, who was far at sea when news came of secession, heard that some young men of the wardroom, who also were Southerners, were asking why the Old Man didn't take down the Stars and Stripes, hoist Confederate colors, and take the ship into a Southern port. Promptly the captain mustered all hands aft, told them that he had been entrusted with the ship, and that he would shoot down the first man who dared to touch the flag. Thereupon, he took his vessel to Boston, turned in his resignation, and then made his way South. And it was one of the pleasant spots in a tragic story of four years of war that when naval officers met after an action was over, victor and vanquished came together again as old classmates or former shipmates.

It was true that to some of these men it was a severe wrench to obey the summons of their state and resign from the Navy, especially since the Navy meant their whole life. Such an officer, who had been one of the first midshipmen to report at the Annapolis school, felt he had to give up his commission and go with his native state, Virginia. I once had the pleasure of hearing him tell how the action between the *Monitor* and the *Virginia* (*Merrimac*) looked from the deck of the little vessel he commanded, the *Patrick Henry,* consort of the Confederate ironclad. He was full of even more interesting yarns of the Old Navy, before the war, when he served on the *Merrimac,* then a new screw frigate and quite the pride of the Navy. This old gentleman was wont to say, when he had a specially bad twinge of the gout, "Oh, damn the Confederacy. If it hadn't been for the Confederacy I'd be a rear admiral!" But no doubt he was careful not to say it when any of the Daughters of the Confederacy—to whom he was a great old hero—were within earshot!

Of course, there still was a town outside the school gates, though by 1861 the Navy was already thinking of it simply as a sort of untidy fringe to their alma mater. Annapolis lay in that part of the state of Maryland which was ardently Southern in sentiment. Admiral Mahan, in his recollections of those days, speaks of only one family in Annapolis society whose heads declared for the Union, and even this family had two sons in the Southern armies. So strong was the contagion of local sentiment that another father sent his oldest boy, then in his early teens, to school in the North for fear he would run away to enlist in the Confederacy. Loyalties were, therefore, not divided as they had been in 1775, between Whig and Tory, but practically unanimous for the South.

Perhaps it was for that reason chiefly that Captain Blake,

then Superintendent of the Naval Academy, feared for the safety of the school and the famous old ship *Constitution,* which at the time was used for quartering the large entering class. There was tense excitement when the Sixth Massachusetts and the Seventh New York Militia came to Annapolis, and there was great opposition to their landing. The midshipmen remaining at the Academy were drawn up on their side of the wall, and Confederate sympathizers assembled on the other. A mild battle followed, in which stones were heaved over the wall, picked up and returned without thanks, but there were no casualties.

Captain Blake was, it seems now, needlessly alarmed about the Academy and its historic frigate, but because the site was too close to the war scene to make it ideal for pursuing studies, the whole school was packed up and taken by ship to Newport, where it carried on as best it might until the close of the war. While the conflict lasted, the buildings and grounds of the Naval Academy, like those of St. John's College, were used as hospitals for the sick and wounded shipped back from the front. Most Annapolitans confidently expected that Maryland would follow the other slave-holding states into secession. Many Maryland officers served in the Confederacy. Buchanan, without waiting to see whether his state would secede, sent in his resignation. Then, when the legislature, by a strong majority, refused to secede, he was left in an awkward predicament by his own state. Accordingly, he wrote again, withdrawing his resignation and requesting reinstatement in his grade. Mr. Gideon Welles, Secretary of the Navy, did not see matters in that light, and Buchanan had to go into the Confederate service.

His old friend, Commodore Isaac Mayo, a famous naval character in Annapolis, sent in his resignation also, couched they say, in no measured terms. But scarcely had he dispatched it when he suddenly dropped dead. Visitors to the Naval Academy cemetery will see a tall granite obelisk bearing the name "Mayo," which marks his resting place. At his burial service the local clergyman took advantage of the occasion to expatiate on the Commodore's resignation, pointing out that he had done it in time to "save his honor" before he died. Whereupon an extraordinary scene took place. A young officer named Flusser, born in Annapolis, but hailing from Kentucky, sprang before the assembly and over the open grave delivered himself of an impassioned speech in behalf of the Union, and intimated that the dead officer had shown a poor regard for his oath to defend his country.

This young man was one of the most utterly fearless warriors who ever faced an enemy. He fought with great distinction, and was finally killed by the explosion of a shell from his own gun, which burst on the casemate of the ram *Albemarle* only a few feet from where he stood directing the fire. The body of "lion-hearted Flusser" lies now within a few feet of the monument to Mayo, on the very spot where he stood forth to defend the Union cause over the old Commodore's grave.

General Benjamin Butler, who came with the Union troops to Annapolis in 1861, had a clash with Governor Hicks of Maryland at the very outset. Nobody wanted any Yankee soldiers in Maryland. The townspeople expected an uprising of the slaves on the arrival of the soldiers from the North, but Butler, whatever his sins committed elsewhere during the war, acted with good sense in announcing that he was there to keep law and order, and if any slaves started an uprising he would put it down with a ruthless hand. This did not please the fanatics of his home state, but it calmed the fears of the Maryland people, and the town submitted quietly to the coming and going of the troops, wounded men, and paroled prisoners, for four years.

Mayor Magruder of Annapolis was as strongly opposed to the landing of Federal troops in the town as the Governor, for he feared rioting like that in Baltimore. At the same time, the Mayor was a Union man—though, by the way, Mrs. Magruder was all for the South—and his position was extremely difficult. The Annapolis negroes, however, seem to have had only the utmost scorn for the blue-coats. A Federal Colonel once knocked at Mayor Magruder's door. The dusky maid opened it. In disgust she turned her back on the caller and announced in loud tones to Mrs. Magruder, " 'Tain't no gemman, ma'am. It's only an orficer."

The sentiment was still overwhelmingly secessionist and the Annapolis boys ran off to join the Confederate army. One lady, like the mythical Barbara Frietchie (in reverse), hung out a Confederate flag from her window on State Circle. But no Union officer gave the order: " 'Fire!'—out blazed the rifle-blast." To her mortification, no one paid any attention to it.

Again war—the most terrible of all in American history—came close to Annapolis, yet passed it by. Not a shot between Union and Confederate armies or ships was heard in the old, slumbering city. The coming and going of troops, and the hospitalization of sick and wounded, made havoc of the campus of St. John's and the Navy Yard. The war-time photographs show an ugly, untidy little city, with rough, cobbled streets, whitewashed board fences, garbage barrels on the curb, and few trees. The fine gardens that gave a green setting to the old brick mansions were either mostly overgrown or built upon. The Civil War period was just about the low-water mark.

Out in the country there had been a camp, in 1861, of a fantastic regiment of volunteers from New York City, composed of Frenchmen. It was known as "D'Epeneuil's Zouaves," from the name of the colonel and the uniform they wore. The baggy red trousers, fez, and the rest of it made an outstanding spot of color by itself but it proved too good a target for the Confederate marksmen, and it was not long before the Zouave uniform vanished. But for a while they brightened the landscape on the outskirts of the town. The colonel was not very successful or happy in his position, and the regiment, after some vicissitudes, was broken up and sent to other units. That Zouave camp was pitched near the Brady farm, at what is now known as Camp Parole, on the road to Washington.

This name of the locality came also from a Civil War encampment that followed the Zouaves. Union prisoners were sometimes paroled until such time as an exchange with Confederate prisoners could be effected. At first the men were sent home to await exchange, but it was discovered that many soldiers had a way of surrendering readily and cheerfully to the foe in the hope and expectation of being sent back home for an indeterminate furlough, which was exactly to their liking. To discourage this practice, the government maintained camps of these paroled men, and kept them together under military discipline until they were due to go back to their regiments or to be mustered out. Such a camp was started on

THE STATE HOUSE, WINTER AFTERNOON

South River and then moved to the site nearer town. The little cemetery one sees beside the road on the outskirts of Annapolis contains the dead of Camp Parole, mournful rows of white stones, all exactly alike, and hundreds of them.

Finally, the war dragged through its four dreadful years to a close. To the intense disappointment of most of the townspeople, at least of the "nice" people, the cause of secession failed. But as Maryland was not a seceding state she was spared the horrors of reconstruction. The negro, the carpet-bagger, and the scalawag were not running wild in the legislative halls on State Circle, as they were doing in sister states only a short distance to the south. Gradually, the old town resumed its normal ways and adjusted itself to new conditions. The constant movement of Union soldiers, the continuous rattle of commissariat and hospital wagons over the cobbles, these all vanished and peace settled down once more. But there was little for the Annapolitans in the spring of 1865 to look forward to. Their slaves had been set free, many a family fortune had been wrecked by its devotion to the Confederacy in both money and men, and the Naval Academy had been banished to Newport. There were no industries, the old-time shipping had long since gone to Baltimore, and the tobacco lands were no longer rich in revenue. If the Revolutionary War had started the downfall of the "Ancient City," it seemed as if its doom were sealed by the "War between the States."

CHAPTER X

THE RETURN OF THE ACADEMY AND THE WAR WITH SPAIN

THE exile of the Naval Academy to Newport was not a pleasant experience for the students, their professors, or the officers. As the transfer was hastily made and the understanding was that Newport would only be a temporary resting place, there was nothing to brag of in the way of equipment. The Navy took over a summer hotel there, the "Atlantic House," a grandly classical structure with six lofty Ionic pillars in front. This was for the upper classmen. For the plebes there was first the old *Constitution,* and in 1862 the frigate *Santee* was added.

The last-named vessel deserves a special paragraph of obloquy. She was famous as a floating monument to politics, a "pork" ship, having been built piecemeal simply to please voters connected with various navy yards. She was started in 1820 and was launched in 1855, something of a record in slow motion. She was found to be useless when sent out on active duty and was placed at Newport to serve as an exceedingly uncomfortable dormitory for the midshipmen. Forty years later, as a dismasted hulk, she lay at Annapolis acting as a prison ship for luckless midshipmen caught smoking, or "frenching." Here the culprits were berthed amid the comradeship of cockroaches and the whiff of bilge water. In January the ice formed in their pitchers, and in June the air was stifling. The *Santee* s not a beloved name in the Navy.

The poor youngsters who were quartered on either the *Constitution* or the *Santee* did not have any bed of roses. They tried to study at long tables on the draughty gun deck, and ate their wretched meals on the berth deck below, in Stygian darkness. In winter there was little to ameliorate either the northeasters or the northwesters, and the boys suffered acutely. Some of the classes were held in hastily-built recitation sheds, where professor and midshipmen alike hugged themselves in their overcoats and recited their irregular verbs or stated the habits of triangles and arcs in clouds of frosty vapor. Every morning at six, the boys arose, lashed their hammocks and carried them to the spar deck; then, just as a jolly, morning eye-opener, they had to scamper up the shrouds to the masthead and down again. This was considered very hygienic, to "start the circulation," and had to be done, even if a blizzard were coating the rigging with sleet and snow. The life must have been about as uncomfortable as the blundering of officials could make it, but as Commodore Ap Catesby Jones once roared at a midshipman who timidly complained of his miseries in the steerage, "Uncomfortable! Why, what damn fool ever joined the Navy to be comfortable?"

The Newport people, especially those who sold ice cream, baked oyster pies, or concocted lemonade, greatly enjoyed the presence of the Naval Academy and worked mightily to keep it permanently in their midst. Then the citizens of Perth Amboy, New Jersey, suddenly discovered that their fair city was much better fitted as a site for the institution, particularly as it lacked the temptations of such a gilded and worldly resort as Newport. In fact, there was no allurement about Perth

Amboy whatever.

Other towns were ready to push their claims, too, but Gideon Welles, Secretary of the Navy, was determined from the first that the Academy should go back to Annapolis. Congress supported him, and in May, 1864, decreed that before October of the following year the institution should return to its original home. However, a move to call it "Severn Point," to correspond with "West Point," died aborning. Only two grim souvenirs of the Newport captivity came to Annapolis. One was the old *Santee,* and the other was the practice of hazing. There was no hazing before the Civil War, but plenty thereafter, and it all began somehow in Newport.

Before October, 1865, the great war had ended, and for the task of restoring the Naval Academy on its old site Welles had the pick of the Navy to chose from. The man he selected, Admiral David Porter, was probably the best that could have been named, an officer with so brilliant a record in the war as to have won four times the vote of thanks from Congress. He was the son of the famous David Porter, of the War of 1812, and the foster-brother of Farragut; in reputation, he stood second only to the latter as the most distinguished naval officer on the Northern side during the Civil War.

What Porter found when he took charge at Annapolis must have been discouraging. Such beauty as there had been in the old days had been wrecked by the Army occupancy. Nothing was left of the lawns but a criss-cross of wagon ruts; the shrubs were gone; the trees mostly killed, only a few around the Herndon monument being left; and the buildings were none the better for having been used as military hospitals. Even the fine old Dulany house, the former Superintendent's quar-

:rs, had been used for recreation purposes and had become ıe "billiard saloon" for the hospital.

Porter, however, was accustomed to hard work. He put a ırge force of laborers on the job and made them step fast, so hat by the time school opened things were fairly shipshape. n addition, he assembled a remarkably able group of officers s a teaching force; outstanding among them was Stephen B. uce, later to become the father of the Naval War College, and he author of what is still the leading text-book on seamanship. t is most appropriate that the Seamanship Building in the Naval Academy today is named after this officer.

The return to Annapolis became a sort of rebirth for the Naval Academy under Porter and his staff. His administration was firm yet human, for he kept an open mind. He was not afraid to do things differently from the ways of tradition, and ıe set the institution well on the road to progress. The memorial window to the Admiral in the present Naval Academy Chapel seems inappropriately designed for this masculine, full-bearded old Triton, but as a memorial it was richly deserved. His personality made a deep impression on the officers and students during his administration.

It is worthwhile at this point to take a look about the Naval Academy as it appeared in the late sixties and seventies. The original Fort Severn reservation had greatly expanded by this time. In 1845 the northern boundary of the lot ran on a line with the spot where "Tecumseh" now stands in front of Bancroft Hall, which was then on the bank of the river. On the west side, the wall ran parallel to King George Street, and extended from the point where "Lover's Lane" ends at Bancroft Hall to the water, which then came up to a spot just inside the southwestern wing of that building. In 1850 a larg tract of land was added to the north, taking in the end of wha was then known as "Northeast Street," but now "Marylan Avenue." During Admiral Porter's administration, a larg dormitory, topped with a cupola, was erected at this end o the yard, a very impressive building indeed for the year 1868 This was called New Quarters. When it was torn down in 190 it was still called New Quarters.

A photograph taken from the cupola of this building in 1870 is an interesting record of the Naval Academy ground of that year. It was a wide, level, and largely treeless plain with a few scattered buildings. The tall trees of today show in that picture as tiny seedlings.

In the following year the Yard was extended toward th western, or town side. This extension took in a famous old mansion, "Government House." This had been the officia residence of Governors Sharpe and Eden, then afterward for all the state governors. For over a hundred years every distinguished visitor to Annapolis was a guest in that house, from General Braddock to President Fillmore. In the Naval Academy, this building was used for a library and Superintendent's offices. Some dreadful additions and alterations were made in the seventies and eighties, but the most inexcusable crime was the tearing down of this historic mansion when the new building program was begun. Anyone interested in communing with the ghost of an old house may stand on the eastern side of Buchanan Row facing the present Superintendent's quarters. This was the site of the dwelling, but the gardens extended as far as the water.

If the man who photographed the Yard from New Quarers had aimed his camera in the opposite direction, his picture would have revealed an exceedingly close and malodorous neighbor of the Naval Academy. This was a section, a suburb, of Annapolis which had the refined name of Lockwoodsville, but which would never have caused the bosom of any Lockwood to swell with pride. It was the dirtiest, smelliest and

OLD GOVERNMENT HOUSE

As it appeared in 1869, when it was taken into the Naval Academy. (*After a photograph*)

slummiest collection of shacks, brewery, gas house and dumps perched on a knoll of the Severn. Still farther to the north, across the creek, rose the low-wooded bluff known as "Strawberry Hill." Then, as now, it was the site of the Naval Academy cemetery, but in that era only an ugly red clay bank, washing away into the Severn with every rain. Lockwoodsville has since become "Worden Field," and, before that, "Oklahoma," because it was considered so far away and wild when it was added to the grounds.

There was another tough neighborhood near the Academy

grounds at the opposite end, namely, the foot of King Georg Street, which was familiarly known as "Hell's Point." Pe haps that name is rough enough in itself to hint at the kin of places of refreshment and the type of gentry to be foun therein.

The photograph already mentioned, of the year 1870, show

STEAM BRIG *ALBEMARLE*

Used as Admiral Porter's barge. It blew up in the Severn, Oct. 19, 1867.
(*After a photograph*)

moored alongside the Naval Academy wharf, the frigates *San tee* and *Constellation,* and the sloop of war *Dale.* These were used for drills and practice cruises for the midshipmen. Too small to appear in the photograph, but interesting as relics of the Civil War, was the launch, oddly enough rigged as a brig which Cushing used in his successful attack on the ram *Albe marle.* Another was one of the Confederate submarines, or

"Davids"—the ancestors of all undersea craft. And, finally, there was the yacht *America,* which after a checkered career had been used as a blockade-runner by the Confederates. The Cushing launch blew up in the Severn, the "David" rusted away from neglect, but after many more vicissitudes the yacht *Amer-*

"CONFEDERATE DAVID"

This submarine, known as the "Confederate David" or "Cigar Boat" was brought to the Naval Academy after the Civil War and set up later on shore as a war relic. A "Confederate David" like this was the first submarine in history to sink an enemy vessel. (*After a photograph*)

ica returned, and she is once more moored at the Naval Academy wharf.

Of the Academy in the eighties there are two illustrated articles in *Saint Nicholas* for the years 1888 and 1889, each written by a graduate. The second was by John H. Gibbons, destined later to be a Superintendent of the institution he described. From these articles one discovers that the name "midshipman" had at that time been abolished. Instead there were "naval cadets," and since there were some officers detailed to the engine room instead of the bridge, the students were divided into "cadet midshipmen" and "cadet engineers." As in the old Newport days, the plebes berthed on the *Santee* during the summer and learned there how to sleep in a hammock, at the cost of many a bruise. The *Santee* was used also for great gun drill, wherein the cadets hauled and swabbed and loaded the old cast-iron smooth-bores as they might have done in 1861. And in the river was the Civil War monitor *Passaic,* still showing the dimples in her round cheeks from the pounding she had received during an attack on Fort Sumter. Except for two small rifled guns on the steam tug *Standish,* there was nothing to suggest that any advance had been made in ordnance since 1850.

One improvement should be noted—that, thanks to Admiral Porter, Fort Severn was transformed into a gymnasium, and there the Academy "hops" were held until well after the beginning of the twentieth century.

One of the cadets' duties, noted in these articles, was that of volunteer firemen for the town. This service also was performed a long time after the eighties, and no doubt would still be offered if a severe conflagration were threatened. The comment on the Annapolis appliances for fighting fire was that "they were of the most primitive sort." Poverty-stricken Annapolis was not buying bright, red, shiny fire-engines in the gloomy eighteen-eighties, and once a house began to blaze, the arrival of the cadets was most pathetically welcome. In those years, the Annapolis fire horses were a pair of mules used ordinarily for drawing the ice-wagon. Whenever the alarm sounded it was necessary to locate the ice-wagon, unhitch the mules and bring them to the engine-house. As for the "kaydets," a fire was usually one glorious lark, in which prodigies of valor were performed, furniture was saved by being hurled headlong from windows, and not one silk hat belonging to a solid citizen was missed by the trusty hose.

The depression suffered by the town was also strongly felt inside the Academy gates. For these years were the lowest ebb of the Navy itself. Congress, having rejoiced in the exploits of the naval men in the war and voted them thanks, cared nothing more about them, their ships, or their guns, once the war was over. The reason the cadets of the eighties were still drilling with obsolete smooth-bores and making their summer cruises in eighteenth-century frigates was because the powers in Washington did not care. Appropriations for the Navy did not bring as many votes as appropriations for post offices. Those were the years when only ten of a graduating class at Annapolis might expect a commission and a naval career. The rest were paid $1000 and turned loose. Promotions were so slow that it was nothing for a man to stay eighteen or twenty years in the grade of lieutenant. And, as for the ships, in a Naval Academy annual called "Fag Ends," of the year 1881, there is an engraving entitled "The Fleet," a pathetic attempt to put the best face possible on the American Navy. This collection of ships included the old *Powhatan,* a side-wheeler that Perry used as his flagship in the expedition to Japan in 1852, the *Constitution,* dating from 1797, and other worm-eaten tubs. Among these there was not one armored vessel, and all the guns on these ships were left over from the Civil War.

Ensign John Gibbons, in his *St. Nicholas* article, says flatly that "hazing is now almost an unknown act at Annapolis, Congress having made it a court-martial offense, punishable by dismissal. Hazing plebes has given place to a mild form of annoyance known as 'running' . . . But even running is considered a form of hazing and is fast taking its place among the lost arts." Somehow, one can almost hear a mocking echo of those words down the corridor of fifty years. Perhaps as a Superintendent, and an excellent one, Captain John Gibbons was in a position to suspect that he had been a trifle hasty in that optimistic statement. But he describes a custom which really has died out, in which the "candidates" who had come

FORT SEVERN AS A GYMNASIUM

After a photograph

to Annapolis to take their entrance examinations underwent a sort of inquisition at their hotel, conducted by a young gentleman from the Academy. By this ordeal, the candidates were compelled to say "sir" ad infinitum, and to solve strange problems in mental arithmetic provided by the lordly young men in uniforms.

The year 1881 proved to be the low ebb of the Navy. Thereafter, things slowly but definitely began to pick up. The new "White Squadron" took the place of the old *Constitution, Powhatan,* and *Hartford* as fighting units of the fleet. Scarcely were these modern vessels in commission when the Spanish-American war came along, which resulted in a tremendous change in the Academy and the town, not to mention the nation's position as a world power.

After the battle of Santiago, which practically ended the war, the Spanish prisoners were brought to the United States. For some reason the enlisted men were sent to Portsmouth, New Hampshire, and the officers to Annapolis. That made a grand to-do in the Naval Academy and a fluttering in the Annapolis dove-cotes. The Spaniards would have to be shown that the descendants of Uncle Sam were no less chivalrous than those of Don Quixote. Prisoners? Perish the thought. "Amigos!" People who had ever studied Spanish blew the dust off their books and the others practiced saying "Car-r-ramba!"

Admiral Cervera and his personal staff and senior officers were to be quartered in Buchanan Row, while the junior officers were assigned to the old cadet rooms in Stribling Row. All should be given their parole. Thus it was ordained.

On July sixteenth most of the Spaniards arrived. Lieutenant W. S. Benson met them with a sheaf of paroles printed in English and Spanish for the prisoners to sign. But there was a hitch at the old *Santee* wharf where they were landed. The officers looked at the paroles but refused to sign anything until advised by Admiral Cervera. That gentleman waved his own paper aside with the remark that he would give his word of honor and nothing more was necessary. Further, he could not see why his officers should do any differently. They were gentlemen, too. That left Lieutenant Benson with a bushel of perfectly good but unsigned parole forms. Captain Parades, for example, said that he thought a verbal parole was enough, and Captain Antonio Eulate wanted the American officer to understand that *his* word, the word of the captain of the *Vizcaya,* was just as good as that of the Admiral. Eventually, all the other officers climbed down off their dignity and signed their paroles, all except Eulate who continued to refuse and, therefore, was obliged for a while to stay on the Academy grounds. Later, Superintendent McNair decided that, parole or no parole, it was just as safe to let Captain Eulate out on the streets of Annapolis as anyone else.

This man stood apart from the rest, gloomy and suspicious. Perhaps some of his emotional condition was due to his having been badly wounded in the back and the head during the Santiago action. Frequently, he was heard to mutter, "I have lost all but my commission and my honor." He insisted that his food be tested by an American orderly first before he would touch it, because he feared the Yankees would try to poison him. Later, a Spanish cook provided his mess table. He was especially worried over the fate of his wife and children in San Juan, Porto Rico, for he could only imagine the worst when he heard that San Juan also had been taken by the Americans. When he learned that his loved ones were safe, he became a much happier man. But he was lonely and silent, and he refused to make any response to the attempted kindness of the American officers and their families. The only time he would unbend was when he saw little children.

There was another incident between American naval officers and their prisoners besides the matter of paroles, which also involved the word of a gentleman. This happened immediately after the battle. One of the Spanish officers taken off the *Almirante Oquendo* was Mellado, the paymaster. When captured he was clutching to his breast a small metal box. Lieutenant Commander Harry P. Huse, the officer in charge of the boat party, told him to turn this box over to him, but the Spaniard refused. On being urged further, he cried that he would rather die than give it up. Lieutenant Commander Huse was in a quandary. Strictly speaking, it was his duty to seize anything which might contain documents, and Mellado's strange behavior made the box seem doubly important, but he could not bring himself to take it by force.

"Will you give me your word," he asked, "that there is nothing there that might be of value to my government?"

The Spaniard eagerly pledged his honor and was allowed to keep the box. Weeks afterward, in Annapolis, Mellado brought the box to one of his new-found friends in the Academy and opened it. In it were some water-soaked photographs of his wife and children, and a packet of her letters. After telling the story of the incident and his admiration for his captor, he asked his American friend to assure Huse at the earliest opportunity that the box did contain only documents that were of intimate and personal value to the owner. Those were the days when even in war a pledge, or a word of honor, was not a mere scrap of paper.

Among the prisoners there was a captain of marines who mystified his hosts by a peculiar custom. He would go up on the verandah of the last house in Upshur Row, just at the time the Short Line train would rumble over the College Creek bridge on its seven o'clock trip to Baltimore. The Spaniard spoke to no one, but took his position on the verandah as if it were the deck of his own ship. As the train passed he would mutter "El tren! el tren!" salute, and walk away, without a word to anyone who might be near him. Finally, an explanation was furnished by a brother officer. This marine officer had a wife and family in Spain. Some day that train would bear him away from captivity and towards home. So he had to offer it a daily salute and an inward prayer.

From Admiral Cervera down, the officers courteously and cheerfully adapted themselves to their captivity. They were scrupulous in obeying all orders. They faced the flag at colors and raised the hand to the salute, like everyone else. Admiral Cervera himself set an example of knighthood in captivity which was followed by the rest.

The one unhappy incident that threatened to mar the whole situation was revealed on the twentieth of July when the *Harvard* arrived with thirty-four more prisoners and the shocking news of a massacre on board ship of six Spanish seamen and the wounding of many others. It was all due to a mistake. The prisoners couldn't understand orders put to them in English; the volunteer soldiers on guard over them got excited, thinking that the Spaniards were attempting an uprising, and fired on them. Cervera could not understand how such a ghastly stupidity could happen and was deeply moved. But he held his peace, and came, no doubt, to realize that no one felt worse about the tragic affair than the Americans themselves.

Meanwhile, the arrival of all the young Spanish officers gave the Annapolis and Naval Academy daughters a thrill that was very welcome in a hot, humid midsummer, when all the local beaux were off at war. There were gay times. The Spaniards and the Americans became acquainted with each other's odd ways. If the young lady admired something that the Hidalgo possessed, he, of course, offered it with a most formal flourish to her, and there being gold-diggers and souvenir hunters even in the gay nineties, some of the enterprising damsels were collecting rings, watches, and what-not with great success, until one of the officers, in tears of despair, went to an American girl who could understand his language. He begged her to explain to the señoritas that offering to give away anything admired by another was just an old Spanish custom. That it didn't mean a thing, really, and would she please make that clear to the other young ladies and collect back all those involuntary presents? It is pleasant to report that by this means most, if not all, of the loot was duly, if sadly, returned.

Naturally, there were lessons in Spanish to be exchanged for lessons in English. There was some extraordinary pedagogy to be sure, but "a good time was had by all." The following note was sent by an advanced pupil, a young lieutenant, to his teacher and pupil:

Miss M——

My dear friend:

I cant go this afternoon to your home at four o'clock because I am a few sick. I am very sorry for that but I hope be well tomorrow and then I go for give you the lection of his panish and receive the of your.

With kind and respectful regards to your grandmother and aunt your very respectfully

Louis de C—— [this name written with elegant circumambient flourishes]

Even as it stands, the Lieutenant's English was probably far better than any Annapolitan's Spanish. It turned out, by the way, that when he reported for his lesson the following afternoon he explained that he had been "a few sick of the knee." This young officer was a strikingly handsome six-footer who made a tremendous hit with the girls. He was also of blood so blue as to be pure cobalt, for his pedigree went back beyond the days of Ferdinand and Isabella. He had a good time, too, and he must have written home about it, particularly concerning a certain officer's daughter whom he found very attractive. Suddenly, his irate mother cabled Admiral Cervera, "Send Luis home immediately!" No designing American baggage should ensnare *her* son. But it never occurred to her that being a prisoner might make it difficult for him to take the next boat to Spain. To her great relief, he did reach home single and unattached and in later years rose to an important position in his government.

The freedom allowed the American girls, even in the nineties, scandalized but entertained these Spanish officers. They had never seen anything like it. On the other hand, they discussed freely certain matters whch in those days Mrs. Grundy did not permit young ladies to know anything about. Babies were tacitly assumed to be brought by storks or found in the cabbage bed. But it was not long before the Spaniards had told all the girls that Admiral Cervera's son, "Angel," was expecting news of the arrival of a baby in his family by any post from Spain. The tidings did not arrive. There was great anxiety and excitement. The postman was mobbed daily. What had happened? Poor Angel was inconsolable. There was no other topic of conversation.

At last the news came that the cherub had arrived and all was well once more; joy knew no bounds, and the Spaniards rushed about the Yard spreading the glad tidings. Happiest of all were Angel and his father, and it was a fortnight before any other subject had a chance in conversation, to the horror of all the old ladies in the community.

Finally, at the end of August, word came from Washington that the prisoners were to be sent home. It had been a strange war, and a still stranger captivity. What had begun with bursting shells and blazing ships ended in ice cream, cake, and moonlight walks. Some naval officers, in fact, who returned to their quarters in the Naval Academy after a nerve-racking experience on blockade duty were not entirely pleased to find their verandahs and drawing rooms cluttered up with the enemy. But they had to make the best of it, for their young people were having a glorious time. It is sad to report that whatever international romances may have begun did not stand transportation. There were no wedding bells in Annapolis.

But the Spaniards went off in a fine frame of mind about the accursed Yankees, and certainly when did prisoners of war ever have such an experience? Admiral Cervera expressed his thanks to Superintendent McNair on departing from Annapolis, and, again, as he boarded the steamer for home he wired his appreciation. The phrase "officer and gentleman" fits particularly well this gallant and courteous man. It is a pity more wars are not conducted after the Annapolis pattern in the brief conflict of 1898! If there were some officers who underwent the constant hospitality "with peril, toil, and pain," and wondered if they had escaped the horrors of battle only to perish with indigestion, they held their peace. Everyone was loath to see these prisoners go, and perhaps some of them would have cheerfully stayed on a while longer.

There was one captive, however, who was obliged to remain.

He did so unwillingly, and certainly no one else desired his further presence on American soil. This was "Cristobal Colon," alias "Lorita," which is Spanish for poll-parrot. This bird was the mascot of the cruiser for whom he was named, the last of the stricken squadron that ran upon the Santiago beach in flames.

While the Americans were rescuing the wounded from the wreck, a Spanish officer who had been mortally hurt, pointed to the bowsprit of the *Colon*. An American midshipman saw what he meant and reached a boat hook up to a queer object squawking furiously, a parrot with every feather burned away. The bird accepted his rescue most ungraciously. Before the Spaniard died, he begged the American midshipman to send the parrot to someone who would care for it. The other promised to do so. He himself liked pets and thought he might make a friend of Don Cristobal. But tribulation, fire, and nakedness had not tamed the proud Spaniard. From time to time he would ejaculate venomously, "Da me un besito," meaning "Give me a kiss." Obligingly the midshipman pursed up his lips. "Nice Polly," he began, but he did not complete the sentence. Cristobal, with one swoop, put his beak through his benefactor's lip.

Thereafter, the fiend resided in a cage, and the owner having had quite enough of him, but wishing to keep his promise to the dead officer, bethought him of an officer's daughter at the Naval Academy who doted on stray cats, dogs, and such, and the more forlorn they were the better she liked them. Accordingly he wrote her a letter, appealing to her kind heart, and without waiting for an answer forthwith sent the winged demon on by express. It was a week after the letter arrived before she accidentally discovered Cristobal in the express office awaiting a claimant. He had chewed up most of his tag leaving only the words "Annapolis, Md." He was still without feathers, and his starboard eye was gone, not an attractive object at best.

After proving her claim to Cristobal, his new owner worked all the resources of her kind heart, but to no avail, for he made it clear that his chief ambition was to nip off the end of a finger, and he wasn't particular whose finger it was so long as it was an American one.

But one day there was a tremendous commotion on the verandah of the house in Upshur Row. "Papa, Papa!" shrieked the bird. A Spaniard, who was passing, stopped in his tracks, and then with three bounds sprang to the cage, threw it open crying "C-r-r-rees-to-bal Colon!"

"Da me un besito!" cried the parrot, imitating the sound of kissing, and putting his beak to the man's face. When the rhapsodies calmed down a bit, the Spaniard explained that he had been the cook of the *Cristobal Colon* and the care of the mascot had been entrusted to him. He had supposed, of course, that the bird was dead and this was like a return of a dear friend from the grave.

Thereafter, every day the cook brought an ear of corn for his precious Lorita and they went through their loving reunion all over again. When the time came for the prisoners to leave, everyone hoped that Cristobal Colon would go with his friend back to Spain. Alas, the Navy Department ruled that the transport was so crowded that no pets could be taken on board. A special appeal was made for Cristobal, but the hard-hearted Navy Department turned the request down.

So this one prisoner lingered behind, the last of the Spanish fleet, in a land and among people that he hated. For he never became reconciled or reconstructed. The sight of a Spanish flag would draw from him a comical imitation of a cheer, but most of his days he spent in gloomy silence, deigning only to mock the voices and laughter of the household. If you drew near to his cage, he rolled his one good eye with such a malignant expression that the wise kept their distance.

At last, about a decade after Santiago and almost on the anniversary of the battle, Cristobal Colon yielded up his sullen spirit, still in captivity. He was entombed with due ceremonies as a soldier, and the New York *Herald* devoted almost a whole column to his obituary. That was a generation ago, but there are some who remember him vividly, notably those whose fingers ventured too near his cage.

Thus, the brief flurry of the war with Spain came and went in a few weeks. The victories at Manila Bay and Santiago had so thrilled our national pride that anything the Navy desired could be had for the asking. Upon this high tide of enthusiasm rode in the new American Navy, and with it the new Naval Academy, the most colossal set of buildings for educational purposes the world has ever seen.

CHAPTER XI

SCENES AND CHARACTERS AT THE TURN OF THE CENTURY

OF course, the transformation of the old Naval Academy into the new, and the accompanying changes in the town, did not come all at once. But, generally speaking, the old era ended about the turn of the nineteenth century, or five or six years after the new century had begun. That era and the people who made it, in town or Academy, had far more in common with the period of the Civil War than it had with the present day.

In 1900, Annapolis was still a sleepy, Southern town, not too spick and span around the curbs and backyards, and rather weak on paint and repairs. The streets were still cobbly, with very rough and edgy cobbles. As for modern improvements, in some parts of the town (as in Baltimore, too, for that matter) one might see a rivulet of dishwater coursing through a little channel in the sidewalk into the gutter. There was no soda-water fountain. A pharmacist still sold drugs instead of sandwiches, soft drinks, books, and tobacco. Mr. Edison's invention of electric bulbs had not yet pushed out gas, or even kerosene, from the Annapolis homes. Going to Washington or Baltimore was an all-day affair. There was one good train to take in either direction in the morning, and one back again in the evening. Going to Washington meant making connections at a junction with the through trains of either the B. & O. or the

Pennsylvania Railroad. Both these junctions were forlorn wooden sheds in open fields, where the passenger sat one hour perhaps two, waiting for the train.

The terror of missing the last train from Baltimore soured all the pleasure of going to the theater, or dining with friend in that city. You either scrambled aboard the last Short Line train around eleven o'clock or spent the night at a hotel. One damsel was escorted by a young man to the play in Baltimore The last act was long, the two were wedged in where they could not escape, and they missed the train. They telegraphed their plight and each went to a separate hotel for the night but when they returned to Annapolis the next morning they found a frigid welcome. All the proper old ladies of the town were happy to suspect the worst. The poor girl had to try to live down the story, but without much success.

The townspeople had two outstanding characteristics, poverty and pride. As many of them had lived through the Civil War they still nursed all the grievances of those days, and clung to the old ways in everything. Longer than anywhere else, perhaps, or at least anywhere in the North, men still wore silk hats and double-breasted frock coats. Probably Annapolis ladies were the last to give up hoops, though on that point I can offer no visual evidence. But certainly there were some bonnets in 1900 that dated no later than Appomattox.

Among these people of the older generation, there were vestiges of the speech of "before the war." "Annapolis," for instance, used to be pronounced "Annawpolis." On a map Spa Creek is actually printed "Spaw Creek," just as it sounded. This "a" in the twentieth century has been flattened out as if crushed to earth by the chariot of progress—"half" is "haff" n Annapolis now, and "laugh" is "laff," but still one refers to Chief Justice Taney, who sits in bronze on State House Hill, as "Judge Tawney," and "Calvert Street" is to this day called "Cawlvert."

Some old-fashioned customs lingered in Annapolis along

From the Annapolis Alphabet

with the silk hats and the rusty bonnets. One of these was the New Year's call. On the first of January, the larger homes were open to entertain friends and neighbors. The ladies "received," and the gentlemen put on their full regalia of topper and frock coat; the officers donned their special uniform, "undress B," which was also a frock-coat costume, and the ladies were arrayed in their afternoon best. The task of "receiving" consisted primarily of ladling out the contents of a huge punch bowl containing egg-nog. There is on the face of the earth no concoction more bilious than this, or more difficult to absorb in large quantities, but custom had made egg-nog sacred to Christmas and New Year in Annapolis. From one port of call to another, the gentlemen cruised, hoisting aboard a mixture of egg and brandy in one house, and brandy and egg in another, until by the time all those hospitable friends had been visited, some of these callers had difficulty in finding their hats and canes, and had to walk down the steps very carefully. But it was a day of goodwill and neighborliness, and no more egg-nog had to be imbibed for another twelve-month.

The general somnolence of the "Finished City" in these days inspired one young stranger connected with the Naval Academy to write and publish an illustrated alphabet of limericks. This was a very reprehensible and irreverent performance. One of his pictures, here reproduced after more than thirty years, purported to represent "Main Street on a Busy Day." The little publication might not have attracted a single buyer but for the fact that the Annapolis Chamber of Commerce was advised by one of their number that this volume of limericks was exposed for sale, and that this picture especially defamed and otherwise damaged the reputation for enterprise of their fair city. It was indignantly pointed out that cows were *not* to be found on Main Street. In short, they declared that the book should be suppressed and something unpleasant should be inflicted upon the author. Further, it was noted that there was another street scene therein, abreast of which was a limerick that ran as follows:

From the Annapolis Alphabet

Q is for Quaintness, that's where
We make other Cities Despair.
There's a good deal we ain't
But as long as we're quaint
For the rest we don't bother to care.

This picture and verse also were held to be a gross slander.

Irreverent midshipmen spoke of the Ancient City as "Crabtown," an allusion to one of the important, if malodorous, sources of income. To them colonial architecture and a historic past meant nothing at all, compared with the fact that from one end of the town to the other one could not get a good ice cream soda. "What a burg!" they used to write home to

Hartford, Toledo, Keokuk and Seattle. But the malefactor who perpetrated the "Alphabet" sits now in penitential sack cloth and ashes for his crime, and an astonishing number of those same scornful midshipmen, when they grew older and desired a permanent home for their family, or went on the retired list, chose "Crabtown" out of all the cities of the United States.

One of the striking differences between the Annapolis of those days and the present is the matter of whiskers. This neglected subject deserves a dissertation all to itself. There was, at the close of the nineteenth century, no such monotony as now of clean-shaven faces, varied slightly by a short stubble under the nose. In spite of the gift of nature to the male sex, men now go about exposing the nakedness of weak chins; prominent noses are left with no visible means of support and ugly mouths stretch open to the ridicule of the world. In the Good Old Days it was otherwise.

By 1900, the gorilla whisker, or "Newgate Frill," which was the fashion earlier, had departed along with the plain mutton chop whisker. But the moustache was in its glory. None of your patches of brush, but an adornment silky and sweeping. Girls still said that "a kiss without a moustache is like an egg without salt," though they willingly made exceptions for midshipmen who were compelled by regulations to shave. Sometimes the moustache stood out sideways in curves of beauty, now called "handlebar" moustaches. With a touch of wax, one could make them stand out to port and starboard like studding-sail booms, or the barber with his iron could put a tight curl in each end after the style affected by the pugilist, John L. Sullivan. Other moustaches curved forward prodigiously and fell in a sweeping arc, like Niagara Falls, to the point of the chin. Adornments like these used to get into the coffee, unless one had a moustache cup, and they certainly dripped soup, "mais il faut souffrir pour être beau."

But the moustache was only one of the types of whisker. Both officers and civilians took pride in an infinite variety of adornment, showing much taste and individuality. There was the "Methodist chin-whisker," so called because it is supposed to have lingered longest among the Methodist clergy, which consisted of a beard with no moustache. There is a bronze bust of Admiral Goldsborough on the stairs going up to the Naval Academy Library, showing this chin whisker blowing to port in a fierce gale. There were retired rear admirals living in Annapolis who fancied this style becoming. Then there were those who cultivated the whisker named after General Burnside, that Union officer who proved so helpful to the Confederate cause in the Civil War. This consisted of a moustache combined with side whiskers. Chaplain Clark, for example, long a beloved figure in the Academy, wore "Burnsides."

Governor Warfield, a familiar personage in Annapolis, especially while the legislature was in session, affected the "Imperial," that combination of moustache and goatee made fashionable fifty years earlier by the late, unlamented Napoleon III. This was particularly popular in the South and became the distinguishing badge of the Southern gentleman of the old school, which was Governor Warfield all over, and very distingué it made him look, too.

There were full beards, also, requiring no shaving whatever and no bother about design. Admiral Worden wore that sort when he came to the Academy, and so at one time did Admiral

Porter. Some beard-bearers, like Chaplain Rawson, parted theirs in the middle; others, like Admiral Sampson, brought them to a point. Admiral Eberle, the last of the bearded Superintendents, not only parted his in the middle but also trimmed it to a point.

But the noblest, the most luxuriant achievement of all, was the "Dundreary," or the "Piccadilly Weeper." The name, "Dundreary," came from a character, Lord Dundreary, who appeared in a popular play of the eighteen-seventies and wore these decorations. "Piccadilly Weeper" was its official title in England. This was like the "Burnside," except that the side-whiskers were cultivated to the extent of billowing down in long cascades to the shoulders. That was the supreme triumph of the whisker. Professor Soley introduced them to Annapolis when he was a young instructor, fresh from Harvard. Admiral Porter at one time affected this style. At the turn of the century, there were two magnificent examples in Annapolis, that worn by Mr. Forbes of the Savings Bank (his portrait may still be seen there), and the other belonging to Pay Inspector Ray, of the Navy. Both these men were tall, handsome specimens of manhood. Ladies, especially those of the younger generation, sometimes complained that in dancing with these gentlemen they used to get lost in the jungle and had difficulty coming up for air. But they lacked appreciation. It took a special gift of nature to grow "Dundrearys."

In short, there were all sorts and varieties of facial adornment that made a collection of males a generation ago much more varied items in the landscape than they are today. Rear admirals, especially, always looked the part, even when in civilian clothes. In this degenerate age, it is sadly otherwise. I know personally a rear admiral whom I first had the pleasure of meeting as a lieutenant. In those days, he was a brown-haired, youthful officer, with smooth-shaven, rosy cheeks, and a pair of humorous eyes that twinkled at you behind their glasses. As a rear

IN THE DAYS WHEN A REAR ADMIRAL LOOKED THE PART—"DUNDREARYS"

admiral today, he still has brown hair and rosy cheeks and his eyes twinkle as kindly behind their windows as those of Mr. Pickwick. Imagine a rear admiral with a kindly look in his eyes! The Navy must be going to the dogs!

* * * *

The comparative isolation of Annapolis, together with its naval atmosphere, tended to develop individual characters such as can be found no more, there or elsewhere. There was no competition in appearances. The town was poor, but unashamed. The most aristocratic families were likely to be the poorest. None but vulgar Yankees cared about money or had the bad taste to mention such a thing. Neither in society nor in the professions was there any scramble to climb at the expense of anyone else. There was no particular place to climb to. You either were, or you weren't, and no amount of struggling to get anywhere did any good. In those days, too, keeping a store was disgraceful enough to disbar one from any social life outside a church "sociable," or the Red Men's Hall. But a lady could keep a boarding-house without losing caste. Indeed, many of them had to.

The naval officers who came to Annapolis on duty, and still more the retired officers who returned there to live, caught the slow tempo of the life, and fell into it. They, too, were secure in their living and not engaged in any cut-throat competition with one another. They could afford to take life comfortably. This security, this lack of ambition to push ahead for one's own advancement, gave play to individualities, even to the point of eccentricities. If there was no goal to struggle for, there was no position to lose, either. You were a rear admiral in the Navy or a descendant of the first families, and that was that. No matter what you said, what clothes you wore, or what you chose to do, this side of high crimes and misdemeanors, you were accepted. This placid security, therefore, was the ideal atmosphere to develop "characters," those people who did not hesitate to be themselves. In this respect, the Annapolis of 1900 had more in common with the atmosphere of 1800 than it had with the present, when Baltimore and Washington are within a short drive in one's car and when so many new people have come in that the old standards, the old memories, and the old prejudices are forgotten, save by a very few.

The personalities of that generation are not comparable, of course, with the men whom one could have seen in the streets of the town one hundred and twenty years before. In 1900, Annapolis could not claim a single figure of national fame. Gone were the Carrolls, Pacas, Chases, Pinkneys; gone, too, all the regal wealth that such names controlled and the corresponding magnificence of their way of life. Even distinguished visitors were rare, and they, when they came, had only a curiosity about the Naval Academy rather than the Athens of America.

Once in a while there was an exception. Among the older men there was a liberal sprinkling of Confederate veterans, like "Colonel" James Owens, who swam the Potomac under rifle fire of Union sentries for the privilege of fighting for Jeff Davis. In the war he rose to the dizzy eminence of Corporal, but, like all other veterans, he was given the unofficial title of Colonel, and thus he was known for forty years. Once I met him in the company of James Ryder Randall, the author of "Maryland, My Maryland," the poem now on exhibition in the author's own hand in the State House. Mr. Randall was as courtly as any chevalier of the old school could possibly be, but it was clear that the Naval Academy was of no interest to him as compared to the "Ancient City." This, he knew, would have cheerfully responded to the appeal of his stirring lines in 1861; but the tyrant's heel came upon its shore so quickly, and the upstate people were so strongly for the Union, that perforce Annapolis had to remain under Yankee rule.

There was a liberal proportion of negroes who had known

slavery, and some of them, no less than their white masters, became well-known characters. There was, for example, Nick Jackson, a living embodiment of slow motion, interspersed by long periods of complete repose and contemplation. Jackson never knew when the urge to rest and reflect upon the universe might come upon him, or for how long, and to protect himself against emergencies of this sort he always carried a lunch in his battered silk hat. Ever and anon, he would sit upon the curb, remove his hat, and proceed with his repast. Usually, he carried a palm leaf fan, with which he soothed his perspiring brow, and this was as likely to be in his hand in January as in August. His favorite resting place was the steps of the Chase Home. Here he would sit and fan himself, muttering "I'm gittin' tired of it!" This complaint seemed to be addressed to the cosmic scheme, for you never could discover precisely what it was that wearied him.

Among the "Cullud" People, another famous character was Dennis. This African spanned more of the Naval Academy's existence than any other man. When the institution began, in 1845, Dennis was hired as a "boy." He continued to work at odd jobs, in quarters or outside, through war, pestilence, and peace. Decade followed decade; it was all the same to him. When the class of '69 were First Classmen they decided that it was high time that Dennis entered the holy state of matrimony, and they undertook to arrange the wedding. They arrayed him in a midshipman's full dress uniform—all except side arms—and conducted the ceremony with pomp and circumstance.

By this time, Dennis had become a Specialist. He was a Raker of Leaves. This became his sacred calling. He grew a straggly, goatish beard, which in time turned white; his black face be-

DENNIS

After a photograph

came seamy with wrinkles, his right eye blind, and his back bent; but he still plied the rake. The children in the Yard used to tease him by jumping into his pile of leaves and scattering them; but, although he pretended great indignation, he really didn't care. All he was interested in was to keep his job, and his only fear was that the leaves would cease to fall, or some hard-hearted Superintendent would take away his occupation.

His technique was maddening to everyone connected with the Department of Buildings and Grounds. Away back in the days of Commander Buchanan, he had discovered that if you rake the leaves against the wind it will prolong the job much more than raking with it. A thousand times he was told better. "Yas, suh," he would answer meekly, but never would he change. He was threatened with dismissal a hundred times, but always he looked the picture of innocent stupidity. He kept on in his own way. He still raked leaves against the wind.

The new Naval Academy buildings took the place of those he had worked in or raked around for sixty years, but he still shuffled about contentedly with his rake and wheelbarrow. There were now many more leaves than in the old days. As the years passed, he became a "Last Leaf" himself, brown and shriveled in the frost of December, until, when he must have been nearly a hundred, the Grim Reaper came along and raked him in at last.

For many years, when Dennis came and went from work, entering the Main Gate, he would raise his hand to salute the erect, dapper figure of a gentleman who lived in the old yellow-painted brick house on Maryland Avenue, only a few paces from the Academy entrance. This was Colonel Tilton (retired) of the Marine Corps, a widower who lived alone and cultivated the art of doing as he pleased and being, at the same time, a good friend and neighbor. The Colonel in those days scorned the sidewalk, but always stepped briskly along in the middle of the street. Automobiles had not been thought of then, but the "seagoing hacks" mentioned in an earlier chapter paused and turned aside for him, as they very properly should.

Once in response to my "Good morning, Colonel," he called

out, "Good morning to you. Do you know that your intestines are twenty-eight and one-half feet long?" That interesting but somewhat intimate fact about myself I had not been aware of, and being very young, I blushed, as some young ladies overheard the remark, looked at me and tittered. "That's just how long they are," he continued loudly and cheerfully, as he joined me and started walking off in the middle of the avenue. Then, with that as a text, he gave a practical sermon on the general theme of diet and its relation to intestines.

In order to keep a feminine note in his house, he hung on the hat-stand, at the entrance where the passer-by could see, a number of ancient and faded sunbonnets. In the front window was a plaster cast of the Venus de Milo. The sunbonnets remained the same in December as in June, but Venus in cold weather was adorned with a little knitted sack which someone had made for her. Out in the trees in his back yard were suspended Eolian harps, because he liked to hear their tinkle, which, he said, kept him from feeling lonely as he dropped to sleep. The cellar was one of his pet hobbies, for this was whitewashed all over. In order not to spoil the perfect purity of that cellar, he also had whitewashed all the ends of the cordwood that showed.

Down in that cool vault he had a particular treasure. Somewhere he had acquired a marvelous recipe for cherry bounce. It was the color of rubies and tasted like nectar. He did not drink it himself, but he would stand on his steps occasionally and invite passing friends in to have a taste. This was a high honor, and never declined.

Colonel Tilton liked the society of the Gentler Sex, and used to entertain them at wonderful "breakfasts." The young ladies would arrive at ten and they would do well if they left by four.

The "breakfasts" would begin with oatmeal and end with delicious ice cream made with real cream. No one was trying to keep thin in 1900! Between courses, he would rise and order every one of his guests to take a run around the house. He used to say this was to give the maid time to wash his one set of dishes, but as his shelves were stocked with china and glass, they all knew it was intended to stimulate appetites for the next course. These same young ladies, feeling under obligation to him for his hospitality, would shower him with slippers, shaving balls, bed-socks, pincushions, and so forth. These gifts he always kept on display, year after year, in his living room, the shaving balls hanging from the chandelier, and he would allow no one to touch them but himself. The room looked rather like a Woman's Exchange.

Also, he gave useful and practical advice to the girls. To one maiden, who was gingerly taking his proffered arm, he said, "You should light on me like a crow, not a canary." To another he observed, "When you say Good Morning, my dear, say it with a smile. Otherwise it has no value. And when you meet people on the street, pause for a moment in passing to ask them about their own affairs to show you are interested. Inquire about Mrs. Smith's rheumatism, and Mrs. Bowie's trip to Baltimore, and congratulate Mrs. Jenkins on the birth of a grandson. Remember that. It all makes life so much more worth living for you and for everyone else concerned." Another one of his favorite bits of counsel was, "My dear, say what you will, but don't write letters. The written word is what makes half the trouble in the world. Thank God for the telegraph!"

One of his foibles was a fussiness about clean clothes. When his underwear came back from the laundress he used to douse it into his tub for another ablution at his own hands. Once, when he was Commanding Officer at the Marine Barracks, he was thus engaged upstairs when he heard the doorbell. The maid was out. He heard through the screen door a voice which he took to be that of a crony of his. "Come right up! Come right up!" he shouted genially down the stairs. Shortly afterwards, hearing many feet mounting the treads, he stepped out to see. He found himself facing the Governor of Maryland, attired in full regalia, attended by his staff of colonels in full dress uniform, who had arrived to pay an official call. The Colonel wiped the suds off his arms, dried his hands on a towel, reached for his shirt and blouse, and led them downstairs away from the wash-tub, with no evident traces of embarrassment.

One story that used to amuse him greatly was that he kept his coffin under his bed. This really was a silver chest. But he did inveigh against the folly of funeral ceremonies and vow that he would have no such nonsense for himself. Of course, when his time did come, he was buried with full military honors.

Colonel Tilton did not mind being regarded as an eccentric. In fact, he got a great deal of fun out of surprising people by the unconventional things he did and said. In particular, he prided himself on saying exactly what he wished. Happily, those things that he wished to say were kindly and wise.

In the story about the Spanish prisoners, it was intimated that everyone in the Yard tried to make them feel like guests rather than captives. But there was one exception, Professor Marshall Oliver, U.S.N. For some obscure reason, neither he nor his wife seemed to have any sympathy for the Spaniards. Indeed, they hinted darkly that anyone straying about the Yard after dusk ran a grave risk of catching a stiletto between the shoulder blades. The Spaniards themselves knew the Oliver quarters on Upshur Road for this antipathy, which they accepted without comment, but also they gathered frequently of an evening on the porches of the neighboring houses to listen to the music. For the Olivers were lovers of music, and they had at least that trait in common with the officers of the defeated fleet. Violin, piano, and voice; music to the Oliver family was not an accomplishment, but the breath of daily life.

Professor Oliver is introduced here because he was so strikingly different from all his brother officers. He was in the Navy, but not of it. Moreover, he took great pride in that difference. Strangers would have described him as a handsome man who carried himself like an actor. Those who knew him better in the Yard might have added that he was a bit affected, a dilettante in the arts and literature, and extremely touchy in temper—frequently they used the word "sissy" to express that idea. He described himself best in a gloomy burst of confidence as "a nightingale in a hencoop."

Poor fellow, he was exactly that, not an American thrush, but a rossignol of the Old World. This foreign quality was accentuated by a monocle, and by a formality of manner, a way of crooking his arm behind his back, on being introduced, with heels together. He used to say to the midshipmen: "There are three accomplishments every gentleman should have—fencing, music, and languages. And," he would add, tapping his chest, "I have all three."

The year 1860 found him studying art with boundless enthusiasm and ambition in Paris—Paris was then at the height of its glory under the Second Empire. There he learned to wax his tender moustache after the fashion of Napoleon the Little, a fashion he continued to follow to the day of his death.

In later years some whirligig of fortune threw him back to New York, where he became a budding actor, winning for himself a role in the company of the great Edwin Booth as he played his tremendous impersonation of Richelieu. That phase passed.

According to a legend now so old that it is past being verified, at some time in his youth he was in Florence in that remarkable group of sculptors, writers, and painters, American and British, that lived and worked there for many years. Chief among them were the Brownings. And, as the legend runs, Robert Browning was very kind to the handsome young American. Once, while they were out walking, they passed an ancient pile on the bank of the Arno. Oliver rapped it with his walking stick and noticed a singularly resonant note that came from the timber. "What a violin that would make!" he exclaimed. Weeks later, with the compliments of Robert Browning, there came, addressed to Marshall Oliver, Esquire, a violin which Browning had ordered made from this piece of wood. "Perhaps," he wrote in his note, "you will have a son some day who will learn to play it." And that kindly wish came true. It is a pretty story anyhow, and let's hope it all really happened just that way.

The next phase reveals young Oliver taking a job at the Naval Academy as an instructor in drawing. He hadn't made his mark at anything yet, and it was necessary to make a living. In time, he entered the commissioned corps of professors and donned a uniform. What little free-hand drawing there was at first gave place to mechanical drawing. For the rest of his life he taught drawing by the use of compasses, rulers, and triangles. It was a far cry from the Paris ateliers, salons, and those ambitions of his youth.

The Naval Academy itself was a still farther cry from his life in those student days. Regulations, uniforms, official reports—the round of official calls, official dinners, teaching and marking papers, the dull talk about orders, chances of promotion, gossip of Washington. There were times when it seemed more than he could stand and he blew up. That was his hencoop.

But at home, despite the ugly government furniture, he had a refuge. His wife shared his tastes and his feelings. She dressed somewhat in the Burne-Jones manner, with her hair parted in the middle, even in the days of pompadours, and with large golden hoops dangling from her ears. Together they created their own life of music and books and art inside their four walls, for themselves and their three children, and Professor Oliver enjoyed the satisfaction of being superior to his Philistine surroundings, including rear admirals. Nor did he make any secret of his superiority, and this did not make him popular.

Although, in general, his seemed to be a career of utter frustration, Professor Oliver's talents won a certain degree of recognition, even at the Academy. He was appointed to be the architect of what used to be called the "New Chapel," and he drew the plans also for a science building. For four years, 1895–99, he was made the Naval Academy librarian, on account of his well-known knowledge of literature, which was unique in the Navy, and his abilities as a linguist. It was pleasant to have these slight tokens of appreciation of his talents and accomplishments, but he was always the nightingale in the hencoop. His heart was in Paris and Florence and New York, with their galleries, theaters, operas, actor folk, and the salons where the men of art, letters, and music gathered and talked. That was life to Professor Oliver. What golden memories he must have had to cherish, such as setting out over the Ponte Vecchio of an afternoon for a walk with Robert Browning and being invited in afterwards for a cup of tea from the hands of Elizabeth Barrett!

There must have been days during a semi-annual examination period when he would look up with tired eyes from his papers and gaze back across the years to see himself in Paris, sketching on the Pont Neuf, or leaning on the Arno embankment, watching the lights of a procession of monks winding up San Miniato in the twilight, or again looking on from the wings at the big scene in "Richelieu" where the greatest actor of his day held the audience breathless while he drew round the heroine the "mystic circle of the Church" in a voice so resonant and beautiful that it thrilled even the alien who could not comprehend the words. Of course, one couldn't expect to have such experiences at the Naval Academy, but the tragic fact was that there was nobody who wouldn't become bored if one tried to talk about them. "Who was Robert Browning?"

Alas, the nightingale never escaped from the hencoop, even in death. For when the last summons came, he was buried with all the pomp and circumstance of a ranking officer's funeral, with honorary pall-bearers, the long procession to the Naval cemetery, led by the Naval Academy band playing the same funeral marches to the grave and the same gay quickstep on the way back. It was all just as every other officer had been buried for fifty years.

CHAPTER XII

SOME TOWNS-PEOPLE

THE Bordley-Randall house, which stands with its back turned on College Avenue, has already been described as unique in Annapolis, because it faces in on its own garden instead of on the street. And it shares honors alone with the John Shaw house on State Circle in having a "Captain's Walk" on the roof. This house was built about 1727, but many changes have been made during the years of its long life. The present front porch, for example, was an addition of the Civil War era, and the west wing has been changed to make a separate dwelling, with a gambrel roof giving a second story to what was originally a one-story structure.

This ancient mansion, which antedates the Golden Age of Annapolis architecture, was built by one Thomas Bordley. His son, Stephen, who had been despatched to London to study law, returned to Annapolis in 1733, and sent back to London for his law library. This was said to be the most complete set of law books in the colonies. He needed them, too, for he once became involved in a legal dispute with no less a person than Lord Baltimore, and had to make the journey to England to fight it out.

Stephen Bordley had become quite a bigwig in his generation. He gave wonderful dinners; he was as famous for being a connoisseur of wines as an expert in law. He enjoyed a reputation as a wit, and was a member of the exclusive South River

Club. He busied himself in good works, and held many public offices. He was one of the prime movers in establishing St. John's College. He should have been a wonderful catch for some girl in Annapolis, but alas, the damsel he loved "rejected his suit." She was Peggy Shippen, of Philadelphia.

Indeed, there seems something peculiar about the atmosphere of eighteenth-century Annapolis that spread a mildew on the most rosy romances. Elsewhere has been told the story of Matthias Hammond and that other stony-hearted damsel from Philadelphia who refused him and his gift of a queenly home. There is that legend also about "Whitehall," of Mary Ogle and Governor Sharpe. Both these gentlemen remained single and their magnificent homes were mere bachelor's quarters. Stephen Bordley, likewise, remained faithful to his blighted love and was a bachelor host in his fine house. His devoted sister, Betty, kept house for him for many years, and the two were inseparable. Poor Betty had her own tragedy, too, for her lover had died in London.

When Stephen passed on, "Sister Bett" inherited a lonely house. The last of the Bordleys died in 1804, and in that year a certain John Randall, who had come to Annapolis after the War of Independence, bought the estate, and thereafter it remained in the Randall family for about one hundred and twenty-five years.

At the close of the nineteenth century, the master of the house was still a John Randall, who, like Stephen Bordley, took a leading part in civic and state activities, and who, with his wife, maintained that other tradition of hospitality which Bordley had begun.

It was a beautiful home and rich in treasures of the past. In the double drawing-room, for example, was a portrait of Washington on horseback by Charles Willson Peale, and in the dining-room two life-size portrait heads by St. Memin of the first John Randall and his wife. At the rear of the house was a large library, its floor three or four steps below the level of the rest. Out beyond, in the eastern wing, there was a roomy kitchen still, as there had been when the house was first occupied, a grand kitchen for oyster roasts and candy pulls.

This was the house in Annapolis above all others that stood for warm and generous hospitality. Officers and civilians attached to the Naval Academy, and a long way from their own homes, as well as townspeople and visitors, entered that doorway, knowing they would have happy hours and a gracious welcome. On Tuesday evenings, the Randalls were regularly "at home" for music and conversation—though some guests had to learn that those two arts should not be practised at the same time—and very informally on Sunday evenings there would be a "hymn sing," a term broad enough to include much music beside the favorite hymns. And everybody piped up, young and old. There was Paymaster Caswell, for example, of the class of '61 at Brown University, who could spin wondrous yarns of the days when he chased blockade-runners off Charleston and who, when the singing began, led off with a tenor voice that was still clear and fine when he was seventy.

The present generation might find it unexciting. No radio, no jazz, no heavy alcoholic content. Only music and conversation. Who in these days has ever heard of conversation in good society? But in those years, not so very far away, after all, the Randall home meant more to the stranger in Annapolis than he ever could express, more than he ever realized until those

Sunday and Tuesday evenings were no more. For a day came when, after prolonged ill-health, Mr. Randall heard a physician pronounce the sentence of death upon him. What he and Mrs. Randall did then was characteristic of them. Invitations were sent out for a reception. Once more, after what had seemed a long interval, the guests came thronging into the old mansion, happy to think that Mr. and Mrs. Randall were opening their doors again to their friends and that Mr. Randall's illness was over. Only those who looked into his eyes as they grasped his hand could guess the truth. But his voice was as cheerful as ever and his smile as warm. As the music began, he went into the library to sit alone by the open fire. What the amateur artists played and sang that evening was a program of his favorite numbers, and finally, after midnight, the guests shook his hand again and said good night, telling him how delightful it was to come once more to his home. That was the last time most of those guests ever saw Mr. Randall.

In after years, Mrs. Randall had a few close friends visit her on Sunday evenings in memory of the old times. Then the day came when the old house lacked its gracious mistress, also, and finally it passed into other hands. No one ever since has taken the place of the Randalls in Annapolis. No one ever could.

In the days when the "at homes" of the Randalls were in full swing, there was a little frame boarding-house on King George Street, snuggled up cozily to a corner saloon. This was not a very prepossessing house from the outside, and inside the rooms were small and cut up on account of the difficulties of making the building do what it never was intended to do, take "paying guests." There was no furnace, because there was no cellar. Heat in winter came from hideous, iron "Latrobe" stoves, messy with coal dust and ashes, and gassy of breath. But the first place one sought for board was "Miss Ida's." That was because her table was so generous, and because she was so charming. Her rooms were usually crowded. "Candidates" studying for the entrance examinations to the Academy, Naval officers and their wives, mothers with marriageable daughters—or at least daughters who it was hoped would be marriageable—civilian professors, mothers of midshipmen determined to keep a loving eye on them; they all came and stayed and, after a time, went.

Since Miss Ida Roget was a lady, she was often imposed upon. Some of her grandest and snootiest boarders would make some excuse and slip out of town without paying their bill. Some of the others did likewise, and her colored servants, though they adored their "Miss Ida," did not scruple to carry off large quantities of provisions in the pockets of their billowy skirts—what they considered their perquisites. And she used to lend here and there to those who were in trouble; some of these so-called loans were gifts in disguise. Altogether, it is safe to say that when she came to figure out her assets at the end of a year she had small prospects of growing rich. Not that she would care about being wealthy. How she would laugh at that idea! But one thing she yearned for with all her heart and mind, an ambition of which she often spoke—a visit to France, and above all to Paris.

For Miss Roget was a Frenchwoman, an ardent one, who had never seen France. Her father was a Frenchman who taught Spanish at the Naval Academy from 1850 to 1873. He had been taken into that corps of "Professors of Mathematics," which included language teachers also. The cadets knew him as the "Don," probably because his subject was Spanish, and he was said to be extremely dignified. He is chiefly remembered now for his difficulties with Midshipman Cushing, who later became famous for his exploits in the Civil War, but who practiced his dare-devil propensities on the long-suffering professors in his Naval Academy years. One story is that Cushing, who had a dreadful time trying to master Spanish, took revenge by the ancient trick of a bucket of water poised on the classroom door, which dowsed the professor as he entered. Another is that when a story was circulated that Professor Roget had been bitten by a cart horse, Cushing drew upon the blackboard a picture of the professor fastening his teeth upon a horse with the inscription, "The poor old Don, he bit the horse." When the Frenchman entered the classroom and saw the work of art, he cried indignantly, "I did not bite zee horse. Zee horse he bite me!" This was too much. Roget laid his case before the Superintendent and Midshipman Cushing was slated for an indefinite vacation from the Naval Academy. But that was January, 1861, and the time soon came when young officers were needed very badly, even those who were disrespectful to their professors. Miss Roget, in her own little room, kept a large oil painting, showing her father in the full dress uniform of his professorial rank, epaulets and all.

Naturally, the language she first spoke and heard was French, and her father saw to it that her accent was perfect. In after years she used to add somewhat to her income by giving lessons in French. But she also learned from her father—homesick for his native land—of the glories of France, and every year she hoped that soon—"in a year or two, perhaps"—she might save up enough to take passage on a steamer from New York, and go straight to Paris. For once she would leave behind the exasperating, thieving servants, the still more exasperating, delinquent guests, the dreadful heat of an Annapolis summer, the tittle-tattle of Navy Yard gossip, and wander through the Paris of her father's memories.

When Du Maurier's *Peter Ibbetson* was published, though Miss Ida had small leisure for books, this one she read and reread. It depicted the Paris her father had described to her, the city of Louis Philippe. "For instance, there was the island of St. Louis, with its stately old mansions *entre cour et jardin,* behind grim stone portals and high walls . . . and that other more famous island, la Cité, where Paris itself was born, where Notre Dame reared its twin towers above the melancholy, gray, leprous walls and brown roofs of the Hôtel-Dieu. Pathetic little tumble-down houses, all out of drawing and perspective, nestled like old spider webs between the buttresses of the great cathedral . . ." Ah, that was *her* Paris! She would see it some day, if people would only pay up what they owed her, and if the price of food only wouldn't keep going up, and if some member of her large "family" did not come begging for a "loan."

But the time never came. In her latter years she had a kinsman to make a home for, and as time went on the steamer passage became much too costly. Meanwhile, everyone who knew her was devoted to her. One young couple who had become engaged in her front "parlor," before a very unromantic and gassy Latrobe stove, used to say, "Some day when we are rich we are going to get that steamer ticket for Miss Ida, then she'll *have* to go!" But, alas for good intentions. There were always other things to be done with such a sum of money, and by and by Miss Ida could not have left her home anyway, on account of her burden of years. Finally, she laid down her tired body for the last time, with the dream of her life unfulfilled.

If there are proper compensations in the next world, as we are led to believe, Du Maurier must have been waiting to greet her. Being an Englishman, of course, he would insist on a formal introduction to Miss Ida, but doubtless some wise archangel arranged that. Then I feel sure that he took her on a tour to Rheims, to Amiens, to Rouen, and, above all, to Paris. Not those cities as they are today, but as they were when Du Maurier's hero was a little boy in Passy; when a major of La Vieille Garde was still spruce and erect, and could demonstrate with his cane in the sand how muddle-headed the English were at Waterloo, and how Napoleon's defeat was due to sheer mischance and bad weather. Du Maurier would enjoy taking her up those crooked little streets near Notre Dame. He would never have found in heaven any other soul so responsive to the things he loved. I am sure it must have happened, because only this would really mean heaven for "Miss Ida."

The famous Hammond mansion on Maryland Avenue has been known for the last seventy years more often as the "Harwood House," after the name of the family that occupied it during the last half of the nineteenth century and the first decade of the twentieth. For that reason, it is sometimes referred to in these pages as the "Hammond-Harwood House." By various ways, the old mansion descended to the Harwoods from the builder and original owner, Matthias Hammond, through Judge Jeremiah Townley Chase.

In 1854 William Harwood became a professor of "English and Ethics" at the Naval Academy. In 1861 he left, along with so many others whose hearts or homes, or both, were with the

Confederacy. He expected Maryland to secede as a matter of course, and, like Captain Buchanan, he did not wait. One legend that used to be told is that he staged his leaving the Academy very dramatically, that he spread out an American flag at the entrance to the Main Gate, jumped up and down on it, to express his sentiments about Mr. Lincoln's government and the people behind it, and brandishing his arms in the air, cried out "Sic semper tyrannis!" Whereupon, the marine at the Gate, who did not know his Latin but did know his flag, seized Professor Harwood by the neck and cast him bodily out into the street. At any rate, it is true that he left the Naval Academy. Thereafter, during the war, he taught school somewhere near Baltimore. In order to take the train home to Annapolis each week he would have had to swear an oath of allegiance to the United States. This he disdained to do. What, crook the knee to a hateful tyrant? Never! So, though not a young man by any means, he used to tramp the thirty miles over rough dirt roads back to Annapolis and thence again to Baltimore every week.

He had another special reason for refusing to submit. His only son was in the Southern army. At last the news came that he was wounded. Mr. Harwood put on a disguise and managed to slip through the lines, but before he could reach his son, the young soldier had died.

To the end of his days, as might be expected, Mr. Harwood was thoroughly unreconstructed. The whole world went dark for him at Appomattox. Before the close of the century, William Harwood had passed on to his reward, the reward of men who have principles and stand by them, no matter what they cost. He left behind him in the old mansion two daughters, Lucy and Hester, and a portrait of General Lee. In his latter years, when their father was too old to earn a living by teaching, these two girls kept up a loving conspiracy never to let him realize how poor they were. Excuses here, subterfuges there, pretenses all the time, and the old gentleman never dreamed of the desperate straits the girls were in to procure food and fuel.

This same fierce pride, in the depths of their poverty, they maintained before the face of all Annapolis. They were not only proud, they were good haters. All the little of their worldly goods which they had inherited was thrown away in fruitless law suits. What they still held of property was mortgaged for more law suits. One of their particular objects of wrath and outraged feelings stood right before their eyes, the Chase Home. This had descended to their kinsfolk, the Chases, but instead of being handed down in time to the Harwoods, had been deeded over to the Episcopal church as a home for old ladies. No one who still remained in the good graces of the Harwood girls dared to be seen going up the steps of the Chase Home, even on friendly calls to some peaceful inmate.

Old Mr. Harwood was hot enough on the subject of the war, but he did not go as far as his daughters did in personal animosities. He was considered a really lovable old gentleman. For instance, Mr. John Randall was counsel on the opposing side in one of the interminable suits brought by the Harwoods to recover rights on some property. As always, they lost. Now Mr. Randall was a neighbor and an outstanding citizen, but thereafter, when they passed him on the street, Mr. Harwood would say courteously, "Good morning, Mr. Randall," but his daughters, walking on either side of him, would turn away stony faces. "Father, how *could* you speak to That Man?" After a while there were very few people left whom the Harwood girls would recognize.

Yet they needed friends so much, for they were in sore straits. Their house was filled with priceless antique furniture, not a stick of which they would sell, even though they had no idea where the next mouthful would come from. Neighbors came stealthily by night and left baskets of food on the steps. Their approach would be as stealthily watched from darkened windows. Then, after a pause, the baskets would be taken in, and hunger overcoming pride, the contents would be eaten. But when the same kind neighbors passed them on the street, Miss Lucy and Miss Hester gave them the cut direct.

A certain very young bridegroom, who had been looking about with poor success for living quarters for himself and his bride in the Annapolis of more than thirty years ago, heard that the Harwoods were considering renting their kitchen wing, which had been made over, after a fashion, to accommodate a tenant. With great difficulty and perpetual calls at the door, he obtained an entry, and with all the humility and deference of one approaching the throne of Queen Victoria, he offered himself as a tenant. It was an ordeal. Miss Lucy looked him over with piercing eyes and dark frown. Medusa herself could not have been more petrifying. Of course, no direct answer could be given at once. There were many things to consider. The young man was a Damyankee, but he was not old enough to bear any personal blame for the War Between the States. His wife, however, saved the situation, having been born in Virginia.

Consent was finally granted, but the new tenants were told most strictly that nothing should be done to the wing that might destroy its Colonial character. The paint, which was needed desperately on the walls, had to be a "Colonial buff." There must be no gas, no electricity, no telephone, and so on, but the young couple agreed on all points and moved in.

One of their earliest "dinners" was given to their landladies. There was room for only four people in the little octagon bay that served for a dining-room, but the meal was conducted in as much state as possible. Miss Lucy, the elder, and much the more terrifying of the two, led the conversation at the same time that she ate her dinner, and you may be sure that the topics were on a genteel plane. For both conversation and eating, she was handicapped by an almost total absence of teeth, but she managed by sheer force of will and an iron jaw.

Her sister, Miss Hessie, was all the while a meek echo. When Lucy declined a second glass of sherry, Miss Hessie primly did likewise. Miss Lucy told a story of how someone, interested in antiques, who had somehow affected an entry into the house, asked if he might look into their Sheraton sideboard. "That showed he was no gentleman," said Miss Lucy, with a toss of her head, "and I replied, 'You may if you insist, but you will find no wine there!' "

"Ha, ha!" laughed Miss Hessie, admiring Miss Lucy, and "Ha, ha," laughed the other two, not knowing what was so funny, but anxious to be polite.

In discussing the problems of housekeeping, Miss Lucy spoke lightly of her "servants" and what a trial they were in these days when slavery was done for. The host and hostess knew that there had not been a servant in the Harwood house for many years. Every week could be seen the pitiable laundry of the two ladies hanging on a string just inside the upstairs window on the south side where the sun could reach it. Miss Lucy touched on politics. She remarked with regret how in the old days "Annapolis always elected a gentleman to be Mayor, but now—Pooh!" "Pooh-pooh!" echoed Miss Hester.

They seemed to enjoy their dinner—all but the grapefruit. They left this uneaten, after a few polite flourishes with their spoons, but the meal on the whole was a success.

The Harwood girls used to stroll out to a dilapidated old arbor in their garden to "take the air." Small boys would come whooping in through a hole in the fence, bang on the sides of the arbor and do wild stunts around the precious old clumps of box. Miss Lucy would be very stern as, in lofty language, she bade them disperse. But as words always proved unavailing, the ladies would beat a dignified retreat to the house and emerge again, on Miss Lucy's arm a huge duelling pistol, at least a hundred years old. Miss Hessie followed breathlessly. Then the two would advance with ominous, if not murderous, looks. "Go away, you bad boys, or I'll shoot!" Miss Lucy would cry. At the sight of the pistol the boys would scamper away, shouting rudely, not quite sure as to whether that old pistol might be loaded after all. Time after time, this little comedy was enacted in precisely the same way, without any variations. Nor were these small boys the only annoyance. There were those architects who, like the boys, got into the garden through the broken-down fence and would try to sneak a sketch of a carved ornament before Miss Lucy and Miss Hester would pounce on them like two furies.

There is no legend about Miss Lucy's ever having had a lover, though she might have been quite pretty in 1860. But Miss Hester had one. He was a midshipman at the Academy. He came from some barbarous outlying Yankee wilderness called "Ohio" on the map. Once a letter from him to Miss Hester was picked up by her older sister. It began "My darling Hessie." That was enough. No gentleman would address a lady in such language, even after they were betrothed. Instantly, Miss Lucy banished the lover and blighted the love affair forever. Whatever protest Hester made has never been known, for evidently she acquiesced, even if in doing so she shed many tears. That was a long, long time ago, when the girls wore their hair in chignons and their skirts had "overdrapes."

By and by, during a Lenten season, Miss Lucy suddenly died. Neighbors declared that she had literally starved to death, and had made the penitential season an excuse for not eating. Miss Hester then left Annapolis for some months. When she returned all expected to see her desolate and crushed. But, on the contrary, she looked younger and more vivacious than she had since the Civil War. She had brought out some of the old family brooches and rings and adorned herself. She had also a fine, new set of teeth and an air of complacency. At last, after seventy years, she was playing second fiddle no longer. But she remained loyal to the old feuds, and the direct methods of Sister Lucy in dealing with people. On one occasion, finding herself at odds with her attorney, she wrote a vitriolic note of dismissal; but, instead of mailing it, she stalked to his office, flung open the door, and without a word cast the missive at his feet. Then bang went the door, and Miss Hessie was gone with her nose high in the air. She knew that Lucy would have been proud of her *that* day!

Hester lingered alone in the old house for several years longer. In her old age she began to talk again about her lover. Once on the list of the Board of Visitors to the Naval Academy she saw his name. It was someone else with the same name, but Miss Hester was satisfied that her suitor had come back after all these years on account of her. He didn't come to *see* her, of course; he couldn't, after she had dismissed him, but she knew he was still true to her.

Further, she believed that this old lover was "high up in Washington," and would take care of her so that she need worry no more about money matters. He came and talked to her in nightly visions. She even tore up her will. He would take care of everything.

Miss Katherine Scarborough, in her interesting book on the "Homes of the Cavaliers," tells a story that writes a mysterious *finis* to Miss Hester's career and links it back to the story of Matthias Hammond, who built the house. She says that long ago, after Miss Hester died, when the work of restoring the old building was going on, Dr. James E. Bordley, Chairman of the Committee on Restoration, noticed in the cellar floor some loose bricks. On working them free, he discovered two large keys, one tagged in faded ink, "To the Secret Chamber," and the other, "To the Secret Burying Place." It was known that all the members of the Harwood family were accounted for in various churchyards. Who could be buried here so mysteriously? When the story of the keys was known, a lady of Annapolis remembered that before Hester Harwood died she had whispered that when she went to her grave she would carry with her a secret that the world would give much to know. But she told no more. Then, a very old lady wrote from Baltimore that as a child she had played with the Harwood girls all over their old house and she remembered well a secret passage, reached by stairs leading from the cellar, which led underground to the little brook at the rear of the garden, where now the guests of Carvel Hall Hotel park their cars. And she said that on the way to the creek in this tunnel one passed a tomb. Then, finally, it was recalled that long ago there had been a legend to the effect that the proud and wilful belle who had broken her engagement to Matthias Hammond had, in her latter years, repented her folly and begged, as a last favor, that she be buried in the garden of the house that her lover had built for her as a wedding gift.

Some digging was done in the garden, but save for finding a few bricks, such as are used in making an archway, no tunnel and no sarcophagus were discovered. The mystery is still unsolved. But the story of this old mansion begins and ends with an "unrequited love."

The death of Miss Hester left the old place vacant and without an heir. An auction sale of the furniture was held. People, dealers especially, came from afar, from New York, Philadelphia, Baltimore, and Washington—everywhere. There was no room for the crowd inside the house. Cars choked the streets. People stood in front and back and shouted their bids through the windows. The old sideboard went for $1200. The chairs brought from $180 to $300 each. A table went for $700. And so the old treasures passed from the home where they had been so much beloved, bringing fabulous prices, treasures that had stood so long in the possession of two old ladies that they had shivered and starved rather than part with a single one. That auction would have broken their hearts. It rang down the curtain on the mansion of the Hammonds and Harwoods. And the passing of these two sisters, with their feuds, their hatreds, their poverty, and their unconquerable pride, marks the close of the *ancien régime* in Annapolis.

CHAPTER XIII

THE OLD ACADEMY AND THE NEW

THE difference between the Naval Academy as it looked in 1900 and the institution of today is like the contrast between the sailing ship *Chesapeake* of that era and the battleship *Wyoming* on which the present-day midshipman makes his summer cruise. Yet anyone who is fortunate enough to have known those little, unpretentious buildings, and the Yard, with its long vistas under the trees, is glad that he can remember the old Academy, just as he recalls with a thrill of pleasure the vision of the old *Chesapeake,* with all her sails spread, and with the sun on her snowy hull and canvas, looking like some great white sea bird against the blue of sky and water.

Of course, this is a different era. A man-of-war has to be a colossal, floating machine shop, and the Academy armory has to be on the scale of the Grand Central Station in order to accommodate the present-day regiment of midshipmen. Everything of this age, apparently, is bound to be scientific, up-to-date, and titanic. The old Academy would be looked upon now with compassionate wonder, and yet, to paraphrase Webster's phrase about Dartmouth, "there be those who love the memory of it."

The Academy has always been growing and changing. In the eighties and nineties, there had been marked advance in general tone and tradition over the era before the Civil War. When the Academy began the job of educating young men for the Navy, the custom of duelling was practised in the fleet, and it happened occasionally in the Yard, though there were no fatalities. There was no provision for the midshipmen in the way of sports or recreation of any sort. Going out into the town on leave usually meant a chance for breaking regulations in ways not always beneficial. One midshipman of the class of '61 told me how he and his room-mate buried a bottle of whiskey in what is now the parking lot of Carvel Hall. When they went out into the town they looked forward to that bottle of whiskey as the chief object of their holiday. From their point of view, there was not much else to do, and the authorities thought that the more closely the Academy resembled a prison the better.

It was Admiral Porter who deserves the credit for starting the idea of athletics, who made a gymnasium for the midshipmen to enjoy, and gave them encouragement to use it. He originated the idea that life might be made more tolerable for the midshipmen without ruining them for the Navy.

Besides the hard liquor tradition, the Civil War generation of midshipmen felt it incumbent on themselves to "chaw terbacker." Only sissies refrained from that manly accomplishment, and a really good marksman could drown a cockroach at five paces. One might outgrow tobacco-chewing, and even find solace in some other diversion than the whiskey bottle, but if one had himself tattooed, that stayed put. It was quite the fashion in the early days for midshipmen to get themselves adorned with goddesses of liberty, American eagles, starry banners, and such pleasing and patriotic emblems across their manly chests, or along their forearms. Sometimes these devices, with their stirring mottoes, excited irreverent mirth in wives of later years. Anyway, the ancient and honorable naval custom of tattooing had also faded out pretty generally in the last two decades of the nineteenth century.

The outstanding difference between the Academy, which trained the men who are at present on the Rear Admirals' list, and the institution as it is now, lies in point of size. The school of the eighteen-nineties was surprisingly small. There were only a few officers on duty, a handful of civilian professors, and a small body of midshipmen. Everybody knew everybody else. For a long time, the prime duty of everyone was to pay a call of courtesy on the newcomer, and all calls had to be returned. If you neglected this you were beyond the pale. This custom died hard. Years afterward, when the list of officers on duty had swollen to unheard-of numbers, all through the golden afternoons of October and November, the Yard would be filled with melancholy officers and professors being dragged by their wives, from one house to another, to pay official calls. Finally, one Superintendent, taking pity on those who wanted to watch football practice or play golf, abolished the whole business of compulsory calls. By that time, the Academy had become so enormous that no one could keep track of the newcomers anyway.

Official dinners were another feature of the routine, the sad part of this rite being that one had to invite not always whom one wanted, but whom one should have, by virtue of rank. There used to be in the equipment of the Naval Academy a large wooden top which could be clamped down over an ordinary dining table and thus accommodate the number of invited guests. A very dark anthropoid had the duty of rolling this table top along the sidewalk of Blake or Upshur Row to the house where the dinner impended. At the first rumble heads would fly to the window to see who was giving the dinner that night, and great would be the heartburning if one considered oneself a "ranking lady," and had not been invited.

For, in those days, at least, the real sticklers for rank were the ladies, and some terrifying sea dogs were married to much more terrifying sea doggesses, who knew to a hair's-breadth who "rated" whom, and exacted reverence most particularly to themselves. The wives of the civilian professors, by contagion, took on rank and rates among themselves. At a civilian reception the ranking professors' wives "poured," and it was a moot point, which was never settled, as to whether pouring coffee ranked above or below pouring tea.

One hard and fast social custom, which probably still survives, is that it must always be the ranking lady who leaves the party first. A lieutenant's wife might be acutely conscious of a baby at home that needed her personal attention, but she dared not stir from the party until the Senior Officer's wife present gathered up her skirts to tell her hostess what a charming time she had had. At the turn of the century, there was a lady whose husband had been a lieutenant for nearly twenty years. In the sudden expansion of the Navy, he was jumped to the rank of commander. At the next official dinner party she was deeply annoyed over the fact that no one made the move to leave, although the clock had struck twelve. Finally, she turned to her neighbor and expressed her sentiment for home and bed. "Well, Mary," the lady tartly replied, "we've all been waiting for you to go for the last hour!" Having been for so many years the wife of a junior officer, she could not imagine that she would ever become a Ranking Lady.

The outstanding fact about the early twentieth century at the

Naval Academy is its sudden growth to unheard-of dimensions. The graduation lists of the school in the eighties and nineties tell the story. In 1886 there were twenty-five. Fluctuations upward continued thereafter until 1899, when the staggering number of fifty-three were granted diplomas. Less than ten years later, 1907, a class graduated in three sections, totaling over 350.

The transformation seems to date from a report made by a Board of Visitors in 1895, which condemned the existing buildings, even to the point of declaring that they were a menace to health and safety. Colonel Robert M. Thompson, of the Class of '68, a great friend of the Academy and a member of that Board, obtained from Mr. Ernest Flagg, an architect of New York, a plan for an entirely new layout for the Naval Academy. This was submitted to the Board of Survey, and approved, but the Navy Department took no official action at the time. Congress was asked to appropriate a million dollars, of which half should be available at once, to build a boat-house, armory, and power plant. When this sum was granted, Mr. Flagg's plan was followed for these first buildings.

The armory of those days was a long, low, brick structure of one story, where indoor drills were held, and the Saturday hops, too, after the Fort Severn gymnasium became too small. This armory, though so low that it would have taken a combination of earthquake and tornado to joggle it, was supported along both walls by the most grotesque flying buttresses, consisting of huge timbers braced against the ground. These would have been strong enough to support the Rock of Gibraltar if it should crack open. The story is that a Machiavellian Superintendent, wishing to impress the Board of Visitors with the imminent peril of collapse, shored up the walls of the armory. "There," he cried in indignation, "our buildings are in such danger of falling down that they actually have to be held up!" This made the Board of Visitors gasp with horror, and hurry back to write their report.

The next year, more money was asked of Congress, and a shift was made from brick to granite. This, it is said, was due to a high-minded senator from New England who announced that he would block any appropriation for the new Naval Academy unless the material used was New Hampshire granite. It would seem as if the style of architecture appropriate to the scene would have been Georgian brick, for that style is not only American, but characteristic of Maryland. Whatever really happened, the new plans were dedicated to granite and French Renaissance architecture.

In 1899 there was a row in Congress over the whole project. Members demanded that the work be stopped until there had been an open competition among the architects of America and a careful inquiry into what the real needs of the Academy were. But this movement was squelched and the work of construction went gaily ahead.

One by one, the little old buildings were torn down, dredges were kept busy making new land out of the mud of the bay, and the instruction of the midshipmen was carried on with suddenly increased numbers crowded into temporary sheds. These sheds were constructed both for recitation and for dormitory purposes. The quiet old yard was transformed into one vast building operation, with derricks and scaffolds, trucks, and board fences. One old brown building after another was torn down, structures that had been landmarks of the institution since before the Civil War. The famous old mulberry tree down near the Fort was almost the only landmark that didn't suffer the indignity of the executioner's ax, for the god of storms had already laid that low in 1895. But the red-brick chapel, which looked churchly, even though it was no marvel of architecture, was broken up and carted away. The "Flats" or "Corrals," where the junior officers lived, and where every baby's cries could be heard in every apartment—those, too, bowed their heads and crumbled into dust. Blake Row, the homes of the ranking officers, Stribling Row, and Officers' Clubs, were cleaned away to make room for the new gigantic structures.

Old Fort Severn was saved, for reasons of sentiment, perhaps, longer than any of the others. Several years after it had been overshadowed by the colossal mass of Bancroft Hall it still survived. There were many who would have preferred seeing it left as a museum piece, a monument to the very beginning of the Naval Academy, just as at Harvard and Yale a few of the old buildings have been carefully preserved as relics in the midst of a welter of new and incongruous Tudor Gothic.

But, finally, the edict came that Fort Severn must go, too. Mr. Elihu Riley, of Annapolis, was so moved with indignation that he composed a poem based on Oliver Wendell Holmes's "Old Ironsides." But his iambics, hot as they were, did not even impinge on the Navy Department's conscience. Of course, the little pill-box had never fired a gun at an enemy, and it is doubtful if its presence had ever influenced a hostile force to keep away. But, here, American naval education was born, and Fort Severn should have been spared for that reason alone.

However, nothing survived the scoop and shovel, save the monuments: Herndon, Mexican War, Tripoli, the Japanese Bell, and "Tecumseh." What had once resembled the campus of a small New England college became an assortment of stupendous granite buildings, decorated in the manner fashionable at the Beaux Arts of 1890. Eventually, considerably over eleven million dollars was sunk into the buildings before the plan was completed. Even that sum was insufficient to cover the use of granite throughout, and the later buildings were made of white brick.

While all this transformation was going on, there were some interesting visits from representatives of foreign navies. In 1906, the remains of John Paul Jones were brought to Annapolis by a French squadron. General Horace Porter, then our Ambassador in Paris, had devoted much time and money to the task of discovering the grave of the neglected hero lying in a cemetery long since built over by Paris tenements. After the body had been found and identification had been made, the French government sent the remains on a cruiser, with an escort of honor, to its final resting place in Annapolis.

The French squadron was joined in Annapolis Roads by an American one. The body of Paul Jones was brought ashore in solemn state, and a ceremonial of honor was enacted in Dahlgren Hall—the new armory—before the flag-draped coffin. Huge as the building is, the audience crowded it to capacity, as it does today for the graduation exercises. Ambassador Jusserand spoke with his characteristic grace and tact. Governor Warfield, quite the handsomest figure present, was on the program to give a eulogy of the State of Maryland, as the land of fair women and brave men. And when President Theodore Roosevelt strode to the speaker's rostrum, even the slightly bored French officers leaned forward to try to catch what he said. The theme that he hammered home with his fists was based on the career of Jones;

namely, "The man who never surrenders never has to make excuses."

After the ceremony, there was an ugly moment when a number of women made a rush for the flag lying on the coffin in an effort to tear off pieces for souvenirs, but, fortunately, the sentries were quick to act and after a few seconds of undignified scramble, in which their hats were knocked down over their noses, the harpies were driven off from the flag they yearned to desecrate. Some of these women were actually wearing large badges of a certain patriotic society!

Since the sarcophagus was not yet ready, the remains rested for a while in Bancroft Hall, until a temporary mausoleum of brick was erected in the Yard near the present bandstand. Finally, on the completion of the crypt in the new chapel, John Paul Jones was interred in his last resting place.

A more festive occasion was another naval visit in 1905, this time of a British squadron under Prince Louis of Battenberg—a name he changed in 1914 to "Mountbatten," to take the curse off a German name. Although the American and British tars never have met, ashore or afloat, without a fight, the officers of the two fleets always get along together better than with any other naval men. The Americans had not forgotten the conduct of the British squadron commander in Manila Bay, when it looked as if there would be shooting between the American and the German ships. The "Yanks" and "Limeys" spoke the same language. It is so much easier to celebrate together when you are not stumped to understand what the other fellow has just said, or to remember whether you must use the subjunctive yourself to reply and can't recall what it is.

So there were high old times in the New Officers' Mess of an evening. The rooms of New Quarters and the temporary dormitories—"Annex A," "Annex B" and "Annex C"—were quite close to the Mess, so that as a midshipman studied his solid geometry at night he could enjoy the chorus roaring from the club about the "High Balls go rolling all around," and by going to his window get a fine eyeful of the fiesta of international goodwill. There was one song that the Britishers soon picked up and chanted lustily with the rest. It ran,

> Here we come, full of rum,
> Looking for someone to put on the bum,
> The Armored Cruiser Squadron!

You could put your whole diaphragm behind that chorus. Oyster men, tonging far out in the bay, must have heard it.

In that epoch, the armored cruisers were considered "great stuff," but the last ever heard of them was at the battle of Jutland, where the German fleet put *them* "on the bum" with horrible speed and thoroughness. Perhaps there were some officers in that strange battle, years afterward, who may have remembered that Yankee song about armored cruisers as they saw the *Black Prince,* for example, suddenly blow up and go down with all hands.

Since the British are supposed to be fond of all sorts of hunting, it was decided that they should have the opportunity of enjoying something they had never experienced before, a coon hunt. Professor Terry, Head of the Physics Department, and an ardent sportsman, was in charge of arrangements. The plan was proposed to the Britishers, but, to Professor Terry's surprise, met with a somewhat embarrassed aloofness. Finally, after much hemming and hawing, the question was put bluntly, "What the hell's the matter with you fellows? A coon hunt is different from any sport in England. We thought you'd like it."

The Englishman thus addressed shuffled his feet in embarrassment. "Ow, I say, reahlly, we don't feel the same color prejudice you chaps have, you know—"

When it was explained that this was not a lynching bee, all was well, and the coon hunt was declared to be topping.

It was about the time of this visit of the British that the famous battle song of the Naval Academy was born. The institution had existed sixty years or so without any peculiarly Navy song to sing at football games and class reunions, or any occasion of the sort. But, in the fall of 1906, "Anchors Aweigh" was composed and sung for the first time. Midshipman Alfred H. Miles, a member of the First (Senior) Class, was then leader of the choir. The bandmaster, Lieutenant Charles A. Zimmerman, wrote a march each year which he dedicated to the graduating class, and played during June Week. Lieutenant Zimmerman was very popular with the regiment. Each class gave him a medal in recognition of his march, so that in full dress uniform he wore enough medals to drown him instantly, had he fallen overboard. But these marches were not often heard outside Annapolis, and seldom were played again after the June Week première. After a while, the midshipmen began teasing him about his marches. Miles told him that his classmates were eager to have a piece of music that would be inspiring, with a swing to it, so that it could be used as a football marching song, and one that would live. Miles offered to collaborate with Zimmerman on this job, and between the two, sitting at the chapel organ, the famous air was composed. When the tune was finally com-

BANDMASTER ZIMMERMAN

From the Annapolis Alphabet

pleted, Miles set the title and wrote the two stirring stanzas which, with the air, have made the song a classic.

Stand Navy down the field,
Sail set to the sky,
We'll never change our course,
So Army, you steer shy.
Roll up the score, Navy,
Anchors Aweigh,
Sail Navy down the field
And sink the Army Grey.

Get under weigh, Navy,
Decks cleared for the fray,
We'll hoist true Navy Blue
So Army down your Grey.
Full speed ahead, Navy,

Army, heave to,
Furl Black and Grey and Gold,
And hoist the Navy Blue.

Words and music of "Anchors Aweigh" were completed and fitted together in November, 1906, and used in the Army-Navy game of that month. For the first time, after a long series of defeats, the Navy team won, and doubtless that fact helped to nail the new song to the Academy masthead. Lieutenant Zimmerman did not at first appreciate the success of this air, which formed the coda to the "1907" march. He had, in fact, another flourish composed to use instead, but the overwhelming popularity of the one that had been used for the football song clinched the matter in the end.

Since that day, "Anchors Aweigh" has steadily grown in favor at the Naval Academy. For twenty years the song was sung only by the midshipmen for their annual Army game, but in 1926 it was published in a collection of Navy songs issued by the "Trident" literary society. After that, through radio and later movies, it became nationally known. It is *the* marching song of the Navy, its "theme" song. Outside of "Dixie," there is no other tune that is so catching or so stirring. It has practically become one of our national airs.

The Army cadets may continue to win at football, as they have had a way of doing, but they have nothing to sing that compares with "Anchors Aweigh." For that matter, there is no college in the country that can boast of a marching song to match it.

A curious and amusing volume might be composed by graduates of various eras of the Naval Academy history concerning the customs, traditions, and ideas which prevailed in their day, and the conventions which were accepted unquestioningly like the laws of the Medes and Persians. Among the Midshipmen, it took only about twenty-four hours for something or other to become an old Navy custom. Some of these have persisted to this day, and others have faded out so long ago as to be remembered only by captains and rear admirals.

As for the officers, they also had iron-clad ideas about what was right and "sea-going." For instance, it was a long-accepted belief throughout the Service that "there's nothing like a sailing ship to teach a man the feel of the sea." Midshipmen still learned to make and furl sail on the practice ship, *Chesapeake,* scampering up and down the shrouds, and "learning the ropes" most literally, just as their forerunners had done in 1845. If an outside person ventured to remark that all that kind of thing was obsolete in a modern navy, he was overwhelmed with arguments. The officers used to quote Lord Brassey: "Sailing ships have been the recognized training school. The length of their voyages at sea compared with those of steamers, and the character of the work on board, give greater opportunity for the instruction of the sailor. Observation is sharpened, energy, endurance, and resource in times of emergency are all stimulated and strengthened."

Now, for many years, the *Chesapeake,* later re-named the *Severn,* has gone the way of other square-rigged ships. All those earlier arguments ought to be just as good today as they were then, but since the World War they haven't been audible. Alas, a new race of officers is growing up who think "sheets" are what you lie on in your bunk; "tacks" are what you hammer; "braces" are an Englishman's word for suspenders; "shrouds" are some-

U.S.S. *CHESAPEAKE*

Renamed the Severn

thing for the dead; and "stays" are what their grandmothers used to wear but never mentioned. The old language of the ship is now getting to be as much of a dead language as Latin. Even "starboard" and "port" have become officially "right" and "left."

Thirty years ago, the idea of discipline was such that a vast number of offenses were tabulated in a regulation book, each with the corresponding number of demerits abreast of it. If you yearned to err from the path of rectitude you knew exactly how much purgatory you were in for, if you were caught. And the old "Reg. Book" drew no distinction between what was wrong in itself and what was wrong by Superintendent's decree. For years, the penalty for snapping a piece of bread across the mess-table was just the same as for copying from your neighbor's work on the blackboard. Smoking seemed to be an exceedingly grave crime, almost the worst offense of all. And, of course, everybody smoked. It was a game of "Cops and Robbers" between the Discipline Department and the midshipmen.

Thirty years ago, there were not many outside interests to cultivate. There were no "Masqueraders," no "Log," and, above all, no leaving Annapolis for athletic contests, except the Army-Navy football game, when all the midshipmen went in a delirium of excitement. Christmas vacation lasted for one day only.

In the eighties, a midshipman's day began at six A. M., with breakfast at six-thirty, when the chaplain had to offer prayer. The study and recitation periods ended at four, followed by drills until six P. M. After dinner, there was a "recreation period" until seven-thirty, for everything under that name, including such athletics as were practised at the Academy in the eighties and early nineties. Imagine going out for football immediately after a full dinner! A midshipman of today transported back into the schedule of a "naval cadet" of 1888 would feel greatly abused.

Apparently in that era the big affair of the year was a sort of "field day" at Thanksgiving, when the cadets chased a greased pig around the field and tried to climb a greased pole as the star events of the day.

Another point of contrast with the present lay in the treatment of the sick. Before the new Academy buildings were erected, the "Sick Quarters" was a small affair tucked away in the shadow of the cadets' dormitory and painted a dismal drab. This establishment was organized like a sick bay on board ship. For nurses, there were enlisted men who had gone into the hospital corps, and whose only knowledge of their duties was a routine which they learned from the doctors. With the best intentions in the world, they could not be very skilful or intelligent as nurses. But the idea of having a corps of graduate women nurses in the midshipmen's sick quarters was regarded as nothing short of scandalous.

Typhoid, at the end of the nineteenth century, was no stranger in Annapolis. The following anecdote may be legendary, but it illustrates the point. A midshipman who was one of the star athletes came down with typhoid. His condition soon became critical. He needed nursing, for the orderlies were allowing him to get out of bed and walk whenever he felt like it, and he required especially a night nurse. Everyone felt deeply concerned. One officer's wife offered to send a trained nurse, whom she had in her home, to take care of the boy. This was refused by the medico. "It wouldn't be decent to have a nurse in Sick Quarters at night." Finally, the point was carried to the Superintendent, who ruled that the nurse might be in the hospital to tend the boy at night, provided there was a chaperon. So a kind-hearted

"THE BEAUTIFUL BLUE DANUBE" IN THE 1880's

lady sat up all night in the hospital, in order to permit the nurse to remain with the patient. By that time it was too late, and the young man died. Nowadays, trained nurses have been so much a matter of course, and for so many years, that a medical officer of today would look upon such an incident as something belonging to the Dark Ages.

While the subject of the proprieties is on the carpet, we must not overlook the Naval Academy dances or "hops." In Owen Taylor's *History of Annapolis,* he says that "these hops are believed to have a refining influence upon the young gentlemen." Elsewhere in the book he remarks that "Annapolis has always been celebrated for the elegance and the beauty of her female population." And thanks to these elegant and beautiful Annapolitans ("Crabs," in the midshipmen's language), assisted by the daughters of the naval officers living in the Yard, who were doubtless elegant and beautiful, too (these damsels being known as "Yard Engines"), the midshipmen couldn't help becoming refined. But the interesting thing to note for the present generation is that these hops began at seven-thirty Saturday evening and they shut down at ten, which is the hour for the modern, fashionable college man to begin to dress for the party. It is only fair to add that twice a year, at the New Year's and the Graduation Ball, the revelry was allowed to continue until eight bells.

But no matter what the closing hours were—and they haven't altered much, even in this enlightened day and age—there never was any reluctance on the part of the girls to attend. These Academy "hops" were considered very fashionable. But, in 1900, whether the girls were "Yard Engines," "Crabs," or the product of a Washington finishing school, hop dresses were no special worry to their parents. The customary frock was a muslin garment which could be heaved into the laundry on Monday and be all ready for the next hop on Saturday, looking quite different with a change of ribbons. Any girl who appeared in a silk, satin or velvet frock at a midshipmen's hop would have been classed with the Serpent of the Nile. In that respect, rumor hath it that the hops are not what they were thirty years ago. It should be noted also that dancing then was really an elegant accomplishment. A young officer and gentleman had his hop card adorned with such dances as "Polka," "Schottische," "York," "Lancers," and, above all, the Waltz. Ah, that last Blue Danube Waltz with your One and Only! That *was* dancing. Nowadays, anyone who can shuffle and jiggle is as good as the best of them.

But the couples of today still stroll out between their so-called dances, along the paths under the trees—when it isn't too chilly—down to the sea wall. The Severn River, and the harbor, and the distant bay look just as they did thirty years ago, or perhaps a hundred years ago, for that matter. And the moon is the same, though there are old-timers who will tell you that even a full moon isn't what it used to be in the Old Navy.

CHAPTER XIV

THE EARLY NINETEEN HUNDREDS AT THE ACADEMY—THE MEMORIALS

THE customs and laws made by the midshipmen ranged over the whole gamut of life at the Academy, and comprised a cast-iron code. One officer, distinguished for conspicuous heroism in the Spanish-American War, dared, from his sense of duty, to go against the code by reporting one of his own classmates who had refused to obey his orders as section leader. Reporting a classmate was considered a major crime by the others, and the one who did so was "put in Coventry" for the entire four years of his course. That is, no midshipman would speak to him except in the line of duty. It took backbone to stick it out as he did, graduating at the head of his class. But, as was proved later, he had the stuff of which heroes are made.

The subject of cheating in class and examinations has given rise to curious ideas and conventions. Park Benjamin, in his history of the Academy, says that when he was a midshipman it was considered dishonorable to cheat in any subject except "Moral Philosophy," but quite permissible in that one, and practically everybody did it. An officer of the class of 1900 told me that in his time cheating was held to be dishonorable unless you were in danger of "bilging" (failing). In that case, it was quite all right to get aid and comfort from surreptitious sources.

Finally, the whole matter was put in the hands of an honor committee of First Classmen, who have been able to accomplish far more in this thorny problem than all the regulations and sharp supervision of the officers could achieve.

The word used by the midshipmen for cheating is "gouging." It is one of the many words peculiar to the institution. Its origin is foggy, but it goes so far back that no one knows when it was first used. Possibly it came from the midshipmen's mess, back in the days before the Academy was even thought of. It was a traditional cry around the mess table when someone stood up to carve the salt horse, "Cut fair now, no gouging!" This was in allusion to the temptation to scoop out some of the softer, fat parts for one's own plate. Thus the word "gouge" may have become associated with any unfair practice.

It is only possible here to touch on a few of the old midshipmen customs and conventions, some of which sprang into full bloom overnight and then withered away, and some of which may be flourishing today. For example, thirty years ago, during "plebe summer," it was considered the proper thing for every plebe to "spike his hat." This was something of a stunt. It involved climbing the shrouds of the *Hartford's* mainmast and maintopmast to the topgallantmast, and, finally, shinning up that spar to the top, where one could whip off his duck hat and slap it down over the iron spike at the very tip of the mast so as to tear a hole in the cloth. This was a dizzy operation for a youngster not used to spars and rigging, and it was a real test of courage. The story is that one poor fellow lost his footing, and thereafter there was no more spiking hats on the *Hartford,* or anywhere else.

In "plebe summer," too, before the arrival of the upper classmen, from time to time there used to be a "company roughhouse," in which members of one company battled to take possession of the "deck" in Bancroft Hall on which the other company was quartered, or to defend their own territory from sudden assault during the small hours after midnight. When the noise reached the officer-in-charge in sufficient volume to awake him, and when said officer had pulled on enough uniform to

OLD "DAMN THE TORPEDOES," THE *HARTFORD*

After a photograph

look awe-inspiring, the plebes were in the rags of their pajamas or nothing whatever, the "deck" was littered with weapons—the brooms and fragments of jars and pitchers which had been used for throwing water on their adversaries. Ten demerits would be assigned everyone for "making a disturbance after taps," but that was a small price to pay for such a rough-house.

Since there was no week of Christmas leave until very recently, all the fun had to be concentrated into Christmas Day. The First Classmen organized their special program of fun-making, the plebes were allowed the full privileges of upper classmen—like the slaves during the Roman Saturnalia—and the hard-hearted authorities gave amnesty to all reprobates no matter how many demerits they had collected. Since Christmas Day was all too brief a holiday at best, everybody "hit the deck" at six A. M., a whole half-hour before the bugle "busted." Then there would be a parade of midshipmen in grotesque costumes, yelling and whooping, and chanting,

> There's one wide river, there's one wide river to cro-oss,
> There's one wide river, there's one wide river to cross.

Santa Claus, the president of the First Class, led the procession around the Yard with resounding cheers and Merry Christmases to Superintendent and Commandant, ending at the Armory for a grand class celebration about a huge Christmas tree. At breakfast, the First Classmen changed places, and also their blouses, with the plebes; and the smallest plebe of all was, on that morning, the five-striper of the regiment. And would he bawl out the upper classmen! So did his brother plebes, likewise, who were for that day company commanders. It was most hilarious. With the granting of the Christmas leave, all that time-honored ceremony vanished.

Another custom following the end of a term and the final examination was the "burial of Math and Skinny," the two most dreaded subjects of the Academy course; "Skinny," for some reason, being the unofficial name for Physics. The interment of these two subjects was the occasion of much burlesque and fun, and the midshipmen enjoyed considerable latitude in their take-offs of both subjects and instructors. The more daring the hit, of course, the louder the applause and the laughter. This custom, too, is no more.

The handling of the cheating problem, "gouging," has already been mentioned, but there is a quaint offshoot of the idea of honor in the matter of work, which is unique. According to the midshipmen's code—at least of a generation ago, though it may still be true—the most dishonorable thing a fellow could do was to study out of study hours. The explanation was that a midshipman's future depended on his marks at the Academy. The ensign's "number" in his class is determined by his standing when he graduates. So to study outside the time assigned for that purpose is to steal a low advantage on your classmates who may be using their recreation period for athletics or some other student activity which redounds to the glory of the Navy. That is the theory, though, of course, many another uses his idle time for a snooze—to "caulk off"—or to call on his best girl. But the feeling used to be so strong that one midshipman, who conceived the idea that he would like to do some reading in the field of philosophy, up in the stack room of the Library, had to square himself with his class by proving that not one page he read could possibly advance him in any subject in the curriculum. Even at that, he told me when he resigned, he was still an object of suspicion, at least for his sanity. "Anyone reading about Plato is bound to be a nut."

Along with this quaint tradition ran another—generally known as the "labor union" idea. The theory was that bright minds must dim their headlights to let the dumb ones have a chance to get by. If a brilliant mathematician walked off with the demonstrations of original problems in a blaze of glory, he would be called on by a delegation who would point out to him the moral obliquity of being too bright. It was really treachery to the poor boneheads in his class. During the following week the instructor, who did not know what was up, would be astonished to have his joy and pride look up at him blankly with "I don't understand, sir," just like the "anchor men."

Thirty years ago, there was in control of midshipman life and thought a curious combination of two codes, fighting and hazing. Day after day, midshipmen would report for recitations with their faces a raw pulp, almost unable to open their swollen lips. A blind man could see that there had been a fight the night before, but there seemed to be a tacit approval of the system on the part of the officers. Nothing, therefore, was done about it, though fighting was forbidden by regulations. Terrific combats over a private grudge or a class privilege were staged, which for sheer dogged endurance and taking punishment make the present-day professional heavyweight fight look ladylike. Some of these fist duels lasted upwards of thirty rounds.

The combats were conducted with all the formality of the prize ring, seconds, timekeeper (with someone's nickel alarm clock) and referee, but usually gloves. All the men concerned would cut supper formation and find a quiet spot where the duel of fists would take place, generally some unoccupied room.

Perhaps the practice would have gone on indefinitely but for one fight occurring in the autumn of 1905 that made headlines in all the newspapers. Midshipman Meriwether, as the story goes, had taken some abuse from Midshipman Branch, of the class above him, in the course of hazing. Meriwether had to wait until he himself was no longer a plebe, and then he challenged Branch. Seconds were chosen, the time set, and the ring formed in an unused room. The two men were both powerful and brave. The battle went to the limit of endurance, until neither could lift his hands any longer but lunged weakly at the other with his head. Neither had been knocked out and neither would give in. At last, Branch swayed and lost his balance. As he fell, he struck his head on the cement floor and became unconscious. His seconds put him under the shower to bring him to, and hastily laid him in bed. They expected that he would be all right in the morning. But he did not respond to reveille, and when his room-mate tried to rouse him he found that Branch was dead.

Other evidences of fighting could be ignored but not a dead midshipman. There was great excitement in the public prints and in Congress. For it did not take long to reveal the fact that the fight was nothing out of the ordinary and that it sprang from the experience of being hazed.

As it happened, right on top of this tragedy burst a particularly brutal case of hazing. The Navy Department had to take notice. It appointed a board of inquiry, and this was speedily followed by a Congressional one. What was the matter, the Congressmen wanted to know? Wasn't hazing strictly forbidden, and fighting, too? There followed some trying weeks. Midshipmen were grilled on the witness stand, trying desperately not to reveal anything and yet anxious not to lie out and out. Some of the testimony that was dragged from them came very close to certain of the officers in the Department of Discipline, indicating that they were well aware that both hazing and fighting were going on.

But, as such things usually do, the whole affair blew over, though eight midshipmen were dismissed and others resigned. The death of a popular classmate probably did more than the investigations to dampen the fighting ardor in the regiment, and for a while hazing was actually suspended.

But, at the time, sentiment among the upper classmen at least seemed to be strongly for the "code" as it stood. One who signed himself "A midshipman of the Naval Academy" wrote a defense of the practice which appeared in the *Independent.* He explained that there were two classes of fights; one, purely personal, and the second, the result of some lower classmen disregarding the rules about class privileges. First Classmen every year set an elaborate schedule of "rates." Plebes had to keep to the side of the walks, or the center of a corridor. They had to maintain a "ramrod brace," they must answer upper classmen with due respect, they must keep out of Lover's Lane, certain stairs, benches, and so on. If a plebe broke one of these taboos, he was first reported to the president of one of the upper classes, who selected a fellow of about the same height and weight from his own class, and then the fight was staged with great ceremony. The president of one class, by the way, used to take on many of these fights himself as a part of his official duties. The rule was that if the plebe won his fight he might go on and enjoy his rates like an upper classman, but this was rarely done, for it made a man very unpopular even in his own class.

The midshipman writer of that article in the *Independent* went on to say that the second type of fight, that for personal grudges, was ardently believed in both by officers and midshipmen, and medical officers were given to understand that they were to ask no embarrassing questions about injuries. What the Commandant thought of that statement when he read it is not on record.

It has been a long time since such a constant succession of fights—official and personal—have been staged in the Academy. But the custom which caused so many of the grudge fights—

hazing—has had more lives than a regiment of cats and more heads to kill than the hydra. Yet it is probably safe to say that the extremes of brutality practised thirty years ago are not known now and have not been for years. I can remember well one little plebe who, on being asked a question in class, was silent. It soon appeared that he couldn't speak. Indeed he couldn't move at all, and he had to be carried over to Sick Quarters to be put to bed in a complete state of nervous collapse as a result of hazing.

Some mothers, being confided in by their sons, would go in a rage to the Superintendent, but the upshot of the matter was always that the other midshipmen soon learned that a complaint had been made, and the poor wretch would suffer a hundredfold what he had gone through before. One trouble has always been that the law is so drastic as to lump together under the head of hazing, good-natured "running," which may be good for a plebe, along with the physical torments which are not good for anybody.

It is hard to make an outsider, at least, believe that hazing has any justification. It has long since faded out of all but the backwoods colleges, and some day it will be ruled out of our naval and military academies as well. But that will happen, not by acts of Congress or regulations of the Navy Department, or periodical investigations, but through the pressure of opinion among the officers in the Army and Navy. In a recent magazine article, a Naval Academy graduate, though defending the Academy against criticism, has only this to say for hazing:

> The hazing problem is one for the executive department. It must be admitted that it has not done a very good job with it. Call it hazing or running or what you will, it is a senseless tra-

dition, and it will be a great and useful work to rid the Academy of such nonsense. It is not worthy of the Navy . . . *

* * * *

In what the older officers sometimes call "the Good Old Days," say, fifty years ago, there was no provision for recreation at either Annapolis or West Point. The idea seemed to be that any fun in life was bad for military discipline. There was no getting away for games, and no visiting by other teams. There were no athletics worth mentioning. Nothing makes such a strong contrast between the Academy of a half century ago and today as intercollegiate athletics, and especially the extracurricular activities. Twenty-three of the latter are listed now and probably every year another is added. There are four publications, four musical clubs, the Masqueraders for dramatics, the "Quarter-Deck" for public speaking, the hop committee, and so on, all the way down to the two gentlemen-in-waiting on the Navy goat at football games.

As for the extraordinary development of athletics, the trips made for contests, even to sending a Navy crew to win the championship at the Olympic games in 1920, all that sort of thing would have had the old-timers snorting with indignation. "Bad for discipline!" The new spirit may be seen even in the watchmen at the gates. In midsummer, as they stand in the broiling sun, they now shine in snowy white shirts with no blouse or jacket. In the old days, a watchman was expected to die of sunstroke like a gentleman. In the Regulation Book of fifty years ago midshipmen were ordered to take a bath "once a week," and probably that luxury was considered sissified by the "old

* James R. Browne, "In Defense of Annapolis," *Forum,* December 1936.

Navy" of that day. "What damn fool ever joined the Navy to be comfortable?"

*   *   *   *

The Naval Academy grounds are naturally the mecca of many a delegation of visitors, for this is a great national school. Most of them trudge about with wide open eyes that see little beside the massive granite structures, and here and there some figure in uniform. (Perhaps the girls don't even see the buildings.) But the place is worth more than a mere hour of sight-seeing. From the bronze or marble tablets in Memorial Hall at one end of the Yard, to those other memorials in the cemetery at the opposite end, it is a sort of Valhalla of American heroes and a record of naval history.

It may be considered very "bourgeois" by our young intellectuals to feel a love for one's country, and it is most unfashionable just now to pay respect to those who fought, bled and died for their country. If an enemy were to invade our shores the proper thing to do would be to sell them suits and overcoats and to interest them in real estate. But there are those that are too old to be young intellectuals and who are not ashamed to get a thrill from the story of the men who died that their nation might live. And they do not mind seeing battle trophies, either, like the flags of French or British ships taken in battles well over a century ago. The most important flag, mounted in the place of honor in Bancroft Hall, is one of blue cloth on which is stitched in roughly cut white letters, "Don't give up the ship," the dying words of Captain Lawrence of the *Chesapeake*. This was Perry's flag at the battle of Lake Erie.

In this connection, a visitor may wonder where the famous

ships are that should be stationed here. The frigates *Constellation* and *Constitution,* the *Hartford,* the *Olympia;* these are far more significant of our naval history than the yacht *America,* which is really the only trophy vessel now at the Academy.

THE U.S.S. *CONSTELLATION*

After a photograph

From the windows of Memorial Hall one would like to see these famous ships riding at anchor in the Roads, where certainly they belong. They would be the most inspiring naval memorial of all.

As for the stories of heroism and devotion to duty enshrined in Memorial Hall, the tablets speak for themselves, but they deserve close inspection. Walking back from Bancroft Hall, one passes the figurehead of an Indian chief between the two walks that lead from Bancroft to the recitation buildings. This is a replica in bronze of the original wooden figurehead, which is now in the Naval Academy Museum, safely housed from the weather. It belonged to the ship *Delaware* and represents a chieftain of the Delaware Indians, but generations of midshipmen have known it as "Tecumseh." This is the "god of the 2.5," or

U.S.S. *OLYMPIA*

After a photograph

the mark of passing. Midshipmen in danger of "bilging" are supposed to offer fervent prayers to "Tecumseh" as they go and come from classes, and offer it sacrifice in the form of pennies. The old chieftain wears an eternal expression of disgust, but the prayers and the pennies might account for that, or perhaps it is because he has to wear that lady-like ruffle round his neck.

Farther down the walk is the little Mexican War monument erected by the midshipmen of 1847 to their brother midshipmen who fell in the war with Mexico; and to the left, in Lover's Lane, rises the simple granite shaft marked "Herndon," with the date "September 12, 1857." At the time, the story was so well-known as to need no further details, but it has long since been forgotten. Briefly, Commander William L. Herndon, detailed to take the mail steamer *Central America* to California and back, lost his life when the ship went down in a gale off Hatteras. A brig stood by to the rescue and managed to save some of the passengers, but over 400 lives were lost. When Herndon saw that nothing more could be done to save the ship and his men, he went below, put on his full dress uniform and cocked hat, and returned to the wheel-house. As the vessel went down, the survivors saw the erect figure on the bridge raise his hat. The manner of his death is eloquent of the dignity of the old tradition. Commander Herndon, knowing his death was imminent, determined to meet his God as he would report for duty to his superior officer, in full uniform. And his last gesture, removing his hat, was the salute reserved for God alone.

In the crypt of the Academy chapel nearby is the sarcophagus of John Paul Jones. This structure, with its heavy dome, is obviously an echo of the Chapel of the Invalides in Paris, in whose crypt lies the body of Napoleon. But there the visitor stands in a gallery looking down on the tomb surrounded by its stately figures and with the names of his victories in gold letters on the pavement. This Naval Academy building, being used as a chapel for the regiment, requires all the floor space for midshipmen on Sundays, with the result that there is no such effective view of the John Paul Jones tomb as it deserves.

The visitor interested in particular relics of naval history should not miss the museum on the ground floor of Maury

Hall, where every conceivable object is displayed, from the breast and back plates of steel worn by Paul Jones in his fight with the *Serapis,* to the gig in which Lieutenant Talbot made his journey of 1500 miles to rescue his shipwrecked comrades in the middle of the Pacific. There is also the raft on which Richmond Pearson Hobson made his daring attempt to blockade Santiago harbor.

In the great glass cases to the right and left of the entrance to Mahan Hall are shown the old battle-flags. These were rotting to pieces, until in 1912 an appropriation of $30,000 was obtained for the purpose of preserving them. This was done by the most skilful needlework. The tattered remnants were stitched on a linen backing, and the threads were carefully dyed to match the colors of the flags so that they should not disfigure them.

Perhaps the most significant memorial of the past is the Naval Academy cemetery on the opposite side of Dorsey or College Creek. From the parade ground of Worden Field, the visitor sees a tall white cross, hung with marble icicles, standing on top of a base of grey stone. This marks one of the great tragedies in peace time, the story of the *Jeannette* expedition, and the cross represents that other cross of wood standing atop of a cairn of stones in Siberia, erected by Chief Engineer Melville, one of the few survivors. In 1879, the steamer *Jeannette* had been sent to find the North Pole via Bering Strait. Starting out chiefly as a piece of publicity for the New York *Herald* and James Gordon Bennett, it turned out to be one of the most tragic stories of death by slow starvation on the part of officers and men.

Near the *Jeannette* monument, to the left of the road, is a grave stone with a hemisphere of marble, once marked with meridian and parallels and a star showing the "farthest north"

NAVAL ACADEMY CHAPEL

reached by the young officer buried there. The marking on the stone is now so weather-worn as to be almost invisible. This was Lieutenant Lockwood, born in Annapolis, a son of Professor Lockwood, already mentioned, one of the first faculty of the Naval Academy. Lockwood, the younger, was in the Army—the only Army officer buried in this cemetery—and he had been a member of that ill-fated Polar expedition headed by Lieutenant Greeley and rescued by Commander Schley, in 1884, after most of the members, including Lockwood, had perished of starvation and cold.

Here, in this God's acre, lie the men who died with their boots on in the performance of duty, either in war or peace, and others who went to their graves quietly after a lifetime in the Service. Out on the very front of the bluff, in the place of honor, lies Cushing, the daredevil of the Civil War Navy. Near him, rests a kindred spirit, the "Lion-Hearted Flusser," and many others. There are graves here, also, of men who yielded their lives for acts of heroism that historians are apt to overlook; for example, that of Lieutenant Roper who lost his life trying to rescue his men from a blazing engine room.

There is still another grave that deserves a word of honor, even in such a brief sketch as this. It is marked by a stone bearing the name "John Halligan." This officer had been a football hero at the Academy in the nineties, and steadily added to his reputation as a fine officer as the years passed. In the nineteen-twenties he was on duty in Washington. There he came upon the astonishing story of the Teapot Dome lease. He was indignant over the matter, and wrote a protest to the Department, forcefully stating his objections. The letter was pigeonholed. He knew that what he said was not to the liking of the Department. He

THE JEANNETTE MONUMENT

wrote again and again, with the same result. Finally, he showed me his last strong letter of protest in behalf of the Navy, saying simply, "I think this will cost me my commission." Probably it would have done so had not the whole subject broken wide open in Congress just in time. Then his despised letters were brought out as testimony, and Commander Halligan, instead of being an "insubordinate" officer, became a patriotic one. This incident is worth a wreath of honor, even in a cemetery containing such heroic dead as this, because there is many a man who would risk his life in a crisis calling for heroism, but who might not risk his career just for a principle.

Enough should have been suggested in the foregoing paragraphs to make clear the difference between the Naval Academy grounds and the campus of one of our colleges. The latter has far more the atmosphere of learning than the school on the Severn. But the Academy, with its countless memorials of the past, emphasizes another tradition—the heritage of action. This action has been devoted, not to the taming of a wilderness or the building of colossal fortunes in business and industry, but to the service of a great nation. All these battle flags and tablets and monuments are a constant reminder to the young men sent here that they are expected to live up to a code, a "noblesse oblige," which exacts self-sacrifice in the conception of duty, a tradition long since established by their forerunners in the Navy, many of them at the cost of their lives.

CHAPTER XV

THE MAKING OF A NAVAL OFFICER

ONE summer day shortly after the Great War, a retired rear admiral, sitting on a bench in the Yard, had his attention arrested by a grotesque figure of a youth entering the Main Gate. He walked on a few paces and then stood, bewildered, at the crossing of the ways. The officer said afterwards that the lad was dressed like a "hick" comedian of the vaudeville stage and was lugging a bulgy "telescope" bag, reinforced by twine. The older man went up to him and, after a little conversation, learned that the stranger had come from a hamlet in the Kentucky mountains. It happened that the admiral was a Kentuckian himself, and he drew the boy out until he had his story. It transpired that he had passed his scholastic examinations for admission to the Academy, and was obeying the order to report for his physical tests. He had never left his mountains before, and had come much of the way on foot. The fact came out that he had prepared himself for his examinations without help from any teacher. The admiral became deeply interested, and was distressed afterward to learn that the lad was rejected by the doctors on account of some kidney symptom. However, the boy took his disappointment like a man. He said now that he had "seen the world" on this trip to Annapolis he wasn't going back to the mountains but would make his own way somehow.

Later, when the admiral told me the name of the boy I recognized it as that of the candidate who had topped all the hundreds of others in the entrance examinations for that year, with marks in all subjects between ninety and one hundred. A remarkable intellect was lost to the Service when the doctors sent him away.

This youth was unique in the fact that he had achieved the amazing feat of teaching himself his algebra, geometry, history, geography, and English so well that he not only passed but did better than anyone else in the country. But he was like many others who try to enter the Naval Academy, taking it for granted that they are "all right" physically, but after much time and labor and expense preparing for the examinations, are thrown out on a physical disability at the very last moment. Sometimes it is on a weakness that might have been cured beforehand. So the boys still come, as they have been doing for years, with hernias, bad ears and teeth, color blindness, and what not, only to be sent home at the moment when they think they have attained their goal. Accordingly, the first thing for a candidate to attend to is to assure himself, by a physician's examination, that he measures up to the bodily requirement.

Another regulation constantly overlooked is that requiring a deposit of one hundred dollars immediately upon being admitted. Year after year boys come who seem never to have heard of this. They are often penniless, not knowing where to turn to get such a sum. At times, officers have chipped in to raise the money, trusting the boy to work during his vacations and pay it back. Sometimes a kind-hearted business man from town will come forward with the money. So far, there has been no case on record of a boy who has tried to dodge his obligation, but the situation is not pleasant to try to deal with. But it occurs so frequently that the regulation governing this deposit should be printed in red ink on the instructions sent to the candidate.

For the youngster who has the ambition to enter the Naval Academy, the first essential is to get an appointment, and this is often difficult. Who may be admitted? At present four midshipmen are allowed for each senator, representative, and delegate in Congress, and the Vice-President. Four are allowed from the District of Columbia. Fifteen are permitted each year from the country at large. These last are appointed by the President who, by custom, chooses them from the sons of officers and enlisted men of the Army, Navy, and Marine Corps.

The law also provides for the appointment of a hundred enlisted men of the Navy and Marine Corps each year to be selected by competitive examination. These candidates must have served aboard a man-of-war for at least nine months before being admitted to the Academy.

A third group comprises twenty-five midshipmen appointed annually by competitive examination from the enlisted men of the Naval Reserve and the Marine Corps Reserve. These must have served in the Reserve at least one year by July 1st of the summer they expect to enter. They must have had a good record, and bring rcommendations from their commanding officers. This, to a youth with no political affiliations, is an excellent road to the Academy. Still another lot of forty midshipmen may be appointed by the President at large from among the sons of officers, soldiers, sailors, and marines who were killed in action or died of wounds or disease contracted in the World War.

Finally, there are twenty midshipmen selected annually by the Secretary of the Navy from among the honor graduates of institutions designated as "honor schools" by the War Department, and the members of the Naval Reserve Officers' Training Corps. These Corps are to be found at Harvard, Yale, Georgia Institute of Technology, Northwestern, University of Washington, and University of California. Here, also, is an opportunity that is not generally appreciated. The appointments from this group are made by competitive examination.

Thus, it is not absolutely necessary to cultivate a friendship with a Congressman or Senator, though it is true that most midshipmen enter the Academy by the benefaction of the gentlemen on Capitol Hill. Each of these Honorables has the right to nominate a "principal" and three "alternates" for each appointment. Frequently they make these nominations from competitive examinations held by the Civil Service Commission. Sometimes they send all four candidates to take the entrance examination, the top man winning the appointment. Others designate the principal and alternates by their own choice. If the principal fails in the examination, the alternates have their chance in order of merit.

Next, if one has the appointment, is physically fit, and is between the age limits of sixteen and twenty by April 1st of the year one plans to enter, it is necessary to scan the entrance requirements. Nowadays the Academy uses a modification of the college entrance plan. This consists, first, of the certificate from the preparatory or high school, showing the work in the fifteen units required. If this is acceptable, "substantiating examinations" must be taken in English and mathematics. Experience has shown a wide chasm between the glittering peaks of high school grades in these subjects and the lowly results in the substantiating examinations. This is the most popular way of entering the Academy, but if one has not graduated from high school one may still take the "regular examinations" in six required subjects.

Another way, still in the experimental stage, is to admit without examination those who have had a year of college work, provided that the high school certificate is satisfactory and the year's record is sufficiently high, the subjects acceptable, and the college itself has an accredited standard.

So much for the dry-as-dust facts about admission to the Naval Academy. A final word should be added as to the fitness of the candidate in temperament and mentality. Many parents move heaven and earth, and badger their Congressman to death, in order to shoehorn their offspring into the Naval Academy, simply because it is a cheap way of providing for the youngster's education and getting him a job. Yet many failures in the Academy and many resignations after graduation are due to the fact that some young men are temporarily unfit for Navy life. If a boy is a shrinking violet, whose interests lie in ideas rather than things, who is by instinct an individualist or a rebel, who loves to write poetry or paint in water-colors, he is just the sort of person to keep out of the Naval Academy. If, on the other hand, he is the "extrovert" type who likes action, the world of things, especially machinery, is practical-minded, delights in mathematics, and doesn't mind dull routine and discipline, he will probably do well and be happy. That is a point not mentioned in the pamphlet issued by the Secretary of the Navy, "Regulations Governing Admission to the Naval Academy," but it is more important than many things that are.

Let us suppose that the young naval aspirant has succeeded in running the gauntlet of all the examinations, including the physical. He walks out of the naval doctor's office and is sent to the Executive Officer in Bancroft Hall. He stands in line with an assortment of other newcomers and holding up his right hand swears "to support and defend the Constitution of the United States against all enemies foreign and domestic." That does seem like taking on something of a contract, but no one has been known to hesitate. Then, perhaps, he goes to the Administration Building to report to the Superintendent. This awe-inspiring official welcomes him in a fatherly fashion, even as it is done in the movies. Next, he may be directed to the Battalion Officer in Bancroft Hall. This gentleman welcomes him, too, but in more of a stepfatherly way. Indeed, it is not long before the new plebe is being told things about his manner of speech, bearing, and so forth, that are not flattering. The process of discipline begins with the first hour. He is given a pamphlet of thirty-eight closely printed pages—his "bible"—which he must study hard, for his whole life is now a matter of regulations.

That same first eventful day he draws his supplies and hauls them up to his room, his uniform, mattress, sheets, towels, shoes, broom, waste-basket, fountain pen, laundry bag—everything, it seems, but the Tripoli Monument—and tries to learn where to stow them all. He has a roommate, or "wife," to compare notes with, someone who has elected the same language course that he has—French, German, Italian or Spanish. Each has a narrow iron bed and a tall oak cabinet, and, in the middle of the room, a double table with a lamp overhead. There are no pictures allowed on the walls, no gay flags or pennants. It is not much like a college room. In fact, it is about as desolate a cell as the most ascetic monk could desire.

During the summer, the upper classmen are away and there

are no formal lessons. But between six-thirty each morning and ten o'clock each night the plebes are kept busy with drills, both on land and water. The "work uniform" first worn is the most unbecoming garb ever devised for a biped. The stiff, baggy

THE GLORY OF THE FIRST UNIFORM

trousers and jumper of yellowish duck wrinkle and bulge in unrhythmic lines; and the little round white hat with its blue border makes any face look foolish. The black neckcloth gives an appropriate touch of grief, but, on the whole, the uniform suggests something in a comic strip. If a plebe has any vanity left he needs only to look at himself in the glass to lose the last grain. The most dashing halfback, when dressed in a plebe's first uniform, presents a picture that only his mother could love.

September brings the upper classmen, and then the real woe begins. The plebe must sit on the edge of his chair at table, bolt upright, never speaking unless spoken to. He may frequently be required to go under the table for the rest of the meal. He must have answers ready for erudite questions. He must mind his

PLEBE DANCING LESSON

table manners most particularly. In the corridor he walks in the exact middle. He must use certain stairs and eschew others. Outdoors, he must keep to certain prescribed walks, and turn sharp corners. He must, on all occasions, maintain a ramrod "brace." He is forever being called by the obnoxious title of "Mister." In short, his sorrows multiply apace.

Still, there are diversions even for plebes, especially the athletics. In particular, there are the excitements of the football games—above all, the annual contest with West Point. And, finally, there comes June Week, bringing the end to his year of servitude. Though he has been having dancing lessons, he has had no opportunity to practice the gentle art until the June Week Ball, when he is considered no longer a plebe. The old rule about hazing was that the hazer never laid his hands on

OFF FOR THE SUMMER CRUISE

the hazee, but whatever the rule about the laying on of hands there is nothing in the code about the laying on of brooms. On the last night of their plebedom, the poor wretches receive from the upper classmen a final chastisement with brooms which induces a preference for standing rather than sitting for some time thereafter. The wise plebe also will sleep in his dress uniform the night before the ball, knowing full well that it stands an excellent chance of being stolen otherwise.

However, the great day comes when at last the first class graduates. Then " 'tain't no mo' plebes" is the joyous cry as the emancipated ones do a snake dance about the Yard, coats inside out and caps hindside foremost. The first year, like the first hundred, is the hardest.

Then follows the first summer cruise. This is a great experience. It means life on a battleship for the first time. Here the midshipmen learn to do all the jobs of enlisted men, and the day's routine is full and yet enjoyable. Shore leave on the cruise means visits, perhaps to London, or Berlin or Paris, as well as the seaport towns, a thrilling experience for many a boy who has never traveled far from home.

There are still three more "rivers to cross"—three more years, and the academic pace tends to tighten up progressively toward graduation; but the greatest number of casualties, "bilgers," come during plebe year.

What about the education itself? This point deserves special emphasis. The Naval Academy is not a college, though in recent years it has granted the degree of B.S., and for many years its "shield" has adorned the University Club in New York. No parent should send his son to the Naval Academy if he expects him to get there a liberal education. It may even be said that the Academy is not an educational institution at all. That is not its purpose. It exists rather to train young men for the Navy; it is a training school, first and last. Its first objective is the habit of discipline; after that come the various acquirements which the Navy demands of the commissioned officer. That is enough and plenty.

These requisites have increased so fast with the mechanization of naval warfare that nowadays the Naval Academy curriculum is only the beginning of the study that lies ahead of the American naval officer. Fifty years ago, a man who squeaked past his final examinations to get his commission sighed with relief that his student days were over. He had only to draw his breath and his pay check for the rest of his life. "Not another book to crack." In this age, the postgraduate studies of an officer have become almost a career-long habit. Besides the Post-Graduate school in Annapolis, naval men are sent to the best technical institutions from Massachusetts to California. The reason is that, as the German navy proved to the British in the World War, mere numbers of ships are not enough if material and personnel fall behind the times.

Let us see how Joe Gish (the time-honored name for the typical midshipman) goes to recitation. Six times a day he steps out to formation in front of Bancroft Hall and marches off with the rest of his battalion to Maury Hall, or wherever else his class may happen to be. The drum and bugle corps—affectionately known by the regiment as the "hell cats"—rend the air with their blowing and thumping. Orders are shouted. The lines wheel in columns. Tramp, tramp, tramp, they go, down one long straight walk, while on the other parallel walk return those who have just attended class. There is a loud scuffling and clumping of feet at the doorway of the building, then a thundrous tramping down the corridor of the recitation hall, a column of midshipmen advancing relentlessly like the German army entering Belgium. Officers and civilian instructors stand in the open doorways of the class rooms. As the head of the column reaches the end of the corridor, the section leaders shout "Sections halt! Fall out!" The men break ranks, hanging up overcoats and caps on the hooks outside, and then, entering the section room, remain standing by their chairs. The section leader reports his absentees or says, "All present, sir." The instructor replies, "Seat your section, sir."

"Seats!" shouts the section leader, and his charges subside into the chairs with one crash. There are usually twelve to fifteen midshipmen in each section. The time-honored procedure is for the instructor to spread upon his table an assortment of slips containing questions or problems on the day's assignment.

"Draw slips," he calls out. "Man the boards!" Whereupon the midshipmen rise, go to the table with a prayer in their hearts, pick up a slip at random, and take a place at the blackboard where they write their answers. Having finished, they face about, standing at parade rest until ordered to go to their seats or to read their work.

When the hour is over, something that sounds like a fire gong clangs outside. The instructor addresses the section leader, "Take charge of your section, sir!" The latter calls out "Section rise, march out!" Out in the corridor they fall in, and the whole procession goes clumping off again to Bancroft Hall.

Often in this routine there isn't much teaching, but merely hearing and marking recitations. There is almost no such thing as a lecture. The midshipman is supposed to dig the thing out for himself, and he has to learn to do it in a short space of time, too, during a period of less than an hour between one recitation and the next, and the evening study time. In any class, they all learn precisely the same lesson from the same books, and two out of four battalions say them at the same hour. It is regimentation of learning with a vengeance, but the whole scheme of a navy career is regimented.

Life for Joe Gish is not, however, merely studying and reciting, and drilling, sweeping his room, making his bed, standing inspection and marching off his demerits. As remarked in an earlier chapter, Naval Academy life today is infinitely richer in fun and activities than it ever was in the old days, especially the extraordinary opportunities offered in athletics for every season of the year, and every type of boy. Here it even goes ahead of the colleges; and there is the relaxation of the occasional Sunday afternoon visit in Annapolis, when, in the society of an alluring "Crab," one may smoke safely and forget that discipline officers exist; or over a drug store counter drown one's academic sorrows or memory of the "pap sheet"—the report—in tall beakers of sickening soda water. There is a lofty wall around about the Yard and hawk-eyed watchmen, or "Jimmy-Legs," stand at the gates to discourage midshipmen from breaking bounds of an evening to disport themselves in Crabtown. But there is a technique of vaulting that wall, or at least there used to be. One present-day rear admiral made the complacent boast to me that he used to do it and "never touch my dress trousers." Also, if one is hopelessly cribbed, cabined and confined by demerits or what not, there are always obliging "Crabs" or "Yard Engines" who will walk about with disconsolate Joe Gishes between drill and dinner formation. Life could be much worse.

Of the various festival events of Naval Academy life, so much has been portrayed in the moving pictures that it would be superfluous to describe them. The ringing of the Japanese bell on a victory over West Point, the hops, boat drills, and dress parades, chief of all the graduation customs—the Ring Dance, the cheering and cap throwing in Dahlgren Hall after the sheepskins are delivered, the presentation of the colors by the pretty girl, who is most spectacularly kissed by the commander of the winning company, the rampage of liberated plebes after graduation ceremonies—all these need no description. They have been flicked before the eyes of millions of fellow Americans these many years by the impresarios of the celluloid.

In fine, the Naval Academy is a great national institution, closely resembling its rival and sister academy overlooking the Hudson. It is true that both these Service schools put the stress on uniformity, on obedience, rather than on originality or initiative. Service men admit that this is true, but insist that this is essential to the first lesson of the officer, which is discipline. Perforce, the mind that leaves these national academies does tend to run in a prescribed groove; that is the drawback. But as we have seen, it is not their business to dispense a liberal education. They are professional schools.

On the other hand, the Naval Academy shares with the Military Academy the unique distinction of being an institution where, somehow or other, manners and moral qualities are inculcated. The phrase which both these service schools revere, "officer and gentleman," involves a sense of *noblesse oblige*. At the head of one of those articles on the Naval Academy, published in the *St. Nicholas* some fifty years ago, was a drawing of Uncle Sam turning the handle of what looked like a gigantic coffee grinder. Into the top were tumbling gawky boys in civilian clothes; at the spout emerged spruce young officers in uniform. There is more in that picture than the difference between ill-fitting civilian clothes and the brass buttons and epaulets. Young men taken from all parts of the country and every walk of life are put through the process and come out not merely with a commission in their hands and a stripe on their sleeves, but with an ingrained respect for courtesy and honor. They also have acquired certain valuable moral qualities, such as obedience, the recognition of duty with the obligation to see it through no matter how unpleasant, the ability to take injustice and punishment without whining, and to bow to the obligation of loyalty where loyalties are due. This may not be a complete catalogue of virtues, but what colleges are doing half as much for their graduates?

CHAPTER XVI

EPILOGUE

THE first score of years that made such a transformation in the Naval Academy brought blessings to the community outside its gates. The rough, cobbled streets, for the most part gave place to pavements; garbage barrels, peeling paint, old board fences, and tangled dooryards disappeared in favor of an almost New England neatness. Even the alleys, where the darkies lived, no longer boasted the same fragrances from various obsolete remains of the vegetable and animal kingdoms. The great increase in Naval appropriations trickled through every street and lane like the waters irrigating a desert farm, and made the town bloom again as it had not done for over a century. It perked up with a new lease on life.

Annapolis had her own excitements and thrills in those days while the building operations were going on in the Yard. Once Mark Twain came, with his white evening clothes to match his mane of tousled hair and moustache. Some Annapolitans can remember the privilege of being in a group around the open fire in the Governor's mansion—Governor Warfield was then the host—listening to Mr. Clemens telling stories. There was that ghost story about the "Golden Arm." It would have been commonplace with anyone else telling it, but he made everybody's flesh creep. "Who's got my golden arm?" he demanded as the vengeful ghost, and at the climax, when he shouted "YOU!" everyone popped up out of his seat.

OLD HOUSE ON TAYLOR STREET

Another distinguished visitor of a different type was Woodrow Wilson, at the time Governor of New Jersey, but seriously considered for the Presidency of the United States. He was austere and professorial in manner, not at all the oleaginous politician. In his speech he upset all local traditions by never mentioning the Land of Pure Men and Brave Women—or perhaps it should be the other way around—and he didn't stretch anything from the rock-bound coast of Maine to the sun-kissed waters of the Gulf. He didn't seem to know anything about God's purposes for our nation, and he never once waved the starry banner. Next day an editorial in the Annapolis *Evening Capital* said of Governor Wilson's effort that "it was a good speech, but not much of an oration."

William Jennings Bryan, also, in his last campaign for the presidency, came to Annapolis to speak. A platform was erected on St. John's campus, and a great crowd assembled to listen to the Silver-Tongued Orator of the Platte. But there was a chairman of ceremonies, the ranking Annapolis Democrat, who had the privilege of introducing the famous statesman. It was the crowning moment of his life and he made the most of it. He lifted the Banner of Democracy, he paid tribute to Lovely Woman, he took the skins off the vile Republicans; in fact, he had so much to do that his introduction lasted about twenty-five minutes. Bryan's placid face took on greater and greater annoyance as the speech dragged on. He had a train to catch, and the result was that his own eloquence had to be curtailed to something less than the speech of introduction. But there was no doubt about it; that introduction was a real oration of the old-time thunder.

The Great War brought its excitements and thrills to Annapolis, though this time there was a united spirit in the town as never before during the other wars. The influx of new people in those hectic months made living difficult. Houses were hard to get and rents were high; so was fuel, and food was rationed. In the Academy there were the Reserve Officers' classes. There were increased numbers of midshipmen, and instructors, more officers on duty, and so on. But patriotic fervor was at high pitch, and no one thought of complaining about trifles. Every now and then some particularly distingué visitor would step off the car from Washington in an unfamiliar uniform, into the arms of a reception committee of officers, and after a while he would review a parade of the Regiment in dress uniform. For example, there was Papa Joffre and there was General Petain, soldierly but grim. Perhaps he still smarted under the Paris nickname of the "Butcher." Still more impressive to the eye was the King of Belgium, accompanied by his son, the present King. The Prince of Wales—later Edward VIII—reviewed the Regiment too, looking as usual, bored. He might not have been as bored if he had known that there was a young bride in the American Navy at that time for whom he would later toss away the proudest crown in the world like a straw hat in September. And the two British admirals, Jellicoe and Beatty, arrived—separately, of course—the latter delivering a speech to the Regiment assembled in Dahlgren Hall. A few years after the war, Marshal Foch came, and also addressed the midshipmen in Dahlgren Hall; he spoke in French, of course, but everyone understood his closing phrase "pour la patrie." Cardinal Mercier was an honored visitor. After a while, a mere Ambassador or Major General from our Allies was a personage of such small importance that Annapolitans would scarcely turn the head to look twice at him.

For their part, these visitors never paid any attention to the town itself. They were hustled to the Academy Gate and out again, and didn't know what they had missed.

A war-time event, which many Annapolitans will never forget, was the pageant staged on St. John's Campus for the benefit of the Red Cross. This was a dramatic rendering of Annapolis history from the Puritans down through the centuries right up to the World War. An army of citizens was drafted to act various parts or fill up the mass scenes.

Happily, the evening was fine. It was expected that as many as 500 inhabitants would be left over—after deducting those citizens who were actually taking part—to pay their dollar and witness the pageant. As it turned out, people came by the hundreds from Baltimore and Washington. It soon became evident that there weren't enough chairs. The ropes gave way, and hundreds joyously trooped in by "crashing the gate." It was estimated afterwards that at least 3000 spectators witnessed the entertainment.

The program began with a procession of Puritans and Cavaliers bearing a large cross—the part of chief Puritan being enacted by a devout Catholic. After singing a hymn, each starting off on the key which suited him best, they all lay down on the grass and instantly fell asleep. Then the "Spirit of Dreams," with her troop of fairies and fireflies (little girls) danced around the pioneers in flimsy garb, and to the strains of the Blue Danube Waltz. (The original Puritans must have turned in their graves.) Suddenly, a young gentleman pranced into view clad in practically nothing. Even that much had been forced upon him by the frantic directors of the pageant. It was before the days of nudism and the shock upon all was electric. He leaped and bounced high in the air, and flung his arms about violently as the "Spirit of Night." Meanwhile, some of the fairies and fireflies were so chilly that they began to wail and had to be rescued by their mothers, who darted out from the audience and gathered up their little darlings.

The episode of the burning of the *Peggy Stewart* was represented by setting off a quantity of red fire, but the Boy Scout who had it in charge was over-generous, and made such a blaze that the leaves of the nearby trees began to scorch and smoke, and hurry calls were sent for the fire brigade, members of which had to be pried loose from the audience.

For the Revolutionary War, a scene was staged where a lady sat at her spinning wheel and sang. There was to have been a bugle at the end of the song to indicate the arrival of her lover, who comes to say farewell before leaving to fight for his country. But the bandsman detailed for the duty was also on the fire brigade and otherwise occupied with the blaze of the *Peggy Stewart*. The beautiful lady sang her song over and over again. At last the man who was waiting for the bugle call found himself violently pushed into the scene without his cue, just as the lady started again on her song. As he bent over to kiss her farewell for the duration of the war, she looked up at him with an angelic expression, and said grimly in his ear, "Where the hell have you been?" This was not in the script, but, being distinctly audible, was a very successful line.

And so the pageant progressed to the final notes of "Over There." Practically everything went wrong somewhere, but afterwards the spectacle was voted a magnificent success. This was the last gayety before the epidemic of "flu" that followed.

In that last year of the war came the plague. Probably no city in the country suffered proportionately more than Annapolis. It was, literally, a stricken city. The pestilence knocked at every door, and too often death came as well. As one walked up East Street to State Circle, one passed daily a heap of new coffins piled

ROOFS AND CHIMNEYS

up on the sidewalk and in the street itself. Those at that time who were going about on their mission of selling the last issue of Liberty Bonds will never forget what they saw in some of the homes, where often the whole family lay sick and helpless. However, nothing like a plague deterred these women from their patriotic campaign, and when it was finished they found that their quota had been well over-subscribed. The epidemic did not last long, though there was a flare-back five months later, but no one who lived through that time is likely to forget it.

So much for the "Ancient City" in the period that ended with the close of the World War. The rest is present-day history. At this point, the chronicler may well wipe his pen and rise, *pour prendre congé* of the reader; but he would like to remark in doing so that a very old town, which was called by a traveler from France, the "Finished City," as far back as the close of the eighteenth century, is by no means finished. *Au contraire,* Monsieur, her cheeks are still blooming and she is still the belle of all ancient American towns. "Finished" indeed! The Frenchman who said that has been dust for over a century. Let us hope his ghost has to walk a mile every night over Annapolis streets, conjugating the verb *finir.*

* * * *

This volume opened with "June Week," the days of graduation festivities for the Naval Academy. It is a very scant week, as all girls will agree, for it never adds up to seven days. Hence, it has a way of coming to an end even more quickly than ordinary weeks. So, by the time the reader has reached this concluding chapter, June Week may be said to be over. And though the visitor was bidden to come at that time to see Annapolis at its gayest, he is now urged to let the crowds go back without him, when the last boatload of midshipmen in their white work clothes pushes off to the waiting battleship. For then he has a chance to see the "Ancient City" in her proper perspective.

Calm broods over the streets. Gone are the pretty girls in their swishy dresses and picturesque hats. Gone are the uniforms, or, at least, most of them. Gone the vast swarms of motor cars that have blocked the streets like a plague of gigantic beetles. The hot June sunshine pours over the pavements. Annapolitans move

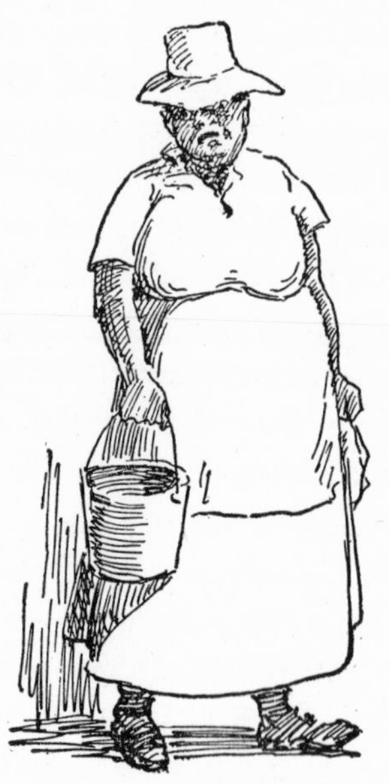

ALLEY REPARTEE

sluggishly in white suits, or brave conventions by shameless display of galluses and necks without collars and ties. Those who spend their days tilted back in chairs in front of fire-engine houses now give themselves up to slumber during the siesta hours. The flies buzz round them. Ethiopian denizens, in particular, fall into an *adagio* or *andante sostenuto* tempo when they move, and droop against a convenient shady wall for indefinite periods of slumber. A drowsy, warm peace broods over the town.

It begins to dawn on the observer that the Naval Academy is, as compared with Anne Arundel's Town, a mere child. To be sure, it has passed its ninetieth birthday, but the city was the capital of Maryland one hundred and fifty years before the Academy was born. Thus, the famous school should be considered not even as the daughter of Annapolis, but rather as the granddaughter. "The Cradle of the Navy" is rocked by an affectionate grandmother who does her knitting the while and lives over the days of her girlhood when she was a famous toast among the colonial towns. And it is a happy circumstance that the venerable lady is now enjoying a serene old age, secure in good days and bad, in the steady stream of Navy Department checks from a certain town nearby on the Potomac. A frightfully upstart, *nouveau riche* town, my dears, but it was planned by and named after a gentleman Annapolis delighted to honor in the Good Old Days, Mr. George Washington, of Virginia. In a way, therefore, she feels that she is now his guest, a happy circumstance indeed. Further, she takes pride in the services rendered by her sons at the national capital, even in the days of her poverty and neglect. There were Pinkney and Johnson, whose records have already been sketched. And the two Hagners, father and son, in their lifetimes, knew every President from Washington to Wilson.

So, thanks to the presence of the Naval Academy, Annapolis is spared the humiliation of sinking into poverty on the one hand, or being vulgarized and exploited as an industrial town on the other. She is permitted to enjoy her memories in peace and plenty. And now, more than ever before, her treasures of the past are appreciated and preserved. An organization has recently been formed for the purpose of the "Restoration of Colonial Annapolis," in order that, in the days to come, such tragic wrecks of old mansions, as the "Randall" house on the corner of Market Square and Randall Street, may never be permitted to sadden the eye.

Very appropriately, that society has its official quarters in the Hammond-Harwood house. And a pleasant place to rest and revive these memories of the past is directly across on the steps of the Chase Home; in fact, just where Nick Jackson sat and fanned himself and remarked bitterly on the universe.

Here, in a long, quiet June twilight, facing one of the most beautiful mansions of the eighteenth century, one need not be unduly "psychic" to conjure up a procession of ghostly memories, the shades of the past. Here is the Chase Home itself, such a tragic disappointment to its builder, who couldn't finish it, but which afterwards became the home of the Lloyds, who lavished hospitality on a princely scale. And, across the way, again, there stands a monument to disappointed hope, for this was to be the bridal gift, which, alas, the bride refused, and where the builder lived alone until his death. Still, there remains the mystery of that secret chamber and that underground path to the tomb!

As you gaze at that doorway, and brood on that romantic story, you will have no difficulty in seeing on that deserted street a return of the spirits who long ago walked this way. There were those early pioneers, the grim-visaged Puritans, winding their way up from the Severn to meet the Susquehannocks under the Tulip Poplar, in order to smoke the pipe of peace. And, after them, the figure of Governor Nicholson, brave in high peruke and long-skirted coat, with tremendous gold-laced cuffs buttoned back to the elbow. He is busy laying out the street plans of his little colonial capital. And, after him, comes a gay succession of governors; among them Ogle with his fine horses, and Sharpe with his secretary, John Ridout, and his physician, Upton Scott. Very handsome gentlemen all, and most elegant in their attire. And there would be the choleric General Braddock, ablaze in scarlet uniform, starting up the Avenue—"Northeast Street," in those days—in Governor Sharpe's coach, amid the huzzas of the Annapolitans, to chastise the French out there on the Ohio and then capture Niagara. A less brilliant figure might be noted, too, because he looks so impressive with his height and breadth and serious mien, George Washington of Virginia. General Braddock is rather curt with him, but Braddock is a Major General of the British army.

Then when the Revolution comes, there is the white of the French uniforms to replace the scarlet; Lafayette appears, the dashing young nobleman, to whom everyone bows profoundly; and General Rochambeau also, who is no less elegant in appearance and manner. Then there follows that great scene in the Senate chamber when, the war being over, General Washington, now Commander-in-Chief of the Colonial armies, reads a stately speech and lays down his sword.

Gradually, all the brilliance fades—the gilded coaches, sedan chairs, and resplendent costumes disappear. Drab decades come, each a bit more shabby than the predecessor. Then a new war brings swarms of ill-fitting blue coats and baggy trousers into the street; bewhiskered young men with Northern and Western twangs to their speech, slouching about on crutches, many of them, and with empty sleeves. Endless processions of supply wagons and ambulances go rumbling over the cobbles. Then, after these pass, there come the courtly Spanish prisoners, among them Cervera, looking every inch an admiral, going out to Mass with his son.

In between these fine gentlemen and warriors, there are the belles of all the decades, flirting outrageously with the officers and the young tobacco princes. And trotting along this self-same avenue are so many other interesting figures—not military men, not even "quality." Oh, dear no! But they are not to be forgotten. There is Mr. Peale, with canvases under his arm. There, too, is Mr. Buckland with his rolls of paper and a pencil stuck in his black wig, watching the new house rise from the ground, and talking with his patron, Mr. Hammond. There comes Shaw, the cabinet-maker; he has forgotten to take off his carpenter's apron, and he pauses to get an earful of gossip from the nosy Mr. Faris. Fie, Fie, Mr. Faris, you should not have repeated *that* story! So they come, in imagination, silently passing back and forth on the same old street, men and women, famous and obscure, young and old, black and white.

Few streets in America can call back such an array of ghosts. They are easy to see if you look for them on such a June night as this, with the soft breeze from the bay stirring the leaves, and the moonlight shining down on the old houses of the Golden Age. They seem to be living again in their prime, these monuments of a day when gentlemen were gentlemen, when one did not hesitate to risk life or property for a principle—when men and women believed in honor no matter what it cost. Anne Arundel's Town stood for these things, a greater glory than even her stately mansions. May that never be forgotten by the generations that follow.

APPENDIX

A LIST OF THE CHIEF HISTORIC BUILDINGS OF ANNAPOLIS

NOTE: There are wide discrepancies in dates assigned to these early structures. Such dates as are given here are based on the most recent researches, but they must be regarded as only approximate in most cases.

ACTON: (v. p. 7) Murray Hill, near Spa Creek. Built about 1790 by Philip Hammond. This house is noteworthy for its attractive façade and the two wide chimneys that face front. Originally the house was surrounded by wide grounds, and it was the last of the Annapolis mansions to surrender its acres to the "realtor."

ASSEMBLY ROOMS: (v. p. 111) Duke of Gloucester Street. This is said to have been erected in 1764 from the proceeds of a lottery. It was the center of much of the social life of the Golden Age. Here George Washington was entertained at dinner by Congress, December 20, 1783, on the occasion of his resigning his commission. During the Civil War the building was used as a guard house, and shortly afterwards was almost totally destroyed by fire. It was rebuilt with three of its original walls still standing. (v. D.A.R. tablet)

AUNT LUCY'S BAKESHOP: (v. p. 87) 160 Prince George Street. Probably dates from about 1730. Aunt Lucy Smith was a famous colored cook of the mid-nineteenth century.

BORDLEY-RANDALL HOUSE: (v. p. 96) Randall Court. Built in 1737 by Thomas Bordley; birthplace of Reverdy Johnson. Originally this property was bounded by the five streets that surround it.

BOUCHER HOUSE: 217 Hanover Street. Built in 1770 and greatly altered since. It was the home of Doctor Boucher, the noted Tory rector of St. Anne's.

Brice House: (v. p. 101) Corner of East and Prince George Streets. Built about 1770. Now the property of St. John's College.

Carroll House: (v. p. 77) Duke of Gloucester Street between St. Mary's Church and Spa Creek. This was built about 1735, with later additions. It was the home of Charles Carroll of Carrollton, the signer of the Declaration of Independence. It is now owned and occupied by the Redemptorist Fathers.

Chase Home or Lloyd House: (v. p. 117) Maryland Avenue, northwest corner of King George Street. Started in 1769 by Samuel Chase, and completed by Edward Lloyd. Now a church home for old ladies. This and the Lloyd-Dulany house on Conduit Street are the only colonial mansions in Annapolis a full three stories in height. Open to the public for a fee of twenty-five cents.

Davis House or Tydings House: Northwest corner of Main and Conduit Streets. Built in 1722. Unusual combination of wood and brick.

Dulany-Duvall House: 179 Duke of Gloucester Street. Built in 1770. This is one-half of the original dwelling.

Forensic Club: (v. p. 54) 170 Duke of Gloucester Street. Built in 1770.

Hammond-Harwood House: (v. p. 119) Maryland Avenue and King George Street, southwest corner. Built by William Hammond, 1774–1782. It was occupied only a short time, if at all, by its builder, who sold it shortly after its completion to Judge Jeremiah Townley Chase, Chief Justice of Maryland. The last owners, the Misses Harwood, were great-granddaughters of Judge Chase. Originally the grounds extended from King George to Prince George Street. The east wing is now the office of the Company for the Restoration of Colonial Annapolis, where the visitor should apply for admission. The building is the property of St. John's College.

Jennings House: 195 Prince George Street. Built about 1740. This is supposed to have been the home of Thomas Jennings, whose daughter married Colonel John Brice of the Brice House. It is said also to have been once the residence of Amos Garrett, who was the first mayor of Annapolis.

JOHN SHAW HOUSE: (v. p. 85) This building, sometimes called the "Brooksbury-Shaw House," the original builder being a butcher named Brooksbury, and once the home of John Shaw, the craftsman, was built originally about 1721 and altered frequently in later years. It is now the club house of the Elks.

JONAS GREEN HOUSE: (v. p. 95) 124 Charles Street. It bears on its D.A.R. tablet the date "about 1680." This was the home of Jonas Green, the editor and publisher of the *Maryland Gazette* in the mid-eighteenth century.

LLOYD-DULANY HOUSE: (v. p. 106) 162 Conduit Street. Built sometime before 1770 by Lloyd Dulany. Washington was a guest there in 1771 and 1773. Now owned by the Masonic Order.

MCCANDLESS HOUSE: (v. p. 93) 139 Market Street. This is one of the oldest houses in Annapolis. It was originally owned by one of the Carrolls. It appeared on a map of 1717, and is believed to have been built before the fire of 1704.

MACCUBBIN HOUSE: 193 Main Street. Built about 1740. This was at one time a tavern. The street entrance has been removed, thus disfiguring its appearance.

MCDOWELL HALL: (v. p. 166) "Bladen's Folly," St. John's Campus. The original building was gutted by fire in 1909, but it was restored on the original lines. It was in the rear of the buildings of St. John's College that Rochambeau's army camped en route to Yorktown.

MARCHAND HOUSE OR DORSEY HOUSE: (v. p. 35) 211 Prince George Street. Built before 1694, said to have been the home of Major Dorsey. In 1695 the Assembly met here, for it served in that year as a residence for Governor Nicholson. In 1704, after the State House had been struck by lightning and partly destroyed by fire, the provincial legislature met in this house again. Later it was greatly enlarged by Judge Hagner. See D.A.R. tablet on wall. It has now been made over into an apartment house.

MARYLAND HOTEL: Church Circle. This curious "flatiron" structure is the present aspect of what was once the grand old Bowie mansion. Later turned into a hotel, it is now an office and apartment building.

OGLE HOUSE: (v. p. 97) 33 College Avenue. Built about 1737 by a Dr. Stephenson, bought by Governor Ogle, and used as his town residence.

PACA HOUSE or CARVEL HALL: (v. p. 105) Prince George Street. Built in 1763 by Governor William Paca, a signer of the Declaration of Independence, and occupied by him until 1780. Since 1899 it has been used as the front of Carvel Hall Hotel.

PEGGY STEWART HOUSE: (v. p. 146 f.) 207 Hanover Street. Built in 1740 and much altered in recent years. This dwelling was the home of Anthony Stewart, the owner of the brig *Peggy Stewart* which he burned off Windmill Point with her cargo of tea, to placate the angry citizens of Annapolis in October, 1774.

PINKNEY HOUSE or PINKNEY-CARPENTER HOUSE: (v. p. 173) 5 St. John's Street. Built in 1737. It was the home of one branch of the Pinkney family. The house was moved from the site of the present Court of Appeals Building to the spot it now occupies. This is the property of St. John's College.

QUYNN HOUSE: 9 Northwest Street. Built about 1750. This is one of the few surviving frame houses of the eighteenth century. It was the home of Reverdy Johnson, the statesman.

RANDALL HOUSE: Randall Street and Market Square. Built in the early eighteenth century. Once one of the show places of Annapolis, with its gardens spreading from Prince George Street to the water's edge, this eighteenth-century dwelling has long been left to decay and desecration. At one time this was the "Middleton Hotel," apparently an inn for seafaring men.

REYNOLD'S TAVERN: 4 Church Circle, corner of Franklin Street. Built in 1735; sold to Samuel Chase about 1771. Now the Annapolis Public Library.

RIDOUT HOUSE: (v. p. 109) 120 Duke of Gloucester Street. Built from 1755 to 1763 by John Ridout. The other block of three brick dwellings to the south of this mansion also was erected by John Ridout for his children.

ST. ANNE'S CHURCH: (v. p. 20) Church Circle. This is the third edifice on the same site, having been built after its predecessor burned down in 1858.

SANDS HOUSE: (v. p. 39) 130 Prince George Street. Built in the last decade of the seventeenth century, it is the oldest frame house in Annapolis and possibly the oldest of any type. It is said that George Washington was so pressed by an admiring crowd of citizens on the occasion of his visit in 1783 that he sought refuge in this house.

SLICER HOUSE: (v. p. 319) Taylor Street. Built about 1740. This was the home and studio of the painter Frank B. Mayer. Mr. Mayer painted the two historical canvases in the State House, the "First Settlement of the Maryland Colony" and the "Burning of the *Peggy Stewart*."

STATE HOUSE: (v. p. 204) State Circle. Built in 1772 from design by Joseph Clarke. The dome was added in 1784. In the old Senate Chamber, on December 23, 1783, Washington resigned his commission as Commander-in-chief of the Continental Army. A public ball was held here in his honor the night before. Here the treaty of peace with Great Britain was signed the following year. In 1786 the Annapolis Convention assembled in this room. The Annapolis capitol and Bulfinch's famous building on Beacon Hill, Boston, are the only two surviving pre-Revolutionary state houses.

TILTON HOUSE: 9 Maryland Avenue. Built in 1750; named after its former owner, Colonel M'Lane Tilton of the Marine Corps.

TREASURY BUILDING: (v. p. 41) State House grounds. Built at some time during Governor Nicholson's term, 1694–1699. It was used as the meeting place for the Colonial Council and court sessions, and also as a treasury, first for the Colony and afterwards for the State.

UPTON SCOTT HOUSE: (v. p. 110) 4 Shipwright Street. Built about 1770 by Doctor Upton Scott. Now occupied by School Sisters of Notre Dame. Francis Scott Key, of Star-Spangled Banner fame, spent much of his youth here. He was a grand-nephew of Doctor Scott.

WALTON HOUSE: (v. p. 37) 10 Francis Street. Referred to sometimes as the "Anthony Workman House." Built in 1696. This has been greatly altered in front, but from the garden it keeps much of its original appearance. Here King William's School is said to have been begun. The structure is sometimes referred to as "Kentish House."

WELLS HOUSE: 131 Charles Street. This early eighteenth century brick dwelling is said to have been the home of William Pinkney, the statesman. Unhappily, the front has been disfigured in recent years by a long narrow porch. The chimneys are interesting for the fact that they are very wide and thin and face the street like those of "Acton."

INDEX

INDEX

INDEX